# Advance Praise for *Evolution's Purpose*

"McIntosh is persuasive in his arguments that the scientific facts of evolution cannot stand alone . . . science shows that historical evolution, whatever its contingencies, is itself on a trajectory of values development. McIntosh has well-researched his sources and integrated them with seminal insight."

—**Holmes Rolston III, Ph.D.**, winner of the 2003 Templeton prize and author of *Environmental Ethics*

"A truly excellent, clear and convincing contribution to our understanding of where evolution is taking us, and in that context, what the deeper meaning may be of the Worldshift we are now facing. Should be read by everyone who is willing to wake up and take a responsible role in shaping our common destiny."

—**Ervin Laszlo, Ph.D.**, distinguished system scientist, President of the Club of Budapest and author of over 30 books on evolution

"Many folks are writing about evolution these days, but few with the vision, intelligence, and even brilliance that Steve McIntosh brings to the table. Thank you, Steve! You are our 21st century Henri Bergson."

—**Allan Combs, Ph.D.**, Professor of Philosophy, California Institute of Integral Studies and author of *The Radiance of Being* and coauthor of *Dreamer of the Earth*

"Steve McIntosh's insightful new book is as readable a "guide for the perplexed" as one can expect to find amidst the many conflicting messages in contemporary thought and culture. Mining the wisdom of traditional philosophies and religions, yet fully conversant with contemporary evolutionary science, McIntosh's fresh synthesis will be helpful to all sincere inquirers."

—**John F. Haught, Ph.D.**, Professor of Theology Georgetown University and author of *God After Darwin*

"*Evolution's Purpose* is a masterpiece! With both uninhibited passion and fierce intellect, philosopher Steve McIntosh deconstructs the materialist paradigm with the precision of an expert neurosurgeon. With gentle persistence and irrefutable logic, he reveals many of the false assumptions in scientific, cultural, and spiritual orientations about our presence in the universe that are less than integral. He takes us on a fascinating journey through the history and evolution of our own conscious and unconscious beliefs, finally delivering us with a truth that is impossible to deny or avoid: We are part of a process that has a direction and through awakening to this life-affirming truth, we discover a sense of purpose that changes everything."

—**Andrew Cohen**, author of *Evolutionary Enlightenment* and founder of *EnlightenNext Magazine*

"It's so easy to feel overwhelmed by the dramatic turn of world events. *Evolution's Purpose* presents another view of the chaos . . . that humanity is evolving in an ultimately purposeful way, lending both meaning and illumination to our individual and collective struggles. Steve McIntosh's brilliant ideas are both stimulating and comforting, as he lays out a theory of our evolution that is both scientifically and spiritually profound."

—**Marianne Williamson**, author of *A Return to Love*

"*Evolution's Purpose* is a moving and profound book that explores the spiritual influences on evolution that are nevertheless consistent with the major tenets of contemporary science. With his clear and accessible prose, Steve McIntosh demonstrates the evolutionary emergence of beauty, truth, and goodness and shows how personal experience confirms the presence of spirit in an evolving cosmos. I highly recommend this book for anyone seeking to make sense of the evolution of cosmos and consciousness."

—**Michael E. Zimmerman, Ph.D.**, Professor of Philosophy University of Colorado at Boulder and co-author of *Integral Ecology*

"*Evolution's Purpose* reaches deep into the living essence of evolution within the cosmos and within ourselves. It gives us strong arguments to carry us beyond the limitations of the neo-Darwinian assertion of no purpose, meaning or direction in evolution; and also beyond the post-modern sense of relativism, by offering a far deeper exploration of the source of purpose itself intrinsic to evolutionary direction. It calls us to become "part of the universal family of conscious evolutionaries who have embarked on the magnificent adventure of experiential perfection." Most important, this seminal book places the

"Evolutionary World View" on the "memetic map" of global culture to guide our generation in the direction of our evolutionary transformation. This is a very important work."

"In an intellectual environment where the mindset of Richard Dawkins and Daniel Dennett dominate all discourse when it comes to evolution, Steve McIntosh give us a scientifically literate, philosophically rich, and spiritually potent alternative. His evolutionary vision is a brilliant light of clear thinking in a landscape dimmed by reactionary atheism and dogmatic materialism. Addressing evolution as a powerful context for meaning and purpose, McIntosh expertly shows us how a new and broader understanding of evolution can revolutionize the way we understand not just physical development but social and cultural progress as well. Deeply considered and tightly argued, *Evolution's Purpose* presents a powerful message of hope to the modern world, one that renews our love for spirit and restores our faith in the future."

"Following in the footsteps of the renowned philosopher Alfred North Whitehead, who questioned the folly of scientists whose purpose was to declare life and evolution purposeless, Steve McIntosh has no such misgivings. He is a man with a purpose, and that purpose is to deliver a positive, progressive message. *Evolution's Purpose* is a timely and enlightened exposition about those supposedly subjective, yet all important intangible values of beauty, truth and goodness and how their appreciation and attainment are an integral part of the evolutionary story. Science and philosophy, and McIntosh is well grounded in both domains, are much enriched by integrating these value dimensions into its otherwise overly materialistic cannon."

"*Evolution's Purpose* is a breakthrough book. It redefines the terms of the rational public debate over evolution. In it, Steve McIntosh articulates, in his lucid original voice, important new ideas and persuasive arguments that clarify a hard-headed rationale for the spiritual implications of our scientific understanding of the story of evolution."

"*Evolution's Purpose* hits me in a sweet spot, where my scientific mind is transcended—and included—into larger, richer and more sacred dimensions. I feel changed and liberated after reading this book the way I did after finishing *The Road Less Traveled* and *Up from Eden:* more awake, heartened, grateful for this gift of existence, and motivated to align my life with the power of loving intelligence that is living in me."

—**Jeff Salzman**, founder, Boulder Integral Center
and CareerTrack Seminars

# Evolution's Purpose

# Evolution's Purpose

**An Integral Interpretation of the
Scientific Story of Our Origins**

Steve McIntosh

SelectBooks, Inc.
*New York*

First Edition

ISBN 978-1-59079-220-9

Book illustrations by Steve McIntosh. All rights reserved.

*Library of Congress Cataloging-in-Publication Data*
McIntosh, Steve, 1960-
  Evolution's purpose : an integral interpretation of the scientific story of our origins / Steve McIntosh.
    p. cm.
  Summary: "Presents the author's view of the scientific story of our evolutionary origins to show how evolution's progressive generation of emergent value reveals a larger purpose within the process. He demonstrates how this purpose can be felt within each of us as the evolutionary impulse to make things better--to grow toward ever-widening realizations of beauty, truth, and goodness"--Provided by publisher.
  Includes bibliographical references (p.      ) and index.
  ISBN 978-1-59079-220-9 (hardbound : alk. paper)
  1. Evolution. 2. Cosmogony. 3. Cosmology. 4. Evolution (Biology) 5. Human evolution. 6. Evolutionary psychology. 7. Human beings--Origin. I. Title.
  B818.M44 2012
  116--dc23
                                    2011039319

Interior book design by Janice Benight

Published in the United States of America
10 9 8 7 6 5 4 3 2 1

Dedicated to my family
Tehya, Ian, and Peter McIntosh

# CONTENTS

# PREFACE

EVER SINCE I WAS A TEENAGER IN THE 1970s I have had a passionate interest in the aspects of science that point to, or otherwise hint at, the existence
of a larger reality. Back then, my scientific interests included quantum
physics, self-organizing systems, and the study of consciousness. Although
my professional development eventually took a different path, I continued
to study and contemplate the intersection of science and spirituality. Then
in the late 1990s I became acquainted with an emerging new form of
philosophy known as *integral philosophy*, which has since become the central
focus of my working life.

Integral philosophy is essentially a philosophy of evolution that emphasizes the evolution of consciousness as a central factor in the process of
evolution overall. This new perspective is compelling and important because
it demonstrates the connection between the personal development of each
person's values and character and the larger development of human history.
Through its insights into the evolution of human consciousness and culture,
integral philosophy offers realistic and pragmatic solutions to the growing
global problems that are increasingly threatening our civilization. That is,
from the perspective of this philosophy, every problem in the world can
be understood, at least partially, as a *problem of consciousness*. So it follows
that the solutions to seemingly intractable problems, such as environmental degradation and climate change, nuclear proliferation and terrorism,
hunger and overpopulation, unregulated globalization and gross inequality,
can all be effectively ameliorated by raising or changing the consciousness
that is continuing to create (or prevent) these problems. Moreover, when
we understand human history from this perspective, we can see how, in at
least some places, human nature itself has developed, values and worldviews
have evolved, and concepts of "worldcentric" morality have come to replace
more narrow ethnocentric sensibilities. As a result of the co-evolution of
consciousness and culture, some segments of the world's population have

increasingly come to reject war, to condemn oppression, and to place a high value on the preservation of our natural environment.

As my understanding of this new philosophy of evolution grew, I was eventually moved to try to make a contribution to the field, which led to my last book, *Integral Consciousness and the Future of Evolution*. The book described the basic contours of integral philosophy and offered some constructive critiques of its leading authors. It also applied integral philosophy's understanding of evolution to politics, psychology, and spirituality in an attempt to expand the scope of this emerging perspective. *Integral Consciousness* was well received by reviewers and readers, and as a result of its success I have established many new relationships and have come to an even deeper understanding of integral philosophy's central subject: the ever-present process through which everything in the universe has come to be—the unfolding epic of evolution. Although I was initially drawn to integral philosophy because it promised to solve real world problems, as my understanding deepened I realized that this philosophy's greatest potential to improve the human condition can be found in its ability to help us better comprehend evolution itself.

Through integral philosophy I have come to see that the evolutionary story of our universe, when understood in its entirety from the flaring forth of the big bang, through the emergence of our solar system, through the evolution of life, and up through the development of human society and culture, carries an unmistakably spiritual message. This message is discovered as we begin to appreciate the unfathomable value that evolution has produced in the course of its development, and how evolution's generation of value discloses its progressive character. And as we come to clearly see how evolution progresses, this reveals *evolution's purpose*. As I will explore throughout this book, the evident purpose of evolution is to grow toward ever-widening realizations of beauty, truth, and goodness; and it is through the generation of these most intrinsic forms of value that evolution expresses its spiritual message.

One of the most compelling features of this conception of evolution's purpose is that it is apparent in the scientific facts themselves. Recognizing evolution's purpose does not require us to adopt a specific belief system or otherwise buy into an authoritative spiritual teaching; the meaning and value of evolution can be readily seen once we carefully consider what science and philosophy have now disclosed. However, although most of the evolutionary science that provides the foundation of our discussion has been around for decades, it is only in the last few years that we have begun to grasp evolution in its fullness. And this breakthrough in our understanding of evolution overall has resulted from the enlarged appreciation of the cultural or psychosocial aspects of evolution brought about by the recent insights of integral philosophy. This new philosophy of evolution helps us directly experience the truth of evolution's underlying purpose because it shows how the personal sense of purpose that we feel in our individual lives is directly connected to the larger movement of evolution as a whole. Stated differently, the evolutionary impulse to make things better that we feel in our hearts and minds is the very same impulse that has been driving the unfolding emergence of the universe from the beginning.

Once this became clear to me I felt the excitement of what seemed like a new discovery. I could sense that if evolution's purpose—both personal and universal—could be convincingly demonstrated, this insight could help bring about further evolution in consciousness and culture. Because once it has been properly pointed out, the purpose of evolution becomes relatively self-evident and self-authenticating. And as more people come to see and agree about this momentous truth, this can help us achieve greater social solidarity and stronger political will, it can make us more effective at addressing humanity's problems, and it can increase our sense of collective well-being by helping us to feel more at home in the universe.

When we begin to appreciate evolution's larger meaning, this does not replace or invalidate the teachings of existing spiritual traditions; rather, it confirms much of what these traditions have been teaching all along, while also refining and improving their essential message. The philosophical recognition of evolution's purpose uplifts both religion and science by better integrating and harmonizing these two indispensible approaches to truth.

Although the meaning and value of evolution does become increasingly evident through philosophical reflection, understanding evolution's purpose in its fullness is not simple or easy. But even though some of the arguments in this book may require sustained concentration to be fully grasped or otherwise appreciated, my ultimate thesis is straightforward: evolution is making things better. Despite the inevitable growth of problems and pathologies, and despite the ongoing presence of suffering and evil in this world, I hope to show how the process of evolution generally moves in directions of intrinsic value. Although our understanding of intrinsic value itself has evolved by dialectical steps and stages throughout history, we can nevertheless detect an enduring current in the cosmos that has been growing from the beginning toward the beautiful, the true, and the good. While this thesis may at first sound lofty or idealistic, the supporting arguments do not rely

## ACKNOWLEDGMENTS

I WOULD LIKE TO THANK AND ACKNOWLEDGE the invaluable support and feedback of my friends and integral colleagues: Jeff Salzman, Michael Zimmerman, Andrew Cohen, Terry Patten, Carter Phipps, Allan Combs, Ross Hostetter, and Wayne Guenther. Also thanks to my friends Lindsay Moore, Boyd Willat, and Doug Doupler, who provided excellent input on the manuscript as it developed. And special thanks to my friend and able editor, Byron Belitsos, whose insights made a significant contribution to the text. I also wish to thank my agent Bill Gladstone, and my enthusiastic publisher at SelectBooks, Kenzi Sugihara. Further, I am very grateful for the endorsements of those mentioned above, as well as for the endorsements of John Haught, Barbara Marx Hubbard, Ervin Laszlo, Holmes Rolston III, and Marianne Williamson. Finally, a very special thanks to my wife Tehya McIntosh, and my sons Ian and Peter, who stood by me through the arduous creative process of giving birth to this book.

# INTRODUCTION

EVEN THOUGH I BECAME A "GROWN-UP" MANY YEARS AGO, I have not stopped growing. While my physical body is no longer growing, my mind and character have continued to develop. And as a result of my ongoing personal evolution I have become increasingly sensitive to the problems of the world. Indeed, many of us who have received the educational and economic benefits of living in the developed world now feel a sense of personal responsibility to help improve the human condition and combat the global problems that increasingly threaten us. Although humanity will most likely adapt to our changing world, as our large-scale problems continue to mount the potential regression of our civilization in the decades ahead is becoming a real possibility. It appears that the challenges of the twenty-first century will test humanity like never before; and the only way we will be able to deal with these challenges comprehensively is through *cultural evolution*.

Cultural evolution, however, is a difficult and problematic subject. A significant number of influential scholars, policymakers, and journalists feel that the very idea that some cultures are "more evolved" than others is misguided and potentially racist. Yet those who deny that human culture evolves are often the same ones who are demanding social change. Although there is widespread agreement about the need to address certain social problems, many of those who define themselves as "progressives" are nevertheless ambivalent about humanity's potential to achieve lasting historical progress. And given the previous failures of progressive ideologies such as Marxism, there are many good reasons why we should remain cautious, or even skeptical, about theories of cultural evolution.

Still, our growing global problems are resulting from the unintended consequences of previous historical developments, and it is only through further positive development that we can overcome these threats. As environmental degradation, nuclear proliferation, the exhaustion of natural resources, overpopulation in the developing world, and hunger and poverty become increasingly dire, we must find a way to outgrow the problems we have created for ourselves. As I will argue in the pages ahead, permanent solutions to the problems we are facing in this new century can only be achieved through the further evolution of consciousness and culture. Therefore, understanding what cultural evolution actually is, how it occurs, and how it can be more effectively brought about is crucial for this undertaking.

In order to achieve a breakthrough in our ability to understand and facilitate cultural evolution, we need to achieve a breakthrough in our understanding of the overall process of evolution as a whole. And as we will see, this breakthrough is beginning to take shape: leading theorists are coming to realize that the cosmological evolution of stars and planets, the biological evolution of organisms, and the cultural evolution of human history are all part of a universal process of becoming that has been continuously unfolding since the beginning of our universe with the big bang. The advance of evolution encompasses much more than the development of biological species. Indeed, evolution is not just something that is occurring within the universe; evolution itself is what the universe actually is—a grand panoply of micro and macro development that affects everything, and ultimately connects everything.

However, the mainstream scientific and philosophical community has not digested or even appropriately acknowledged the staggering fact that evolution is universal. Yet once we accept that all forms of evolution—cosmological, biological, and cultural—are part of the same overarching process, despite their significant differences and discontinuities, this leads to a deeper recognition of evolution's meaning and value. And as we begin to discover the underlying meaning and value of evolution, this reveals *evolution's purpose*. A scientifically informed philosophical recognition of the underlying purpose of evolution can be very powerful because, as my arguments will show, a better understanding of evolution's purpose can lead directly to a more evolved world.

Evolution's purpose, however, cannot be discovered through science alone. In fact, scientists have not even been able to "discover purpose" in humans—neurologists have yet to pinpoint a specific mechanism or network in the brain that is responsible for will power or decision-making. Moreover, many scientific materialists argue that free will is an illusion and that all human choices are predetermined by social and environmental factors. Purpose is thus a subject that remains elusive to science. And this is because purpose is primarily a function of values, and values must be understood through philosophy rather than science.

## The Role of Philosophy

Although professional philosophy had only a marginal social impact in the last half of the twentieth century, there have been times in history when philosophy served as a powerful lever for social progress. For example, the philosophies of Socrates, Plato, and Aristotle were a significant factor in the flowering of ancient Greek civilization during its golden age. In ancient Greece the contemplation of philosophical questions occupied the minds of all the best citizens and the work of professional philosophers was indispensible to the social fabric of the community. Then again during the Enlightenment of the seventeenth and eighteenth centuries philosophy provided a new way to think about the world. It supplied a framework for the rise of science, and it described new ideals of freedom and morality that contributed to the overthrow of feudalism and the inauguration of democratic forms of government.

Now in our time in history a new form of philosophy is emerging—an expanded perspective that promises to help us solve our world's problems through an enlarged understanding of evolution. Just as Enlightenment philosophy helped give birth to science, which led to a significant improvement of the human condition through scientific medicine and other technological innovations, this new philosophy of evolution has the potential to produce similarly dramatic improvements. These advances will be achieved as we increasingly recognize how fundamental values such as beauty, truth, and goodness influence evolution at every level of its unfolding. As I will argue, by coming to understand the "gravitational pull" of values on the process of evolution we can more clearly see why and how cultural evolution has been achieved in some places and why it has stagnated or regressed in other places. Once grasped, this enlarged appreciation of the evolutionary process can be used to produce sustainable cultural evolution on every front of its development. This new understanding of evolution reveals how both our personal progress as individuals and our collective progress as a society are directly connected to the creative unfolding of the universe as a whole—a process that has progressed by emergent steps from matter, to life, to mind, to spirit. This new philosophy of evolution links the individual sense of purpose that courses within our own minds and hearts to the larger cosmic purpose of evolution overall. And when we work to feel and cultivate this universal evolutionary impulse within ourselves, this kindles our motivation and improves our ability to give our gifts to the world.

Most people think of evolution as a scientific subject. Indeed, one could argue that the discovery of evolution is the most useful and important scientific insight of all time. Not only is it central to biology, it has become a cornerstone of many other scientific fields as well. In fact, there are now very few branches of science that do not make explicit use of the discoveries of evolution in one way or another. Every year thousands of books and scholarly articles are published on the subject, and it remains an ongoing focus of intense interest in the media and popular culture in general. Yet despite its enormous impact on science this powerful and overarching theory has had an even greater impact on our society's understanding of itself. As philosopher Mary Midgley observes: "The theory of evolution is not just an inert piece of theoretical science. It is, and cannot help being, also a powerful folk-tale about human origins. . . . Evolution is the creation myth of our age. By telling us our origin, it shapes our views of what we are. It influences not just our thought, but our feelings and actions too."[1]

Part of the appeal of the subject of evolution comes from the tremendous controversy it provokes. Controversy about evolution is found not only in the well-publicized battles over public school curriculum but within science itself, where heated debates on a wide variety of details have characterized the development of the idea from its beginning. The great passion the subject of evolution evokes adds to the intensity with which the concepts have been both championed and critiqued. But beyond its abundant scientific utility, and beyond its evident power as a lightning rod for passionate debate, the subject of evolution also appeals to us because it seems that there is something very meaningful and profound about it that has yet to be fully realized or discovered. In fact, many sensitive thinkers are beginning to feel a tantalizing intuition that what science is increasingly revealing about our evolving universe represents a monumental truth that transcends the boundaries of scientific inquiry.

As I will argue in the pages ahead, the scientific facts of evolution cannot stand alone. These powerful facts can only exist within a reality-defining frame of reference or worldview that situates these truths within our understanding of the universe as a whole. Even those who deny that there is any greater meaning or value to evolution beyond its physical facts are nevertheless situating these facts within such a framework. As the scientific discoveries accumulate we are coming to see that evolution is not just a characteristic of life, but is an overarching process that encompasses every aspect of the cosmos. And once we acknowledge that evolution is influencing everything we can begin to see the spiritual implications of this recently discovered truth. In other words, there is no getting around the metaphysical connotations of evolution as a ubiquitous cosmic process.

Those who reject evolution on religious grounds do so because they can find no room for these discoveries within their pre-existing, reality-defining framework. But even those who hold that evolution is simply the result of chance and necessity within a universe devoid of larger meaning must nevertheless admit that such a pessimistic assessment is also inescapably metaphysical—that such conclusions extend beyond what can be observed in the physical world. Alternatively, if we accept the facts of evolution but feel that no one can really know the ultimate origin or destiny of this process, this is likewise a metaphysical framework. Or if we maintain that evolution is a technique of creation used by spirit to bring forth the manifest world, this too is a metaphysical framework. Once we recognize that the universe is, somehow, in the process of becoming, this existential truth cannot help but connect to some kind of metaphysical explanation. Even anti-metaphysical explanations, which argue that the only reality is physical reality, are nevertheless inescapably metaphysical; the all-encompassing facts of evolution create a container of one sort or another no matter what you do. So at this point the question is not *whether* evolution has metaphysical implications, but rather *what* metaphysical framework most adequately accounts for what science has now disclosed.

The philosophy of materialism (also known as physicalism or naturalism) that has served as a container for evolutionary science for most of its history has fulfilled a valuable purpose. Strict methodological naturalism (an investigative approach that rules out any metaphysical interpretations) has been a useful incubator for our emerging understanding of the natural process of evolution. And this approach remains an important tool of scientific inquiry. But we have recently come to the point where the *scientific facts themselves* increasingly demonstrate that a purely physical explanation of the phenomenon of evolution, one that can only include empirical data gathered from sensory observation, is now relatively exhausted. Such an explanation can no longer adequately contain the discoveries of science. Thus, because the science of evolution, whether scientists admit it or not, always has a *philosophy of evolution* attached to it, it is time to work toward an enlarged philosophy that can better account for what we now know.

The current climate within the academic study of evolution can be compared to the branch of psychology known as *behaviorism* that was influential in academic psychology up until the 1970s. The behaviorists maintained that humans could be studied and understood in their fullness by simply observing their external behaviors; there was no need to postulate a mental life or hypothetical internal states—all could be explained by behavior alone. Of course, we now look back at psychological behaviorism as woefully inadequate to the task of explaining human psychology. The apparent absurdity of trying to understand the mysteries of consciousness by running rats in a maze borders on the humorous. Yet the academic professionals who are recognized as our official experts on evolution are currently using an essentially behaviorist approach to our understanding of the cosmos. These scientists and philosophers have concluded that evolution can be completely understood by simply observing its external phenomenon.

However, the accumulating facts of cosmological, biological, and cultural evolution are now giving rise to a deeper philosophical understanding of evolution that recognizes how interiors—agency, sentience, subjectivity, consciousness, and mind—play a central role in the universe's unfolding development. This new integral philosophy is not yet fully recognized by the academic mainstream, but it is nevertheless grounded in science and its arguments are intellectually rigorous. The emerging perspective of integral philosophy provides fresh insights into how consciousness itself actually evolves and why this form of evolutionary development is a primary feature of the process of evolution overall. Consciousness can evolve in a wide variety of ways. It can be raised or evolved by increasing empathy and compassion, by cultivating knowledge, understanding and forgiveness, and by building political will and the determination to achieve social and environmental justice. Consciousness can also be raised by enlarging people's estimates of their own self-interest, by expanding their notions of what constitutes "the good life," and by persuading them to appreciate new forms of beauty and truth. The developed world's relatively recent acceptance of women as the social equals of men provides a good example of how the human condition can be improved through the evolution of consciousness.

Examining what science has revealed about our evolving universe from the perspective of integral philosophy shows us how evolution is not random, accidental, or otherwise meaningless. On the contrary, its progressive advance reveals the presence of *purpose*—not an entirely preplanned or externally controlled type of purpose, but rather a creative generation of value that has been continually building upon itself for billions of years.

When we come to understand the grand panoply of evolution as a unified, overarching process of development that has been unfolding since the beginning of the universe 13.7 billion years ago—when we see how the seemingly distinct evolutionary domains of matter-energy, life, and mind are actually just different aspects of a larger, universal process of becoming—we begin to sense the spiritual implications of this momentous truth. And despite its vigorous use as a weapon against spirituality, as our understanding of evolution deepens I believe the subject of evolution will increasingly come to be seen as a profound and sacred teaching in its own right. By illuminating the spiritual implications of evolution and by describing how we can use this understanding to solve problems by raising consciousness, I hope to bring the insights of integral philosophy to the attention of the educated mainstream.

## Where I Stand

Practically all writers on evolution have a philosophical reality frame in which they situate evolution. And this can result in a hidden agenda. Therefore it is important to state my position up front. Although I am not an academic, my arguments and conclusions are being made within a framework that strives for academic respectability. I have a high regard for the tremendous accomplishments of the sciences of biology, geology, physics, and cosmology (among others), through which the facts of evolution have been brought to light. My aim is thus to be as faithful as possible to the scientific facts and argue only with some of the philosophical interpretations that have become closely associated with these facts. Although I maintain that purpose can be detected in the unfolding of evolution, I reject the assertions of creationists and "intelligent design" proponents. Distinguished philosopher of evolution Henri Bergson clearly understood that "nature is more and better than a plan in the course of realization." The philosophical discussion that follows seeks to appeal to the scientific community as well as to the larger audience of those who are intrigued by the subject of evolution. The contemporary evolutionary scientists who have influenced my thinking include Stuart Kauffman, Paul Davies, Lynn Margulis, Simon Conway Morris, Ervin Laszlo, and Eric Jantsch. From the field of philosophy, my influences include Pierre Teilhard de Chardin, Alfred North Whitehead, Ken Wilber, Holmes Rolston III, Philip Clayton, and John Haught. And of course, no credible philosophy of evolution can avoid giving credit to the father of evolutionary philosophy, Georg Hegel.

Although I hold that evolution has unmistakable spiritual implications, I do not subscribe to any organized religion. Nor do I intend to argue philosophically for any particular form of spiritual belief. If I must have a label for my spiritual position, then I will accept the tag of "panentheist," which means that I recognize spirit as both immanent and transcendent. However, I also believe that science, philosophy, and religion must be afforded a degree of separation. So it is my sincere intention to keep our discussion at the level of philosophy (with the exception of chapter 8), and to thus make use of the most minimal metaphysics possible to account for the facts. Moreover, recognizing the kind of purpose that I argue can be found within evolution does not necessarily require that one believe in God. This philosophical interpretation of evolution is thus compatible with a wide variety of spiritual paths and belief systems. While I will avoid a tedious dialogue with atheistic philosophies, I will not presume any particular beliefs on the part of the reader. When it comes to the meaning and value of evolution no one can be completely objective, but I do hope to make my beliefs transparent and to strive for an inclusive philosophical agreement that can accommodate multiple worldviews.

## The Evolution of Worldviews

Here at the beginning it is also necessary to introduce a central concept of integral philosophy that we will be returning to and elaborating upon throughout our discussion. This conception recognizes the sequential emergence of values-based stages of human cultural development. Integral philosophy's view of cultural evolution sees history as unfolding according to a clearly identifiable *developmental logic* or cross-cultural pattern that influences the growth of human society. This developmental logic need not be construed as a "deterministic law of history" or as implying a strictly unidirectional course of cultural development, but it does reveal a recurring theme in humanity's narrative story. The unfolding of this theme or pattern results in a dialectical structure of conflict and resolution, which is created by the interaction of specific worldview stages or levels of historical development. The most obvious and widely accepted example of this stage structure can be recognized in the distinct, historically significant worldviews known as *modernism* and *traditionalism*.

As most readers know, prior to the Enlightenment the majority of the world's population was divided among the great religious civilizations. These are the cultural worldview structures identified as Christianity, Islam,

Hinduism, Buddhism, Confucianism, and others. While there were, of course, major differences between these civilizations, there were also many remarkable similarities. And these similarities allow us to now classify these diverse religious worldviews together under the general heading of the *traditional* stage of development. Contemporary traditionalists value family life, lawful authority, self-sacrifice, and the sanctity of their beliefs. Although every traditional worldview has been significantly impacted and modified by the developments of ensuing centuries, this stage of cultural development continues to define reality for billions of people alive today. Even in the developed world the traditional worldview remains the cultural center of gravity for significant minorities who give more credence to scripture than to science.

Most readers will also acknowledge that beginning in the seventeenth century a radically new, reason-based worldview structure emerged, which we now identify as the *modernist* stage of cultural evolution. Like the traditional worldviews that preceded it, modernism is a complex structure of value agreements that frame a well-defined view of nature, history, and what it means to live a good life. Modernist values include personal achievement, financial prosperity, individual liberty, democratic government, scientific reasoning, and higher education. The values of the modernist stage are distinct, and in many ways antithetical to the values of the traditional stage. And the ongoing tension between the enduring traditional level and the spectacularly successful modernist level reveals the structure of these dialectically related stages of development.

Yet the historical record also reveals that there are more than just these two stages. Prior to the emergence of the traditional stage, which arose through innovations such as written language, law, and feudal forms of government, there were several *pre-traditional* stages of cultural development. These pre-literate, indigenous cultures used kinship-based forms of social organization and employed time-honored survival strategies that kept them closely connected to nature. And remnants of these ancient cultural structures continue to exist in parts of the world today.

Although there are many ways to divide up the course of human history, and although there are a variety of competing stage theories, few will disagree that the recognition of the pre-traditional, traditional, and modernist stages of cultural development represents a valid reading of the historical record. Like practically all forms of evolution, cultural evolution unfolds by discrete, emergent steps, rather than along a seamless continuum of growth. To paraphrase Jean Piaget, "there is no development that lacks a structure" and the development of human civilization is no exception. The veracity of this stage conception will become increasingly evident as our discussion unfolds, but it needs to be briefly introduced here at the beginning because we will be using the words "pre-traditional," "traditional," and "modernist" as defined terms to describe these stages of cultural evolution. And to this list we must add one additional defined term: the controversial concept of *postmodernism*.

Unfortunately, the word "postmodern" has become a battleground of meaning. Although the term has been used to describe art movements and critical forms of academic discourse, integral philosophy uses the term as a general description of the distinct cultural worldview that has emerged beyond modernism in many parts of the developed world. The large demographic group that comprises this worldview, also known as the "cultural creatives" or the "green meme," adheres to a different and distinct set of values that contrasts with both traditionalism and modernism. Although this group includes a great diversity of outlooks and beliefs, it does cohere as a recognizable worldview structure, showing many similarities to the historically significant worldviews that have preceded it. Like modernism and traditionalism, the postmodern worldview provides people with a sense of identity and thus creates strong loyalties to its perspectives. And following the pattern of the rise of previous worldviews, postmodern values stand in antithesis to the values of the existing culture from which they arose. Postmodernists are generally united by their reverence for the natural environment, by their concern for social justice, and by their desire for self-actualization or spiritual growth. With the rise of postmodern values comes a rejection of the stale materialistic values of modernism and the chauvinistic and oppressive values of traditionalism.

However, like the rise of modernism and traditionalism, the emergence of the postmodern worldview has also brought new problems and pathologies. Postmodernists can be prone to narcissism, value relativism, a return to magical or mythical thinking, and intense forms of anti-modernism that threaten to undermine the social foundations upon which the postmodern worldview ultimately depends.

Here in America the worldviews of traditionalism, modernism, and postmodernism each vie for the allegiance of the population, with modernists comprising a majority of approximately fifty-percent, traditionalists approximately thirty-percent, and postmodernists perhaps as much as twenty-percent. These demographic estimates have been arrived at through extensive research on both the psychology of individuals and the sociology of large groups. Yet we don't need social science to confirm these cultural realities. Our country's "culture war" is evident on practically every evening's news broadcast. A simplified overview of the characteristics of these major developmental stages is provided in Chart 1.

It is important to emphasize that these worldview structures are exceedingly subtle and complex. And it is possible for the same person to hold more than one worldview, depending on the circumstances. According to integral philosophy these stages of historical evolution represent an unfolding trajectory of *values development*. Yet integral philosophy also recognizes additional lines of development, such as cognitive or emotional development that are not directly tied to the evolution of values or worldviews. Admittedly, describing the culture of the developed world in terms of a vertical scale of values development is certainly controversial. And claims that postmodern values are somehow more developed or evolved than the values of previous stages may be especially difficult for some readers to accept. Integral philosophy, however, does not claim that later appearing stages of development are absolutely better in every way. Accordingly, in chapters 5 and 9, I will carefully argue that the values of each of these historically significant worldviews are evolutionarily appropriate for a specific set of life conditions, that the accomplishments of earlier levels are prerequisite for the achievements of later appearing levels, that the core values of every worldview have a crucial and ongoing role to play within our larger culture, and that every one of these perspectives deserves consideration and respect.

But regardless of their relative position within the spectrum of cultural evolution, each of these worldviews has developed certain erroneous views of evolution that we shall do our best to avoid. Within the traditional worldview many are persuaded by the arguments of creationism, which either deny evolution altogether or claim that it can only be explained through supernatural intervention in the process. Modernism can also be dogmatic about the subject of evolution. Some modernists insist that the science of evolution proves that the universe is pointless and has thus overthrown the legitimacy of every religious outlook. Postmodernists too can sometimes have problems with evolution, uncritically accepting New Age appropriations of the subject, or otherwise buying into pseudoscientific accounts of its structure and function. Acknowledging these problems, I will attempt to transcend the limitations of each of these previous worldviews, while also including their positive contributions to our understanding of nature and history.

Again, the "developmental logic" that has formed these distinct worldviews does not represent a deterministic blueprint that all psychosocial

## Stages of Worldview Development

Historical Timeline ⟶

← Earlier
"Pre-traditional"
Worldviews

Future ⟶
"Post-postmodern"
Worldviews

| | | Traditional Worldview | Modernist Worldview | Postmodern Worldview |
|---|---|---|---|---|
| | | Faith in a higher order, black and white sense of morality, self-sacrifice for the sake of the group | Birth of reason, progress through science and technology, rise of democracy | Birth of environmentalism, multiculturalism, and a new spiritual sensitivity |
| Cultural Contributions | | ■ Sense of duty<br>■ Honors traditions<br>■ Strong faith<br>■ Focus on family<br>■ Law and order | ■ Science and technology<br>■ Meritocracy<br>■ Middle class<br>■ Belief in progress | ■ Environmental priority<br>■ Race and gender equality<br>■ Worldcentric morality |
| Examples in Culture | | ■ Traditional religions<br>■ Patriotism<br>■ Conservativism<br>■ Military organizations | ■ Corporations<br>■ Modern science<br>■ Mainstream media<br>■ Professional sports | ■ Progressive culture<br>■ Critical academia<br>■ Environmental movement |
| Types of Organization | | ■ Feudalism<br>■ Dictatorships<br>■ Bureaucracy | ■ Democracy<br>■ Corporations<br>■ Strategic alliances | ■ Democratic socialism<br>■ Consensus committees |
| Exemplary Leaders | | ■ Winston Churchill<br>■ Pope John Paul<br>■ The Dalai Lama<br>■ Billy Graham | ■ Thomas Jefferson<br>■ Charles Darwin<br>■ Thomas Edison<br>■ John F. Kennedy | ■ Mohandas Gandhi<br>■ Martin L. King, Jr.<br>■ John Muir<br>■ John Lennon |
| Potential Pathologies | | ■ Ridgedly intolerant<br>■ Dogmatic<br>■ Fundamentalist<br>■ Chauvinistic<br>■ Denies scientific truth | ■ Materialistic<br>■ Nihilistic<br>■ Unscrupulous<br>■ Selfish<br>■ Exploitive | ■ Value relativism<br>■ Narcissistic<br>■ Denies hierarchy<br>■ Dislikes modernism and traditionalism |

*Chart 1.1* Stages of Cultural Evolution

evolution is bound to follow. Nevertheless, these value structures do continue to reappear cross-culturally through time, and their existence has been established by over a century of research.2 Moreover, these stages can be seen in the development of both internal values and external economic modes of production. For example, pre-traditional societies made a living mostly through hunting, foraging, and horticulture, the economies of traditional societies are based on agriculture and trade, and modernist economies are industrial and increasingly informational. Understanding the dynamics of the *internal cultural ecosystem* that is formed by these stages of social development is a primary focus of integral philosophy. However, a full account of the subtleties and complexities of these systemic cultural structures is beyond the scope of this introductory overview. I will revisit integral philosophy's understanding of these stages of development throughout this discussion, with chapter 9 devoted to exploring the practical applications of this new *philosophical technology*.

## Overview of the Chapters

Chapter 1 describes *the new picture of evolution* that has emerged from the physical and social sciences in the last several decades. This new picture shows how evolution is not just "descent with modification" in biological species; it is actually an overarching process of *becoming* that has been affecting everything in the universe for billions of years. In other words, evolution is now understood as a universal phenomenon, one which is actively shaping the physical universe of matter-energy, the biological realm of life, and the cultural domain of human history. Chapter 1 provides a definition of evolution and then goes on to describe science's growing recognition of the phenomenon of *emergence*, which ties all forms of evolution together. The chapter concludes with a discussion of the evolution of human consciousness, where arguments are presented for why the development of consciousness is an authentic form of evolution, and how a better understanding of the evolution of consciousness provides insight into the nature of evolution overall. As we will see, it is our growing understanding of the evolution of consciousness that most clearly demonstrates the need for a new account of the evolutionary process—an account that transcends the purely materialistic explanations with which evolution has been associated from the beginning.

Chapter 2, entitled *Necessary Metaphysics for an Evolutionary Worldview,* shows how the science of evolution is inescapably bound up with a variety of philosophical interpretations regarding what is real and what can be known. After discussing how these philosophical or metaphysical interpretations influence the current science of evolution, chapter 2 extends the argument for why the emerging facts of universal evolution now require an enlarged philosophical conception of the evolutionary process. The chapter then discusses the evident yet unexplained influence of *information* and *value* on all forms of evolution, showing how these influences demonstrate that reductionistic and materialistic philosophies can no longer adequately explain the phenomenon of evolution in its fullness.

Chapter 3, *Eros—Value Gravity,* focuses specifically on the central role of values in evolution. This chapter traces the history of the idea of values and considers arguments that show how values are real entities which have an existence that is at least partially independent of our subjective perspectives. Chapter 3 explains why values are best conceived as *relational structures* that bring subject and object together in the course of seeing and being seen. The chapter then explores the way in which values exert a kind of *gravity* on evolution through their influence on consciousness. Next, the "gravity of disvalues" is briefly examined. This leads to chapter 3's concluding section, which describes evolution's dialectical pattern of development and sets the stage for our discussion of the beautiful, the true, and the good in the next chapter.

Chapter 4, *Primary Values—Beauty, Truth, and Goodness,* continues the examination of values with a discussion of the *most intrinsic* forms of value. These "primary values" have been influencing the evolution of human culture for thousands of years, even while our conception of these values themselves has evolved through a series of historically significant worldview stages. The chapter concludes by proposing that the recognition of the evolutionary efficacy of beauty, truth, and goodness provides a form of perfectly minimal metaphysics that harmonizes both the scientific truths and the spiritual truths that we are continually discovering about evolution.

Following the investigation of the role of values in evolution in chapters 3 and 4, chapter 5, *Evolutionary Progress in Human History,* and chapter 6, *Evolutionary Progress in Nature,* will cover the concept of evolutionary progress overall. Taken together, chapters 5 and 6 argue that all forms of evolution result in net progress in the long run. Although every progressive step forward brings new problems and pathologies, evolution has nevertheless managed to continuously generate value throughout the course of its unfolding—value that has built on itself and increased exponentially over billions of years. This discussion of evolutionary progress also addresses the objections to the idea that have been raised by both modernists and post-modernists, countering arguments that notions of progress in evolution result from ethnocentric biases or anthropocentric projections.

After examining progress in the evolution of human culture, progress in the evolution of life forms, and even progress in pre-biotic cosmological evolution, our consideration of progress concludes in chapter 6 with a discussion of integral philosophy's understanding of teleology. The theory of teleology presented in chapter 6 argues that evolution does not move strictly toward a pre-set goal; it is rather the creatures of evolution themselves who increasingly determine the directions of relative improvement.

Then in chapter 7, *Purpose in Evolution*, we come to the heart of our philosophical inquiry: the meaning, value, and purpose of evolution overall. This discussion shows how the purpose that we each experience in ourselves is intimately related to the purpose that produces the rising flow of creativity through which we have come to be. Chapter 7 addresses both the instrumental purpose of each level of evolution and the intrinsic purpose found within every whole entity of evolution. Although evolution is "more and better than a plan in the course of realization," this does not preclude us from finding evolution's purpose in its evident growth toward the beautiful, the true, and the good. Chapter 7 then ends with a brief discussion of how recognition of purpose in evolution can be reconciled with the presence of evil and suffering in the world.

Chapter 8, *Spiritual Reflections on Evolution's Purpose*, goes beyond the "minimal metaphysics" of the scientifically informed philosophy presented in the first seven chapters by closely considering the spiritual implications of this enlarged understanding of evolution. Chapter 8 presents an evolutionary theology that is consistent with science but nevertheless compatible with a wide variety of spiritual orientations and worldviews. This theology of emergent evolution is unpacked through *ten tenets* that follow a logical sequence. These tenets reach the conclusion that the ultimate purpose of evolution in the finite universe is to bring forth an *experiential* form of perfection—not a predetermined kind of perfection, but rather a perfection that has been directly experienced and personally chosen and achieved through the faithful travails of evolutionary free will creatures. Chapter 8 then concludes with some personal reflections on the nature of evolution's first and final causes.

Finally chapter 9, *The Promise of a New Evolutionary Worldview*, explores how this enlarged philosophical understanding of evolution leads to a new frame of reality and a *post-postmodern* ability to evaluate that transcends and includes the best of what has come before. This emerging "evolutionary worldview" provides meaningful and practical solutions to our global problems through the advent of a new kind of philosophical methodology. Chapter 9 goes on to explain how this expanded evolutionary perspective can be used to raise consciousness and build the political will necessary for the further evolution of our civilization. This discussion of the newly emerging evolutionary worldview then considers the impact this enlarged perspective may have on national and international politics.

This leads to the concluding section on evolutionary spirituality, which explains that the "spiritual teachings" of evolution are not a fixed doctrine. Our understanding of the meaning and value of our universe's ceaseless process of becoming will undoubtedly continue to deepen in the ages to come. But even now, our growing understanding of the meaning and value of evolution reveals how evolution's larger purpose can be personally experienced by each of us as the *evolutionary impulse* to make things better. And through the practice of cultivating this evolutionary impulse within ourselves, we become increasingly assured that we are spiritual beings living in a universe of ongoing spiritual growth.

• • •

THROUGH THE MOMENTOUS ACCOMPLISHMENTS of the physical sciences, we now have a relatively comprehensive picture of the history of our evolving universe. And when we view these findings of science through the lens of a philosophy that is willing and able to recognize the value of what evolution has accomplished, these facts disclose a universe of progress and purpose—a universe wherein purpose is found externally and internally, and from beginning to end. Contrary to the assertions of materialistic philosophies that seek to control the story of evolution for their own cultural purposes, the unfolding history of evolution does reveal a rising flow of value generation—a current of creativity—that moves toward ever-widening realizations of beauty, truth, and goodness. And as we come to better understand the underlying purpose of evolution, we will begin to see how this philosophical appreciation of the story of where we have come from and where we are going is not only compelling and significant in itself, this knowledge can also assist us in the task of building a more evolved form of civilization—a more compassionate, prosperous, and sustainable world that works for everyone.

# CHAPTER 1

# The New Picture of Evolution

THE FRONT LINE IN THE BATTLE over the meaning and value of evolution can often be found in the struggle over the definition of the word itself. Indeed, many of the controversies and debates that have arisen around the subject have resulted from the disputants holding slightly different definitions of evolution. Many biologists want to use the term exclusively to signify the descent with modification of organisms. But as this chapter makes clear, the phenomenon of evolution transcends biology and can now be recognized as a process that influences everything in the universe. How we define evolution, of course, is very important in our attempt to understand its deeper meaning. However, exactly what evolution is or how best to define it is not a straightforward question.

This investigation of evolution's larger significance begins by carefully defining evolution and by showing how it is a unified process that encompasses the cosmological evolution of matter, the biological evolution of organisms, and the psychosocial evolution of human consciousness and culture. After defining evolution and recounting its history as an idea, the discussion then turns to an exploration of science's growing recognition of *emergence*. Science's meta-theoretical understanding of evolutionary emergence reveals how all of evolution's various forms are tied together in a nested sequence of development that extends all the way from the big bang to our current global civilization. Recognition of the phenomenon of emergence thus reveals a new picture of evolution, overturning previous conceptions which characterized it as a mechanistic and essentially accidental process. This discussion of emergence then leads to a consideration of the evolution of human consciousness, which has demonstrated the remarkable ability to evolve beyond its biological foundations. Ultimately, it is the evolution of consciousness that refutes the claim that the overall unfolding of evolution is nothing more than a purely physical, mechanistic process with no larger meaning. Further, it is the evolution of consciousness that points most directly to the truth that this universal process is somehow being animated or activated by an underlying aim or purpose that we are only just beginning to understand.

## Defining Evolution

The English word "evolution" dates from the seventeenth century and is derived from the Latin *evolutio*, which literally means "unrolling," as in the unrolling of a parchment scroll. At the most basic level of meaning, evolution connotes *becoming*, the tendency of most forms of being to unfold and develop over time. However, it is important to distinguish between the idea of mere change or growth and the more complex process we can identify as authentic evolution. Although one might expect a clear definition of evolution to be a rather simple matter, it actually presents a thicket of conceptual problems.

By the end of the Enlightenment and the beginning of the nineteenth century many scientists and philosophers had come to realize that both living things and human society were subject to gradual development over time. It was during this period that Hegel described the unfolding development of history and Lamarck introduced his theory of the gradual modification of animal species. However, although various theories of evolution had been around for decades, it was not until 1851 (eight years before the publication of Darwin's *Origin of Species*) that the actual word "evolution" would be used as a scientific term of art by the controversial English philosopher Herbert Spencer. And notably, Spencer first employed the term to refer to the cultural evolution of human civilization rather than to biological evolution. Spencer, however, was quick to make the connection between Darwin's theory of biological evolution and the development of human institutions over time. Three years after Darwin (and Wallace) explained the process of natural selection, wherein slight variations between the offspring of organisms are selected for fitness by their environment, Spencer advanced a more general definition of evolution that encompassed both biological and cultural development: "Evolution is a change from an indefinite, incoherent homogeneity, to a definite, coherent heterogeneity; through continuous differentiations and integrations."

Spencer became one of the leading lights of the Victorian movement known as "evolutionism," which sought to link Darwin's biological theories with ideas of social progress. Although the Victorian evolutionists were apparently motivated by a genuine desire to make the world a better place, they ended up distorting the concept of evolution by employing it to justify their own ethnocentric sense of cultural superiority. This led to the rather dark theory of social Darwinism, which used the concept of "the survival of the fittest" (a phrase also introduced by Spencer) as a justification for British imperialism and colonial oppression.

These Victorian ideas of evolutionary progress in human society fell out of favor in the early part of the twentieth century as the horrors of World War I made the scientific and industrial development of Western civilization seem decidedly *regressive*. This rejection of the concept of "progress," and cultural evolution in general, was echoed in the social sciences as anthropologists such as Franz Boas condemned the idea that cultures could be ranked in a hierarchical order. Margaret Mead, Boas's most famous student, would later summarize their position: "We have stood out against any grading of cultures in a hierarchical system which would place our own culture at the top and place the other cultures of the world in a descending scale according to the extent that they differ from ours. . . . We have stood out for a sort of democracy of cultures, a concept which would naturally take its place beside the other great democratic beliefs."[1]

Yet as the idea of cultural evolution came into disrepute, the study of biological evolution thrived in the early twentieth century, achieving a major breakthrough in the 1930s when Darwinian natural selection was combined with Mendel's theories of genetic inheritance to form what became known as the "modern evolutionary synthesis." Once the idea of cultural evolution had fallen out of favor, this left the subject of evolution in the exclusive control of the biological sciences. And for most of the twentieth century, it was thought that authentic evolutionary development only occurred in the context of changes in biological organisms. Scientists accordingly developed a technical definition of evolution, which narrowed the concept so as to exclude the evolution of human history. This neo-Darwinian definition of evolution is well stated by prominent biologist Douglas Futuyama:

> Evolution . . . is change in the properties of populations of organisms that transcend the lifetime of a single individual. The ontogeny of an individual is not considered evolution; individual organisms do not evolve. The changes in populations that are considered evolutionary are those that are inheritable via the genetic material from one generation to the next. Biological evolution may be slight or substantial; it embraces everything from slight changes in the

proportion of different alleles within a population (such as those determining blood types) to the successive alterations that led from the earliest protoorganism to snails, bees, giraffes, and dandelions.[2]

Given the powerful cultural impact of the theory of evolution, it is certainly understandable that biologists would seek (perhaps unconsciously) to tightly possess and control the conceptual definition of this phenomenon. Although belief in the evolution of human history remained an accepted element of Marxist philosophy, for the first half of the twentieth century the majority of scientists held to the conviction that the subject of evolution was the exclusive province of biology. But despite the attempts of biologists to narrow the definition of evolution to changes in biological organisms, and despite the attempts of some anthropologists to discredit theories of the evolution of human history, by the mid-twentieth century the idea of cultural evolution began to be cautiously reintroduced within academic discourse. A notable landmark in the rehabilitation of this concept in the social sciences was the influential book *Evolution and Culture*, published in 1960 by a quartet of prominent anthropologists at the University of Michigan. These authors argued that the development of human culture shows more than an analogous resemblance to the evolution of life; they maintained that cultural development is in fact parallel to, and indeed *homologous* with, biological evolution.

Since the 1960s recognition of the evolution of human societies has made increasing inroads within anthropology and sociology. Although the social sciences remain fragmented, with some academics continuing to deny that culture evolves, many contemporary social theorists now acknowledge the authentic evolutionary interaction between cultures and their environment, even as they reject earlier Victorian notions of general social progress or simplistic, unilinear models of civilization's upward advance.

But despite growing academic recognition, the evolution of human history and culture remains a difficult concept for many people to accept. Those who dispute the notion of cultural evolution often point to the evident increase in threats and pathologies that inevitably accompany social development, such as disintegration of the extended family, exploitation of workers, and destruction of the environment. Other objections contend that any standard by which cultural evolution could be measured will be biased in favor of the group claiming to be more developed. These valid concerns must be addressed by anyone arguing that the evolution of human society and culture is an authentic form of evolution constituting an ongoing continuation of cosmological and biological evolution. These objections, however, are addressed in the context of the discussion of evolutionary progress in human history in chapter 5.

At the same time that the concept of cultural evolution was being gradually reintroduced to the social sciences, the physical sciences were rocked by the startling discovery that the entire universe was the product of evolution. Although the theory of the "big bang" originated in the 1930s, it was not until 1964 that the discovery of cosmic microwave background radiation confirmed that the universe was not in an "eternal steady state" as had been previously thought by the majority of scientists. And perhaps the most astonishing aspect of this discovery was the finding that the universe is less than twenty billion years old, which in cosmic terms is a very short amount of time. Since the confirmation of the big bang, the age of the universe has been continuously revised downward, with the current consensus placing the universe's age at 13.7 billion years, which is only three times older than the earth itself. These discoveries revealed that the unfolding of cosmological evolution from its primeval origins has been very rapid indeed.

Recognition of the pre-biotic evolution of the physical universe has now become a standard feature of astrophysics, with the periodic table of elements being understood as a kind of "fossil record" of cosmic evolution. Many astrophysicists, however, have tended to resist making too much of the evident connection between biological and cosmic evolution, opting to confine their investigations within their own narrow field. As of this writing there is no formal, distinct, interdisciplinary "science of general evolution" that seeks to study this overarching universe process as a macro-phenomenon. And this can perhaps be explained by the fact that the philosophical implications of universal evolution are inevitably unsettling to the contemporary academic culture of scientific materialism and reductionism. The gradual realization that everything in the universe is subject to evolution can actually be an embarrassment to the more philosophically minded materialists who are discomfited by the evidently spiritual connotations of these facts.

Some scientific materialists, however, have embraced what they refer to as the overarching *paradigm of evolution*. The emergence of this relatively new evolutionary paradigm was described in 1999 by atheistic philosopher Loyal Rue:

> Fifty years ago the only science to speak seriously about evolution was biology. But today the paradigm of evolution is rapidly becoming the organizing principle for all the sciences—the physical sciences, the life sciences and the social sciences. Astronomers, physicists, chemists, biologists, psychologists,

anthropologists—these researchers have come to recognize that they can no longer think constructively in their disciplines apart from the paradigm of evolution. The unifying insight behind this integration of the sciences is that the entire universe is evolving. The universe is a single entity—one long, sweeping spectacular process of interconnected events. The universe is not a place where evolution happens, *it is* the evolution happening. It is not a stage on which dramas unfold, *it is* the unfolding drama itself. If ever there was a candidate for a universal story, it must be this story of cosmic evolution. And it is only within the past two generations that the narrative features of cosmic evolution have come sufficiently into focus so that the story can be told.[3]

Rue's enthusiastic sentiments are, however, only representative of the relatively small minority of scientists who have paid much attention to the fact that evolution is universal. Most professional scientists have preferred in general to remain compartmentalized within their respective specialties. And this, of course, is understandable given that dealing with the "big picture" of evolution quickly becomes more philosophical than scientific. A noteworthy exception to this reluctance to recognize the universal nature of evolutionary development is systems scientist Ervin Laszlo. Laszlo has written extensively about what he characterizes as the "Grand Evolutionary Synthesis"—a holistic understanding of evolution which identifies "basic regularities that repeat and recur" across cosmological, biological, and historical forms of development, and which shows how all the domains of evolution are systemically related. However, Laszlo's penchant for holism and his affinity for progressive forms of spirituality have prevented his ideas from receiving adequate attention from the scientific mainstream.

In the humanities the accumulating scientific facts of universal evolution have given rise to the field of historical study known as *Big History*, which looks at the past across the maximum time-scale from the big bang to modernity. But this sub-discipline remains relatively obscure, being taught at only a handful of universities. In the field of philosophy itself there have been numerous, albeit sporadic, attempts to frame the significance of the big picture of evolution, with integral philosophy being the most recent. And as promised, the insights of integral philosophy are touched upon throughout this book, with a detailed discussion of its contours in chapter 9.

Returning to the thorny problem of defining evolution, we are still faced with the question: What makes the evolutionary unfolding of stars and planets, life forms, and human history, all part of the same process, despite the significant differences in their respective methods of development? Although certain scientists have attempted to identify a variety of common elements that supposedly tie together the distinct developmental domains of cosmological, biological, and cultural evolution, most of these proposed "unifying factors" have been disputed or otherwise criticized as being unscientific. For example, some scientific writers have argued that each of these evolutionary domains exhibits directional development. Other scientists, however, have argued that evolution shows no directionality and is merely a "random walk." Another popular proposal for a common element in all forms of evolution is "increasing complexity"—the idea that unfolding evolution results in forms of organization with more parts, or more complex behaviors. Yet in the realm of biology, arguments for even this seemingly obvious unifying trend have been criticized for ignoring the growth and persistence of simpler and more numerous species, such as bacteria, in favor of less numerous but more complex organisms that are more similar to humans. The recognition of increasing complexity in evolution has thus been disputed as resulting from a "sampling bias." Claims for increasing complexity in evolution have also been criticized as being too impressionistic and not subject to accurate scientific measurement. (These objections are examined in greater detail in chapter 6 in the discussion of progress in biological evolution.) So it might seem that science's search for larger, unifying themes within evolution overall has not revealed any significant common elements. There is, however, at least one clearly unifying factor that connects all the developmental events in our universe's 13.7 billion year history—from isolated atoms of hydrogen to our globalized society. And the structural connection that unites all these domains of development is the phenomenon known as *emergence*.

## Emergence and Transcendence

A remarkable feature of evolutionary history is that it has consistently produced *qualitative novelties*—entities that exhibit entirely new properties. These qualitative novelties can be distinguished from developments that result from merely the quantitative addition of new parts. For example, increasing weight is a quantitative result of the aggregation of matter, but the liquidity and surface tension that arises from the combination of hydrogen and oxygen in water molecules represents a new, qualitative feature not found in these elements in isolation. The scientific term used to describe evolution's generation of qualitative novelties is *emergence*. Biophysicist Harold Morowitz describes emergence as follows: "When the whole is greater than the sum of its parts—indeed so great that the sum far transcends the parts and represents something utterly new and different—we call that phenomenon emergence. When the chemicals diffusing in the primordial waters came together to form the first living cell, that was emergence. When the activities of the neurons in the brain result in mind, that too is emergence."4

The scientific interpretation of evolution known as *emergence theory* began in the 1920s with the work of a group of British scientists who recognized that nature consists of a nested hierarchy of ontological levels, which form a structure of encompassing envelopments, like Russian dolls. These early "emergentists" saw how evolutionary levels have arisen in a specific sequence wherein each new level depends and builds on the levels that precede it in time. For example, cells include the preexistent level of molecules, and molecules include the preexistent level of atoms. Early emergence theory showed the inadequacy of the prevailing reductionistic accounts of evolution, which sought to explain every evolutionary development as resulting exclusively from "bottom-up" microphysical causation occurring at molecular and atomic levels. Emergentists countered reductionism by pointing to various forms of "top-down" causation resulting from the influence of higher levels upon lower levels. However, although emergence theory showed great promise in its explanatory power, this branch of science was largely ignored and sidetracked from the 1930s through the 1960s because it cut against the grain of the staunch scientific materialism which prevailed in the academic culture of the period. But beginning in the 1970s, the rise of systems science and complexity theory led to the "re-emergence of emergence" as a valid form of theoretical science as researchers came to recognize the need to account for the evident fact that unpredictably novel entities continue to appear in the course of evolutionary development.

Since its rehabilitation within the scientific community the theory of emergence has increasingly revealed a new picture of evolution, which shows how cosmological, biological, and cultural forms of evolution are all part of the same process of universal development. Emergence theory reveals how these distinct types of evolution are tied together through the nested sequence of emergent developments that form a kind of ladder or chain that connects these evolutionary domains: from cosmological evolution there emerges biological evolution, and from biological evolution there emerges psychosocial evolution.

Moreover, the development of each of these macro-levels of emergent evolution themselves proceed through a series of distinct emergent steps: from the primordial matter existing shortly after the big bang there

## Emergent Structures of the Human Brain

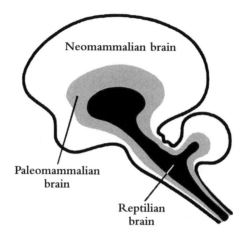

Neomammalian brain

Paleomammalian
brain

Reptilian
brain

*Figure 1.1*
The structure of evolutionary emergence embodied in the human brain
(After MacLean and Wilber)

emerges the first generation of stars, which is followed by the emergence of the heavy elements, then by solar systems and planets. As biological anthropologist Terrence Deacon describes, each new step represents "complex dynamical ensembles that spontaneously assume ordered patterns of behavior that are not prefigured in the properties of their component elements or in their interaction patterns."[5] Following this structural pattern, we can see how biological evolution also unfolds through a sequence of creative emergences: from single-celled bacteria there emerge multicellular organisms that reproduce sexually, and from these emerge vertebrates, with emergence continuing with the appearance of reptiles and then birds and mammals. This emergent sequence is embodied in our own anatomy. For example, as shown in figure 1.1, the very structure of the human brain reveals the emergence from reptiles (represented by the brain stem) to mammals (represented by the limbic system) to humans (represented by the outer encompassing complex neocortex). And this same emergent pattern is also found in the domain of cultural evolution: from hunting and gathering there emerges organized agriculture, and from feudal forms of political organization there emerges democratic forms of government.

The scientific account of emergence describes how each emergent level arises out of and *depends* on the constitutive elements and characteristics of the level below it—each level of emergence always *includes* the lower level as a foundation. Yet a truly emergent system also *transcends* the level out of which its novelty springs. This transcendence can be seen in the way emergent levels exhibit a certain amount of autonomy from the processes that underlie them. For example, we all experience the relative autonomy of our emergent minds over our physical bodies. Although our consciousness depends on the functioning of our brains, we are also aware that we possess degrees of freedom through which we transcend biological determinism. The simultaneous existence of both partial dependence and relative autonomy among evolutionary levels demonstrates how emergence achieves a balance between the new and the old—evolution builds on and uses the competencies and accomplishments of earlier appearing levels while simultaneously going beyond the limitations of these foundational levels in the quest for new evolutionary achievements. The structural sequence of emergence thus forms an interdependent hierarchy of development wherein the relationship among levels of emergence is characterized by both continuity and discontinuity.

Evolutionary biologist Peter Corning defines systemic emergence as "the arising of novel and coherent structures, patterns and properties during the process of self-organization in complex systems."[6] However, while this definition may be technically correct, it fails to convey the *radical novelty and creativity* that accompanies the appearance of an entirely new level of reality, which the most dramatic instances of emergence represent. For example, out of the "singularity" (the theoretical state of things prior to the big bang), all at once there emerges space, time, energy, matter, and the laws of physics! In other words, at first there was practically nothing, and then in an instant there was something—something very big. It doesn't get more radical than that. Similarly, during the early eons of our young planet there were originally only inorganic materials, yet somehow, life forms emerged—reproducing organisms constituting an *entirely new level of ontological being*, featuring what are arguably new natural laws and new types of causation (as explained in the next section). When you think about it, the philosophical significance of these macro-events in the history of the universe is staggering.

As noted, scientific explanations of emergence represent a distinct departure from the reductionistic approach customarily favored by most scientists. In the traditional way of doing science, one seeks to explain the phenomena being studied using the laws of a lower-level discipline: Human phenomena are explained according to the laws of biology and biological phenomena are explained by the workings of the laws of physics, with the laws of physics being understood as the fundamental basis for all scientific understanding. However, the new scientific account of the operation of emergence challenges this reductionistic, physics-based approach—not by positing the emergence of new physical substances per se, but by nevertheless recognizing higher levels of organization that cannot be reduced to lower-level explanations. Moreover, within the understanding of emergence known as *strong emergence*, these higher levels of organization result in new forms of causality—new natural laws—under which a higher level exerts *downward causation* on the level from which it emerged.

While the idea of downward causation may seem obvious from the way that we all experience the causal influence of our consciousness on our bodies (downward causation of mind upon matter), this type of causation poses difficulties for a purely physicalist description of reality. Indeed, the evident facts of emergence in natural history show how the metaphysical reality frame (materialism) that currently contains (and constrains) the academic study of evolution, as well as the larger symbolic use of the theory of evolution in our culture, can now be seen as exhausted and inadequate. Philip Clayton, a leading figure in the movement to harmonize science and spirituality, and a proponent of "emergence theology," observes:

> Emergence, then, is the hypothesis that reduction, or rather "reductionism," is false. An emergent theory of human thought and action, for example, argues that the reduction of human sciences to biology is false. A non-reductive theory of religious belief argues that the reduction of religious belief to its psycho-social functions is false. . . . Three general claims undergird emergence theory in the philosophy of science. First, empirical reality divides naturally into multiple levels. Over the course of natural history, new emergent levels evolve. Second, emergent wholes that are more than the sum of their parts require new types of explanation adequate to each new level of phenomena. Third, such emergent wholes manifest new types of causal interaction. Biological systems are not "nothing more than" microphysical interactions. Nor are the mental experiences that you are having right now "nothing but" complicated brain states. In a real and important sense, one mental state can indeed cause another.[7]

Despite its initial rejection by the scientific community, emergentist accounts of evolutionary growth have now become a central feature of the scientific discourse on evolution. We will thus use the insights of this important theory of evolutionary science as a foundation for our exploration of evolution's progress and purpose in the chapters ahead. But before moving on to the consideration of the evolution of consciousness, we cannot avoid inquiring into the underlying causes of this ubiquitous phenomenon. Again, science's growing understanding of evolutionary development shows how the structural connections produced by the pattern of transcendent yet inclusive emergence ties together both the major domains of evolution and the steps of development that occur within these domains. Yet this enlarged recognition of evolution as a universal phenomenon presents new problematic mysteries for scientists, such as: What is producing this ordering pattern of nested hierarchy? And why does evolution continue to produce qualitative novelties?

## What Causes Emergence?

Emergence *is* a scientific theory, but it is one with a lot of unanswered questions. Among these, the most obvious question is: what causes evolutionary emergence? It is debatable whether the question: "what 'caused' the big bang?" is a scientific question in the first place. This is because concepts such as cause and effect do not make much sense without space and time, which did not exist prior to the big bang. On the other hand, the question: "what caused the emergence of life?" has been the subject of intense scientific investigation for many decades. And the fact that the origin of life remains an ongoing mystery to science provides a good illustration of how the retention of materialist metaphysics now prevents scientists from getting at the larger truths of the natural world.

Throughout the twentieth century scientists thought that it was just a matter of time before they would be able to synthesize life by reproducing the conditions of the early earth. Yet despite a mammoth investment of time and resources on the project researchers remain stymied, having been unable to produce life from non-living materials. In 1988 prominent evolutionary scientist Klaus Dose concluded: "More than thirty years of experimentation on the origin of life in the fields of chemical and molecular evolution have led to a better perception of the immensity of the problem of the origin of life on Earth rather than its solution. . . . We do not actually know where the genetic information of all living things originates."8

The ongoing failure of this research program, after decades of sustained effort, is connected to science's larger failure to come to grips with the fact that life represents a new level of emergent reality. Although the *substance* of life is nothing other than matter and energy, the emergent form of organization found in living systems nevertheless results in something more. With the rise of life comes a new kind of *causation*, a force that cannot be reduced to bottom-up microphysical causation. This emergent form of causation in life is seen in the way living things *strive* to survive and reproduce. Even the most primitive forms of life *try* to survive; they actively seek to fulfill their needs and reproduce themselves. By contrast, nonliving forms of evolutionary organization do not strive or try; they do not make choices or have aims. Pre-biotic, self-organizing dynamic systems such as ocean currents or weather systems may exhibit complex behaviors, but these systems do not possess *agency*, they do not act on their own behalf. That living things strive and choose may seem commonplace or otherwise obvious, but it is important to reflect on the philosophical significance of this fact because it provides a key to understanding the meaning and value of evolution overall. And this is because with life appears the momentous emergence of *purpose*. As we will discuss further in the next chapter, the agency possessed by all living things is unmistakably purposeful—all life forms have a purpose, and can thus fail to achieve their purpose.

Darwin noted the striving of life forms in *The Origin of Species*. Describing what he called the "principle of fecundity," Darwin wrote that all living things "strive to seize on every unoccupied or less well occupied space in the economy of nature." Indeed, Darwin's theory presupposes organismal striving as a necessary precondition for the action of natural selection; because if life did not strive to fill every niche, it would produce no surplus of itself, and so there would be no competition and thus no selection. Recognizing this, ecological psychologist Rod Swenson observes that Darwin's principle of fecundity "refers precisely to the intentional dynamics of living things. . . . Darwinian theory begs a theory of intentionality; [but] it does not, and cannot, by its own definition provide one."[9] And to this day biologists have neither explained, nor adequately explained away, the intentionality possessed in increasing measure by all living things. The appearance of organismal striving and purpose can accordingly be recognized as a novel form of emergent causation that drives the evolution of life.

The evident purpose inherent in the urge to survive and reproduce shared by all forms of life might be characterized as "first-order purpose," recognizing that this urge is instinctual or semi-automatic in most animal behavior. This first-order type of purpose found in plants and animals can be contrasted with what we might call the "second-order purpose" possessed by humans. Humans not only have purposes, we have purposes for our purposes; we have relative freedom of choice regarding the urges or impetuses we want to act on and the appetites we want to resist. Moreover, humans can have purposes that require a lifetime or more to fulfill, we can have highly creative purposes, compassionate, loving purposes, and world-changing purposes that improve conditions for everyone. Just as the emergence of purpose in life forms represents a new aspect of reality that results in a new form of evolution, the emergence of self-conscious free will in humans likewise represents a new level of reality that results in a new form of evolution—the psychosocial domain of development in which the evolution of consciousness and culture transcends our biological origins.

Along with the original emergence of matter and energy in the big bang came the laws of physics, such as Newton's laws of motion, Einstein's relativity, and the laws of thermodynamics.[10] These laws, or principles of behavior, continue to hold our universe together and shape its basic character. Scientists generally do not ask where these laws come from or why they are so supremely efficient at making our universe coherent and intelligible; the laws of physics are regarded as simply fundamental. Similarly, along with the emergence of the first life forms came the uniquely biological phenomenon of agency and the purpose to survive and reproduce. This too is regarded by scientists as simply fundamental—evolutionary biologists usually do not ask why or how purpose appeared in the universe. The problems this "accidentally-on-purpose phenomenon" causes for a physicalist reality frame is well articulated by philosopher Robert Godwin:

> A huge conceptual problem for biology . . . is that it is completely organized around the paradigm of natural selection, which turns out to be metaphysically incoherent. Natural selection does not bear on the problem of Life itself, but on the origins of *species* of life. As such, orthodox biologists are committed to the view that any and all changes in life forms occur absolutely blindly, governed by chance mutations presided over by an environment which selects the winners whose genes will pass on to the next generation. At no point, according to the standard model of biology, is there a violation of any known physical principle. But whereas the ongoing evolution of life is completely random, the origin of life itself is supposedly not; rather, the origin of life is to be explained mechanistically, as an inevitable consequence of "simple downhill reactions," of underlying chemical processes. Here we are being asked to accept a stark contradiction; that is, despite no unambiguous evidence, it is assumed that life as such must be a necessary outcome of chemical properties, potentially present at the outset of the universe. But once life appears, it is then regarded as completely contingent, guided only by random, unpredictable and accidental mutations, with no purpose or necessity whatsoever. Here we are confronted with an incoherent, ad hoc metaphysical dualism of the first order. . . . It is logically impossible for a true novelty (such as life) to arise from a chemical necessity.[11]

The emergent origin of the big bang and the emergent origin of life remain mysterious. But most biologists are confident that the long series of lesser emergences (such as the appearance of vertebrates or mammals) that characterize the evolutionary appearance of new species can be fully accounted for through the accepted mechanisms of standard neo-Darwinian evolution. However, it is worth mentioning in this regard that Darwin originally introduced his explanation of natural selection through a discussion of the changes in animal forms produced by the selective breeding of dogs and livestock. Yet even after millennia of the accelerated selection of animal breeding, no viable new species has ever emerged.

But even if we accept the proposition that the emergence of radically novel species of animals can be fully explained by the gradual accumulation of random mutations selected for fitness by the changing environment, this explanation breaks down when it comes to the emergence of human consciousness and culture. The brain of anatomically modern humans appeared between 200,000 and 150,000 years ago. Yet paleontologists have discovered that the original emergence of *Homo sapiens sapiens* changed little in the fossil record in terms of tools or social practices. For several thousand generations, the culture of anatomically modern humans was virtually indistinguishable from their Neanderthal contemporaries or from previous species of hominids, such as *Homo erectus*. But sometime between 60,000 and 40,000 years ago, an extraordinary event appears in the archeological record. Known by many names, such as the "creative explosion," the "great leap forward," the "upper paleolithic revolution," and the "big bang in the mental universe," after tens of thousands of years of evolutionary stasis, there appears fine tool making, sophisticated weaponry, sculpture, cave painting, musical instruments, body ornaments, and long-distance trade. There is thus strong evidence that many of the cultural universals that distinguish humans from animals resulted from an emergence that cannot be tied to any anatomical changes in the human brain.

But even if we discount the evidence of any "great leap forward," attempting to explain the appearance of human self-consciousness through the simple methods of natural selection remains extremely difficult. As the great polymath Arthur Koestler wrote: "The evolution of the human brain not only overshot the needs of prehistoric man, it is the only example of evolution *providing a species with an organ which it does not know how to use*; a luxury organ, which will take its owner thousands of years to learn how to put to proper use—if he ever does."[12] The inadequacy of natural selection as a sufficient explanation for the emergence of humanity was previously recognized by Alfred Wallace, the nineteenth century English naturalist who co-discovered the process of natural selection. Wrote Wallace: "Natural selection could only have endowed savage man with a brain a few degrees superior to that of an ape, whereas he actually possesses one very little inferior to that of a philosopher."[13]

The mystery of the emergence of human self-consciousness provides a good illustration of how the stark facts of emergence, as they are now being faced by science, reveal a new picture of evolution which cannot be accounted for through physical forms of causation alone. That is, there is clearly more to the story than physical reactions or mechanistic processes. So in order to begin to understand the underlying causes of emergence, we need to reflect on causation itself. In fact, the idea of "causation" is inescapably philosophical. And much of contemporary philosophy's current understanding of causation can be traced back to the philosophy of the ancient Greeks.

The great Greek genius Aristotle described four essential kinds of cause, which he termed material causation, efficient causation, formal causation, and final causation. The operation of these four distinct causes, shown in figure 1.2, has been traditionally illustrated through the example of the building of a house: The *material* cause of the house is its bricks and mortar (the construction materials), and the *efficient* cause of the house is the workers who built it. These two types of straightforward causation are physical and directly observable to the senses. However, there are many cases in which material causes and efficient causes by themselves cannot provide a full account of why a given effect (in this case the house) comes to be. As Aristotle realized, a full explanation of the causes of things requires that we also recognize the causative effects of purposes—the power of plans and reasons to affect outcomes and produce results. Continuing with the example of the house, we can see that the house's *formal* cause is the plan or blueprint which served as its design, and the *final* cause of the house is that its owners needed a place to live. Science has traditionally ruled out notions of formal causes (plans or designs) or final causes (reasons or purposes) in its explanations of natural phenomena, and this strict methodological naturalism has served as an important part of the scientific method. However, as we will explore in the next chapter, as the new picture of evolution comes to be increasingly understood, it is forcing us to expand the scientific method by adopting a new metaphysical framework wherein what counts as "natural" is no longer limited to "physical."

**Aristotle's Four Kinds of Cause**

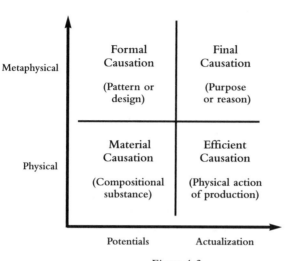

*Figure 1.2*
Four Essential Types of Causation as Described by Aristotle

Thus the fundamental question: "what causes emergence?" turns out to be a question that cannot be answered without addressing the evident operation of formal and final causes in the process. In other words, in the case of the evolutionary domain of life, and even more so in the evolutionary domain of human culture, the new picture of evolution includes the scientifically heretical idea of *purpose*. We will return to the examination of purpose in emergent evolution in chapter 7. This chapter's preliminary discussion of the new picture of evolution, however, would not be complete without an account of the evidence for the evolution of consciousness itself.

## The Evolution of Consciousness

As we have seen, there is now strong scientific consensus for the proposition that there are three major domains of evolution: cosmological, biological, and cultural. Although each of these domains unfold in different ways, we have also seen how they are all nonetheless authentic forms of evolution connected by the nested sequence of emergence that can be traced all the way back to the big bang. There is, however, a kind of evolutionary development that often goes unrecognized in discussions of the macro-picture of evolution, and this is found in the evolutionarily unique features of human consciousness. Knowledge of the methods and processes by which human consciousness evolves is central to the understanding of the meaning and value of evolution as a whole because it is in the evolution of consciousness that evolution's larger purpose is most directly revealed.

Although the concept of consciousness is easier to illustrate than define, a common sense definition of "human consciousness" includes our thoughts, feelings, intentions, values, memories, and sense of self. Our consciousness can be understood as the *inside* of our experience, what it is like to be and know ourselves; and this sentient personality, this original identity, is also the unique subjective presence through which others know us.

Among the factors that distinguish human consciousness from other kinds of animal consciousness is the fact that humans have demonstrated the ability to evolve our consciousness in ways that are partially independent of the evolution of our brains. Whatever biological evolution the brain may have gone through in the last 10,000 years, this cannot by itself account for the tremendous evolution of human consciousness during this same period. Although our bodies have changed very little, human mentality and awareness have exhibited tremendous growth and development over the course of recorded history. Indeed, one of the most profound and amazing features of human consciousness is that it can evolve in ways that are not dependent on biological evolution. Before the appearance of humans, an animal's interior mind and exterior brain evolved together in lockstep. In their natural environment, animals can only become appreciably smarter by evolving biologically. But with the advent of humans, the interior domain of consciousness is partially liberated from its biological constraints and is able to embark on the path of an entirely new type of evolution—mental, emotional, and spiritual evolution. And for the last several thousand years the sentient subjectivity of ordinary men and women has become increasingly more complex, more perceptive, more sensitive, more moral, and in many ways more free.

However, the evolution of consciousness has not been evenly distributed. In some parts of the world consciousness has developed dramatically in the last 350 years; but in other corners of the globe human awareness has changed little, being hardly distinguishable from the consciousness that prevailed in these places 1,000 years ago or more. Today, humanity's state of development remains spread out over the last 5,000 years of human cultural evolution. Even though we are all alive here at the beginning of the twenty-first century, not all of us live at the same "time in history."

Whether those who live in developed societies have minds that are "more evolved" than humans who lived in the Stone Age is certainly controversial. But there is no question that the amount and complexity of information—the sheer number of words and images—processed by the average citizen in the developed world is orders of magnitude greater than the quantity of information processed by our prehistoric ancestors. And not only are most modern humans conscious of a greater quantity of information, they are also conscious of fine distinctions of quality that would have been lost to their forebears. A modern human's sense of smell or ability to recognize animal tracks may be less than her ancestors, but her ability to discriminate the myriad types of experience available today is unquestionably more complex—her access to food, music, art, media, travel, and technology give her a range and degree of choices that are significantly greater than those available to people who lived in prehistoric times. Further, the enlarged perspectives available to moderns result in increased powers of perception. For example, unlike our ancient ancestors, who perceived the rising of the sun as a miraculous event requiring the intervention of the gods, through science modern humans can now perceive the rising of the sun as the result of the turning of the planet.

In addition to this, educated moderns have a conceptual ability that is not found in tribal peoples; moderns are able to think about themselves and their society from enlarged perspectives that are usually not found in Stone Age cultures. Numerous studies involving extensive interviews with contemporary indigenous tribal peoples confirm that their thinking and perceiving is largely "representational"; that the words they use can usually only match individual objects, not entire categories or larger, more general types of phenomena.[14] This research indicates that the consciousness found in most tribal peoples is not ordinarily capable of thinking in syllogisms or logical types. Comparisons between objects are generally made on the basis of physical attributes, with functional or conceptual similarities being largely ignored. This research does not suggest that there are any biological or racial differences between peoples who live "in different times in history," but it does provide evidence that there are significant, detectable differences in the development of their respective forms of consciousness.

The reason why human consciousness can evolve over time is explained by the simple fact that, unlike other animals, humans can evolve their culture.[15] As described by neuropsychologist Merlin Donald:

> Human beings are cognitive hybrids, tethered to both biology and cultural environment. Another way of phrasing this is that humans were the first

species to evolve a truly "distributed" cognitive system, that is, a system in which thought and memory are carried out in a community of minds. In a network, individuals are joined to a larger cognitive architecture that can have powers (e.g., deep memory resources and diverse expertise) that are not available to single individuals. Networks can also serve as generators of novel and powerful cognitive tools (e.g., languages, instruments, and symbolic notations). Languages in particular are network-level phenomena.[16]

As Donald's analysis suggests, human consciousness is bound up with human culture—when humans evolve their culture through new agreements or new forms of organization, this results in a corresponding growth in human consciousness. Through the "network effect" of cultural transmission, when one person has a conceptual breakthrough or new realization, this advance can be shared with others. And as new discoveries or new skills are adopted within a larger cultural context, such advances become refined and reinforced.

However, it is important to understand that culture does not evolve by itself—culture and consciousness co-evolve together. The sustainable evolution of a new level of human civilization almost always requires correlating evolution in the underlying forms of consciousness that correspond to that cultural level. Although the artifacts or technologies of more advanced cultures can often be effectively learned and used by people living in less developed levels of culture, the ability to actually produce such technologies usually remains beyond the powers of such earlier levels.

Yet the co-evolution of human consciousness and culture proceeds by more than the simple accumulation of greater knowledge or more learned skills; the development of civilization also depends on the evolution of values. Over the course of recorded history, *human nature itself* has evolved through the series of values-based worldview stages first described in the introduction. For example, as a result of the emergence of new value systems, the human value of morality has evolved so as to encompass larger and larger estimates of the scope of those worthy of moral consideration—from the tribe, to the nation, to the world, and eventually to all sentient beings.

But again, because consciousness and culture necessarily co-evolve together, the evolutionary efficacy of the emergence of higher values in individuals depends on the corresponding existence of cultural structures to provide the agreements and social contexts wherein such higher values can make a difference. For instance, even if values such as liberty and equality are held by many individuals in a given culture, without democratic forms of government and the rule of law, these personally held values cannot create a just society by themselves. Conversely, the lack of values development within the consciousness of individuals can prevent or retard progress within their larger culture. This can be seen in the case of many developing nations—where higher education and the accompanying modernist values of personal achievement and individual initiative are scarce, attempts to develop modernist economic systems often result in failure, despite significant outside investment. The dismal success record of developmental aid efforts in the twentieth century demonstrates that the existence of a certain degree of *modernist consciousness* is a necessary prerequisite for the development of first world economies.

However, before resting in the conclusion that consciousness and culture co-evolve together, I must address the distinction between the idea of individual development—the growth of a person's mind and character over the course of their lifetime—and evolution proper, which according to some theorists requires multiple generations before it can be counted as authentic evolution. Under this multi-generational definition, one could argue that cultures may *evolve* but individuals themselves merely grow or develop more or less within their respective cultures. Perhaps this is just a matter of semantics. There are, however, some very bright people within the field known as developmental psychology who do recognize the growth of individual consciousness as an authentic form of evolution.

## Developmental Psychology

Developmental psychology is the branch of social science that deals most directly with the evolution of consciousness. This field of study began with the pioneering work of American psychologist James Mark Baldwin at the turn of the previous century. But the twentieth century's most famous and influential development psychologist was Jean Piaget, whose vast body of empirical research into human cognitive development now serves as a foundation for the field. Piaget's research has been carried forward and expanded by several generations of developmental psychologists, and after over a century of investigation there is now broad consensus among developmentalists that the psychological growth of individuals, from childhood into adulthood, proceeds through a series of cross-cultural "major stages" of evolutionary development. Piaget identified these universal stages of development as "sensorimotor, preoperational, concrete operational, and formal operational." And while the opinions of contemporary developmental psychologists often differ as to the specific contours or definitions of these stages, the basic fact that psychological growth involves major stages of development is usually not disputed.

Each of these major stages of cognitive growth provides a kind of developmental "center of gravity" that generally serves to orient a person's overall psychology and outlook. Yet it is important to emphasize that despite the overarching influence of these major developmental stages, human consciousness has also been found to develop along a variety of trajectories. That is, in addition to their recognition of general levels or overall stages of consciousness, developmental psychologists have now discovered a wide variety of "developmental lines" within the human mind. Within this branch of psychology, a line of development is defined as an aspect or capacity of consciousness with a distinct trajectory of growth that can develop with a degree of independence from other components of the mind.

For example, distinct developmental lines in consciousness include ego or self-sense, cognitive reasoning, moral reasoning, linguistic ability, and interpersonal skills. Developmental psychologists have demonstrated that the growth of consciousness is more than just the accumulation of knowledge or experience. These researchers have shown how consciousness can grow in a wide variety of cognitive and emotional dimensions. However, although different aspects of consciousness can grow at different rates, the general development of a person's consciousness can be either significantly helped or greatly hindered by the major stage or level which serves as the center of gravity or "psychic location" for that person overall. In other words, even though developmental psychologists have identified a variety of distinct lines of growth, the mental growth most often recognized as authentic "evolution" is development that involves a transcendence from one major stage of consciousness to another.

This conclusion stems from the observation that the major stages of individual psychological development show a loose correspondence with the series of distinct ages or eras that have marked the development of human history. That is, the evolution of both consciousness and culture generally proceed through the same general stages of development. Harvard developmental psychologist Robert Kegan, for example, characterizes these stages of human development as "evolutionary truces," or symbolic constructions of subject/object relations, which have arisen in history and which come to define reality for those who participate in a given stage. Developmentalists often point to the Enlightenment as the most obvious example of a distinct emergent stage in the evolution of culture which corresponds to an identifiable structure within consciousness (Piaget's formal operational stage), and which continues to be used by individuals to make meaning in the present. The Enlightenment resulted in a new way of thinking and knowing that we now identify as the modernist worldview. And today, contemporary modernism is recognized as a distinct stage of both consciousness and culture that can be clearly distinguished from the traditional worldview, which precedes modernism in both history and in the sequence of an individual's psychological evolution.

The existence of an evolutionary *recapitulation* between the development of a single individual and the development of its species as a whole was originally posited in biology by Victorian zoologist Ernst Haeckel. Haeckel coined the phrase "ontogeny recapitulates phylogeny" to describe the way human embryos appear to pass through the stages of the entire biological tree of life as they develop in the womb. Modern biologists now reject the literal and universal version of Haeckel's theory, but many (including prominent biologist Stephen Jay Gould) nonetheless acknowledge that a loose correspondence between the development of the "onto" and the "phylo" can indeed be found. Literal or strict interpretations of the onto/phylo parallel have also been criticized in the assessment of psychological development, but a large body of scientists and philosophers nevertheless continue to recognize that there is a connection.

The widely respected social philosopher Jürgen Habermas has used the evident "homologies" between psychological and historical development as the basis for his moral philosophy. Habermas takes great care in distinguishing his understanding of these onto/phylo homologies from the more naive and fallacious interpretations of earlier theorists. He nonetheless finds that culture and consciousness do generally progress by employing what he calls the same *developmental logic*. According to Habermas, "If one examines social institutions and the action competencies of socialized individuals for general characteristics, one encounters the same structures of consciousness. . . . All provisos notwithstanding, certain homologies can be found."[17]

The point here is that even though individual development and cultural evolution are not identical, the developing mind does reveal patterns in its unfolding, and these patterns resonate with the historical unfolding of culture that occurs on an evolutionary time scale. And, as we have seen, what ties all forms of evolution together is the phenomena of emergence, which can be clearly recognized in the development of human history. As noted, dramatic forms of cultural emergence can be traced all the way back to the paleolithic great leap forward 40,000 years ago. Evolutionary emergence can also be recognized in the appearance of agriculture and writing; it can be seen in periods of cultural florescence such as the widespread religious and philosophical awakening of the fifth century B.C.; and it occurs again during the European Renaissance and subsequent Enlightenment. And as these forms of evolutionary transcendence appear in culture, they simultaneously occur in consciousness.

Yet these dramatic periods of historical emergence are not just past events, they continue to exist in the present as stable worldviews—distinct cultural agreement structures, also referred to as "natural epistemologies" or "evolutionary truces"—that persistently shape both the spectrum of evolving human consciousness and the contours or our contemporary culture. Thus, once we begin to see that as each individual grows up from childhood, their path of development roughly recapitulates the cultural evolution of human history, this provides evidence that the growth of human consciousness is an authentic form of evolution in the universe.

Here it is worth reemphasizing that the evolution of consciousness is not simply a matter of maturation into adulthood; mental evolution by stages has been shown to continue in the development of adult consciousness. When a person adopts a new worldview and thus transfers her allegiance to a form of culture that is more developed than the one in which she may have been raised, she is participating in a form of emergence that constitutes real evolution. For example, if through religious conversion a person raised in a tribal setting exchanges a pre-traditional worldview for a traditional worldview, she is reenacting an evolutionary emergence that first occurred several thousand years ago. Continuing the example, if as a result of higher education, a person raised in a conservative religious culture exchanges her traditional worldview for a modernist worldview, this too is a form of emergence that represents the authentic evolution of consciousness.

However, evolving one's consciousness by participating in a larger cultural emergence need not be limited to reenacting the already existing advances of history. As discussed in chapter 9, we are witnessing a novel cultural emergence in our own time. The enlarged understanding of evolution embodied in the integral perspective is emerging as part of a larger, historically significant new worldview—one which provides a real opportunity for the further evolution of human consciousness and culture.

For some, the evolution of consciousness is obvious, but for others the notion that the consciousness of certain people is more evolved than others may at first seem troubling. Those who object may argue that "people are people" and human nature does not change, so even though some of us may have more relative knowledge or experience, we're all *Homo sapiens* and thus we're all at the same level of evolution. Moreover, objectors may argue that any criteria by which we might try to judge the relative scale of evolution in consciousness will be subjectively biased. Some may also contend that estimates of relative "progress" between human individuals or groups are both offensively condescending and inevitably ethnocentric.

Yet from the perspective of integral philosophy these egalitarian concerns are, ironically, actually evidence for the evolution of consciousness. This new philosophical understanding of evolution recognizes that our estimates of what counts as progress are themselves progressing. And the postmodern rejection of ethnocentric estimates of cultural superiority is, in fact, a progressive step forward. But as explored in subsequent chapters, while the rise of cultural relativism in academia served to remedy many of the hubristic pathologies of traditionalism and modernism, taking this viewpoint to the extreme can result in an opposite kind of pathology. The progressive thinking that sees how no value system is final or absolute can end up falling into a kind of value paralysis, becoming blind to comparative excellence. However, the discussion of the limitations of relativism will be saved until chapter 5. There we will see how integral philosophy provides a path beyond strict cultural relativism, rehabilitating our hope for a better world through an understanding of progressive evolution that carefully includes but also transcends the postmodern perspectives which deny that some forms of consciousness and culture are more evolved than others.

The developed world has indeed made important moral strides by discrediting the ethnocentric perspectives that once colored its understanding of less developed peoples. And these multicultural sensibilities have come to inform the field of developmental psychology, even as it seeks to understand the evolution of consciousness. Robert Kegan is especially sensitive to these issues, writing:

> [Developmental psychology] tells a story of increase, or greater complexity. [It is] thus more provocative, discomforting, even dangerous, and appropriately evokes greater suspicion. Any time a theory is normative, and suggests that something is more grown, more mature, more developed than something else, we had better check to see if the distinction rests on arbitrary grounds that consciously or unconsciously unfairly advantage some people (such as those who create the theory and people like them) whose own preferences are being depicted as superior. We had better check whether what may even appear to be an 'objective' theory is not in reality a tool or captive of a 'ruling' group (such as white people, men, Westerners) who use the theory to preserve their advantaged position.[18]

# CHAPTER 2

# Necessary Metaphysics for an Evolutionary Worldview

THE DISCOVERY OF EVOLUTION HAS PROVEN to be extremely useful for the advancement of science, and for the advancement of other forms of human knowledge as well. But among all the uses of evolutionary theory, arguably the most useful application can be found in its central role in replacing the false metaphysics of traditional creationist explanations with an empirical account of human origins. Therefore, the idea that scientific descriptions of evolution are somehow in need of metaphysics may strike some as a conceptual contradiction. But as we will explore in this chapter, empirical systems cannot stand alone in isolation; every empirical system of explanation necessarily employs certain kinds of metaphysics in both its foundational presumptions, and in the process of its investigations.

For many, the word "metaphysics" connotes New Age or occult beliefs, yet the term is more accurately defined as the branch of philosophy that examines the nature of reality. This category of philosophical investigation can be traced all the way back to the pre-Socratic Greek philosophers. But the first formal exposition of the subject can be attributed to Aristotle, who referred to this line of inquiry as "First Philosophy." And we can see in these ancient Greek origins how metaphysics has been intimately related to science from the beginning. Notwithstanding the important contributions of Plato and other early Greek philosophers, who advanced a kind of proto-science through their questions about the constitution of the world, Aristotle is arguably the original father of Western science. That is, one could argue that the empirical study of nature really began with the *Physics*, Aristotle's great scientific treatise. Yet Aristotle was more than a scientist; his thinking and writing primarily concerned matters that we would now identify as entirely philosophical and even spiritual.

Following his teacher Plato, Aristotle's explorations went beyond inquiries regarding the physical world into what he called "the knowledge of immaterial being." And this line of Aristotle's thought would later be identified by his followers as *metaphysics*, which literally means "that which comes after, or goes beyond physics." Thus, from the beginning, the category of human knowledge known as metaphysics has been defined as that which falls just outside the border of science, and this shows how the subject of metaphysics is related and connected to science. Metaphysics, however, is not anti-science. Rather, it *frames* science and provides interpretation and contextualization for scientific investigation. As Aristotle and his Greek forebears clearly recognized, there is more to the world than physics, and the rational investigation of what can be known about that which is *extra-physical* has been an important aspect of human knowledge ever since.

This chapter briefly recounts the development of the subject of metaphysics since its origin in the ancient world. It then examines how metaphysics remains woven together with the study of evolution as it is currently understood by mainstream science. Next, it considers the possibility of a more comprehensive approach to the subject of science-based evolutionary metaphysics. This leads to a discussion of the influence of *information*, and the influence of *value* on evolution. These evident, yet nonetheless "extra-physical" influences affect evolution in unmistakable ways, and thus demonstrate the need for an expanded scientific framework that can account for the causal power of these realities.

## The Evolution of Metaphysics

Although metaphysics is an ancient and venerable branch of human understanding, the field did not fare well in the twentieth century. For at least the last hundred years, one of the chief pursuits of professional philosophy has been the attempt to do away with metaphysics all together. As described by philosopher John Heil:

> In the English-speaking world, metaphysics was deflated by neo-Kantians, logical positivists, logical empiricists, as well as by philosophers who regarded the study of ordinary language as a fitting replacement for traditional philosophical pursuits. Elsewhere, philosophers promoting phenomenology, hermeneutics, and existentialist and deconstructionist creeds showed themselves equally disdainful of tradition. Metaphysical talk was replaced by talk about metaphysical talk; concern with conceptual schemes and patterns of ontological commitment supplanted concern with ontology.[1]

However, it eventually became obvious to many that one could not denounce metaphysical philosophy without appealing to a version of metaphysics in the course of making such a denunciation. In other words, even the most anti-metaphysical forms of philosophy could nonetheless be shown to be relying on a form of metaphysics in their arguments. As deconstructionist philosopher Jacques Derrida observed: "There is no sense in doing without the concepts of metaphysics in order to shake metaphysics. We have no language—no syntax and no lexicon—which is foreign to this history; we can pronounce not a single destructive proposition which has not already had to slip into the form, the logic, and the implicit postulations of precisely what it seeks to contest."[2]

Futile attempts to do away with metaphysics of every kind have produced a variety of definitional errors, including: 1) the identification of the general category of metaphysical knowledge with a particular type of metaphysical system; 2) the equating of metaphysics with pre-scientific thinking; 3) the conflation of metaphysics and ideology; and 4) the assertion that all metaphysical sentences are meaningless. But despite the vigor with which this category of knowledge has been assaulted, the fact remains that some form of metaphysics is indispensible to human thought. When we distinguish between general and particular, when we hold another person responsible for their actions, when we expect that the universe is intelligible and that truth can be known, and when we assume that our beliefs about the world have some relation to a reality which is at least partially independent of those beliefs, we are using metaphysics. The truth is that we can no more get away from metaphysics than we can get away from the concept of the real. Even if we hold that there can be no valid questions or answers about what is real, we are nevertheless employing a metaphysical thesis in the holding of this opinion.

For the vast majority of people, the most immediate and familiar use of metaphysical principles is in the often unconscious construction of what is known as a categorical framework or reality frame. Almost every human being organizes her beliefs around certain axioms through which she can determine what is true, what is good, and what is beautiful. These categorical frameworks are rarely "home-grown"; reality frames are most often contained within historical worldviews that are received from one's family and the larger society. Moreover, we can observe how reality frames or worldviews have developed in history through the series of steps or stages we have discussed. For example, in pre-literate, indigenous or tribal cultures, animistic or magical worldviews are often used to frame reality.

In traditional cultures reality is framed by scripture and the mythology of a particular religion. In modernist culture reality is largely framed by the explanations of science, which are occasionally supplemented by existentialist or atheistic philosophies. And now, we can even recognize a postmodern worldview, in which the truth about reality could be characterized as "whatever is true for you."

Although it is not always obvious, each worldview structure accomplishes its role of building cultural agreement and social solidarity by using metaphysics to explain what is real and what is valuable. Indeed, historically significant worldview structures are most often inaugurated through metaphysical breakthroughs. Practically all the world's great religions began with the new revelation of a prophet or seer; and all of these revelations assert a version of metaphysics. Similarly, the subsequently appearing modernist worldview was also originally framed largely by Rene Descartes' dualistic insights regarding the objective and subjective nature of reality. In fact, it is generally agreed by historians that the advent of Cartesian metaphysics was an essential factor in the development of science and the ascendency of the West.

Yet the metaphysics that originally gave birth to the modernist worldview came under attack by practically every school of twentieth century philosophy. This eventually resulted in the field of philosophy being plagued by the lack of any coherent agreement about what was real or what could be known. Although the battle over the fate of metaphysics is still raging in academia, one point of agreement can increasingly be found regarding the inadequacy of what has been termed "naive realism" or the "myth of the given"—the presumption that an "outside observer" can know reality "as it is." In other words, one of the accomplishments of late-modern philosophy was the demonstration that a knowing subject always imparts characteristics to the object being known. Every perception of "reality" is therefore always partially constructed by the perspective of the observer. It was through this insight that the concept of a pre-given, independent ontology was deconstructed, as philosophers demonstrated that all assessments of reality are inevitably colored by culture-bound interpretations, or by the intrinsic limitations of human cognition. But perhaps predictably, this "constructivist" approach was taken to extremes by some postmodern philosophers who sought to undermine every theory of reality and the veracity of every worldview. Yet these radical deconstructionist philosophies were themselves undermined in the way that their staunch denial of all "truth" denied the very possibility of the truth of their own statements.

Recently, however, some thinkers have tried to transcend philosophy's metaphysical muddle by attempting to steer a path between the "myth of the given" on one side, and what philosopher of science Karl Popper has called the "myth of the framework"—the assumption that reality is arbitrarily constructed by the observer—on the other side. These thinkers recognize that we are both finders and makers of reality.

In this chapter's examination of the metaphysics that is necessarily implied by the new picture of evolution we discussed in chapter 1, we must keep in mind that the definition of metaphysics is itself evolving. And this requires us to hold onto the concept of metaphysics very loosely, recognizing that "every attempt to define metaphysics is itself dependent upon a metaphysics, so that every definition of metaphysics as well as every metaphysical question is itself circular."[3] For example, within the modernist worldview, metaphysics is defined as "that discipline which addresses the question of what is reality." But from a postmodern perspective we can see how the very structure of this modernist definition presupposes a strict separation of the knower, who is asking: "what is?" and the object to be known: "reality." Postmodern philosophers might reformulate this definitional question as: "what can I know of the reality I am apparently knowing?" But this only begs the question. Perhaps we can find some relief in the humorous definition of metaphysics advanced by F.H. Bradley as: "the finding of bad reasons for what we believe upon instinct."[4] So even though the concept of metaphysics is subject to a variety of definitions, we will use the term broadly to refer to the aspects of reality that are "extra-physical," or otherwise beyond the physical realm.[5]

In light of these considerations, it bears repeating that despite the paradoxical and partially circular nature of metaphysics, and despite the fact that metaphysical systems are inevitably bound-up with historically situated worldview structures, there is no getting away from metaphysics. Although the definition of metaphysics is a moving target, estimates of what is true and what is real remain essential for the advancement of human knowledge. Although we now know that reality is not *simply given*, this does not mean that reality has been *taken away*. Despite the difficulties, we *can* continue to use philosophy to expand our knowledge of our selves and the universe. And as I am arguing, an important key to the growth of our overall understanding of the world can be found within the subject of evolution. So if we want to advance our knowledge about the "reality" of evolution, if we want to achieve a deeper understanding of evolution's facts, meanings, and values, we must recognize that despite the "mobility of the real," progress in truth is still possible.

As we have seen, over the last 150 years, science has gradually revealed the staggering fact that everything in the universe is subject to one kind of evolution or another. And as both the grand scope and minute details of this evolutionary picture now loom into view, we are faced with the challenge of devising a new metaphysical frame that can adequately hold these facts. This new metaphysical framework need not go entirely beyond the bounds of science; rather, it needs to carefully and modestly expand the bounds of science so as to better account for what we can now see. So keeping this general and preliminary discussion of metaphysics in mind, we turn to a more specific consideration of how metaphysics is employed by science in its current description of the facts of evolution.

## How Metaphysics Is Used in the Science of Evolution

The theory of evolution in all its forms has always been a combination of science and metaphysics. However, this is not a criticism of evolutionary theory, because it really couldn't have been otherwise. In fact, the enterprise of science as a whole depends on an orientation to truth and a commitment to make things better that are grounded in metaphysical premises. For example, all science is founded on faith in reason, logic, and the conviction that the universe is intelligible. Scientists necessarily proceed on the premise that the truth about nature can be discovered and reliably known, and that what is true in our part of the universe is true throughout the universe. Scientists also presume that their minds can be dependably used to investigate the reality of the world, and that their sense perceptions provide accurate descriptions of the subjects of their inquiries. Science also rests on the *a priori* principle that mathematics is real and can be used to model and describe physical reality. Indeed, the presumption that matter itself is real is ultimately metaphysical.

We can also detect the use of metaphysics in the way scientists rely on the premise that scientific knowledge is a good in itself. This faith in the value of scientific truth is connected to the conviction that humanity will be benefited by science's free inquiry and progressive discovery of the truth about the universe. Similarly, the longing for greater perfection in knowledge and the hunger for discovery that motivates most scientists are also grounded in a metaphysical premise regarding the very possibility of increasing perfection. All of these foundational value assumptions thus generally presuppose a transcendent ground of ultimate value or goodness.

Beyond these specific uses of metaphysics, we can also see how the vast enterprise of science itself is supported and sustained by the metaphysics of the modernist worldview, which originally gave rise to the notion of an objective reality that could be progressively discovered using scientific methods. Prior to the advent of modernism, it did not generally occur to people that carefully controlled experiments or empirical investigations might yield greater understanding of the natural world. For example, the basic act of cutting open a cadaver to learn about the human body for the advancement of medicine was abhorrent to premodern sensibilities. Thus, the very activity of scientific investigation is a product of the modernist reality frame, which firmly rests on the metaphysical foundations of the Enlightenment.[6] Without these forms of foundational metaphysics, science would be impossible. And it is worth saying here that I am in firm agreement will all of the general metaphysical principles stated above.

However, when we examine the metaphysics that is bound up with the theory of evolution, we find assumptions about reality that are far less inspiring. Today, the "experts" on evolution generally recognized by mainstream academia and the corporate media are a closely-knit group of scientists known as "neo-Darwinists." Neo-Darwinists are firmly committed to the metaphysical principle that, like physics, biological evolution is essentially a mechanistic process that can be completely explained using reductionistic methods. For example, neo-Darwinists hold that macroevolution (major transitions in species or taxa) is to be understood entirely by the processes involved in microevolution (accumulation of variations in populations). Douglas Futuyama, for instance, declares that "the known mechanisms of evolution [provide] both a sufficient and necessary explanation for the diversity of life."[7] Although it has never been proven as a matter of scientific fact, contemporary neo-Darwinists insist that the mechanisms of random genetic variation and the genetic drift of allele frequency, coupled with environmental filtering, can account for practically all forms of biological evolution. Moreover, neo-Darwinists maintain that genetic variations must always be completely random and can never be directed toward an advantageous mutation. Process philosopher David Griffin writes:

> This doctrine that mutations are random [in the non-advantageous sense] is important to Darwinists for several reasons: The idea that the organism's purposes could influence evolution would contradict the ideal of making biology a purely mechanistic, deterministic science. Also, the idea that purposes

could give a bias to genetic mechanisms seems impossible to most Darwinists. (Richard Dawkins, for example, says that "nobody has ever come close to suggesting any means by which this bias could come about.") And, perhaps most important, the idea that variation is somehow directed toward adaptation would reduce the importance of the central Darwinian conception, natural selection. . . . We do know that some mutations are caused by cosmic rays; but we do not know that *all* mutations are due to these or analogous causes. Many neo-Darwinists, nevertheless, express great confidence in the truth of this speculation—a confidence that, in light of the number of confidently held ideas that have in the past turned out to be false, is somewhat awe-inspiring. For example, Jacques Monod, argues that random mutations "constitute the *only* possible source of modifications in the genetic text," so that "chance *alone* is at the source of every innovation, of all creation in the biosphere."[8]

This insistence on the "scientific reality" of something that has not been proven is a clear example of how metaphysics and science are frequently mixed together. Similar examples of reality-framing metaphysical assumptions can be found in evolutionary science's commitment to the philosophical doctrine of *nominalism*, which insists that there can be no forms, archetypes, or preexisting information involved in the process of development. Despite the facts of *convergent evolution*, wherein evolutionary solutions are repeated almost exactly in different evolutionary categories or phyla, the experts are adamant that the mysterious process of organismal development (morphogenesis) cannot involve any kind of "morphic fields" or nonphysical inputs or influences.

Related to this metaphysical commitment to the exclusivity of physical causation is the premise that evolution must always proceed gradually through a step-by-step accumulation of minute changes. This gradualism is essential for neo-Darwinist accounts of evolution. Darwin himself wrote: "If it could be shown that any complex organ existed, which could not possibly have been formed by numerous, successive, slight modifications, my theory would absolutely break down."[9] The fossil record in Darwin's time contained few transitional types, but in the last 150 years abundant transitional species have been discovered. Yet even as the fossil record has been filled in, enough gaps remain that theories such as "punctuated equilibrium" are still needed to explain transitions at the species level. Moreover, paleontologists have found that "once a species appears in the fossil record, it tends to persist with little appreciable change throughout the remainder of its existence."[10] This finding underscores that at some point in the appearance of every major new form or evolutionary innovation, significant novelty enters the universe. In other words, evolutionary scientists now agree that *emergence* is a ubiquitous characteristic of biological evolution, and emergence by definition signifies that there has been a jump or a surge—that something more has come from something less.

Thus, when we face the facts of evolutionary emergence, we can begin to see that the underlying assumption that evolution must *always* occur randomly through tiny steps and without the influence of any "outside information" is not a scientific fact, but rather a commitment of faith held for the sake of the consistency of the theory. Unproven theoretical conclusions in science do not necessarily amount to metaphysical premises, but when these theoretical conclusions contradict the weight of evidence and are held primarily because they preserve *a priori* metaphysical commitments to materialism, they are more metaphysical than scientific.

Among the many philosophical principles used in the evolutionary sciences, perhaps the most radically metaphysical of all is the assertion that evolution is not progressive and indeed pointless. Today, it appears that the majority of biologists think that evolution does not progress, and that the development of species over time is merely a "random walk." Stephen Jay Gould went so far as to call the idea of progress in evolution "noxious," maintaining that there are no criteria by which improvement could be measured. Gould wrote: "If an amoeba is as well adapted to its environment as we are to ours, who is to say that we are higher creatures?"[11] And despite the basic moral intuition shared by most people that a dolphin or an elephant is "higher" (and thus worthy of greater moral consideration) than an ant or a bacterium, Gould's repudiation of the notion of evolutionary progress is accepted by many biologists without question. This "scientific proposition" can be found not only within the field of biological evolution, it is also echoed by cosmologists. In an oft-quoted passage, Nobel Laureate in physics, Steven Weinberg, writes: "The more the universe seems comprehensible, the more it also seems pointless." But by this stage of our discussion, I hope it is obvious that science has not "proven" that evolution is unprogressive, let alone pointless. These pessimistic assertions are based on the philosophy of *scientism*—the materialistic belief system that has become an embedded feature of the institutional culture of science.

The discussion of evolutionary progress will continue in chapters 5 and 6. The point to be emphasized here is that within the academic study of evolution, including cosmological, biological, and cultural evolution, the metaphysics of the scientific worldview plays a major role in determining the boundary conditions under which evolution can be studied or even understood. These metaphysical commitments are for the most part unconscious, and thus they are usually held uncritically. And because the metaphysics of the modernist, scientific worldview is generally *received* by scientists in the course of their training and held unconsciously, this metaphysics is passed on to others far more readily by insinuation rather than by direct argument. Despite the fact that the metaphysics of the modernist worldview has been severely questioned by professional philosophers, professional scientists continue to use this reality frame as a definitional container for the institutional study of evolution.

However, from an integral perspective, modernist metaphysics is not "all wrong," as some postmodern philosophers contend. The naturalistic spirit of the scientific enterprise has been responsible for many of science's greatest achievements. Integral philosophy thus seeks to include the advantages of methodological naturalism within its purview, even as it transcends the limitations of scientific materialism. As we look at the history of science we can see how the various philosophies of materialism and positivism have served the important function of cleansing our thinking about nature by ridding it of superstition and all kinds of fallacious assumptions. In a world that was once dominated by traditional consciousness and state-sponsored religious political authority, mechanistic materialism served as the protective shell out of which the "chick" of science could be born. But now the chick is hatched and science has become the new politically empowered authority on the truth. And this has resulted in the accompanying metaphysics of scientism becoming a new kind of state-sponsored belief system, used by materialists as a quasi-religious power base in academia and the mainstream media.

As we have seen, there is no getting around metaphysics—if we want to investigate reality we must have a categorical framework with which to organize both our investigations and our findings. Historically, the metaphysics of materialism served science well because it was the most minimal form of metaphysics available. Scientists wanted to get at the bare facts, and it was presumed that a philosophy of materialism would interfere the least in their apprehension of these facts. However, scientists adopted materialist metaphysics not only because it seemed to interfere least with the process of getting at the facts. In practice, the primary use of materialistic accounts of evolution was found in their symbolic role of overcoming the cultural power of traditional religious worldviews. Throughout the nineteenth and twentieth centuries the theory of evolution was used as an effective tool for recruiting people into the modernist worldview because it provided a creation story that was more rational and more satisfying than Biblical, or other scriptural accounts. Thus, despite its abundant utility for science, the theory's greatest power was found in its ability to produce *cultural evolution*. As Stanford scholar Robert Wesson observes: "Darwinism became the banner of those who would overthrow what they saw as an irrational, superstitious view of human origins. . . . The theory of evolution became the focus of the confrontation of science and religion."[12]

However, as a result of their ongoing battle with Christian fundamentalists, ironically, many scholars of evolution have themselves become "Darwinian fundamentalists." Wesson continues:

> The faith that all things can be attributed to analyzable material causation is, in the end, only a faith like more candid faiths. The contention that reality consists of only material particles and their modes of interaction is not even a clear-cut theory. . . . But are the laws of nature not real? Are mathematical theorems real? Are patterns real? Are thought and consciousness? It is paradoxical to deny their essentiality, for science could not exist without them.[13]

In the last decade or so, some biologists have begun to question the strict doctrines of neo-Darwinism, which insist that random changes in genes selected by a changing environment provides a sufficient explanation for practically all forms of biological evolution. These more open-minded biologists have begun to see that evolution is a multi-level process of co-evolution that occurs between genes and ecosystems. These scientists recognize additional evolutionary mechanisms besides natural selection, such as group selection, symbiosis, and horizontal gene transfer. Within this vein, the recent reintegration of developmental biology (which studies the growth of individual organisms) with evolutionary biology has led to the new field known as evolutionary developmental biology (referred to in the literature as "evo-devo"). Discoveries in the field of evo-devo have shown how vast differences in organismal forms can arise from the same set of genes through variation in the timing or pattern of gene expression, rather than through changes in the genes themselves. These discoveries suggest that biological "evolution is not so much the result of wholesale genetic variation in terms of mutation . . . as it is a matter of changing when and where genetic switches will be turned on and off in the development of an organism."[14] Related to the field of evo-devo is the new science of epigenetics, which studies the impact of the environment on an organism's epigenome. Discoveries in epigenetics (discussed further in this chapter) are showing how changes in gene expression can be caused by mechanisms other than changes in an organism's underlying DNA sequence.

These new approaches to the study of biological evolution, sometimes collectively referred to as "holistic Darwinism" or the "extended synthesis," are helping to soften some of the rigid doctrines of the neo-Darwinists. However, despite their recognition of new mechanisms of biological development, these expanded conceptions of evolution remain within a strictly naturalistic framework wherein only material forms of causation can be recognized or accepted.

Outside the realm of biology within the larger scientific community there are a growing number of scientists who are beginning to question the wisdom of a strict commitment to metaphysical materialism. Yet it seems that this trend is least evident among evolutionary biologists, who, for the most part, remain staunchly loyal to the physicalist creed. But this loyalty to a strictly mechanistic account of evolution among many biologists can perhaps be explained as the natural defensiveness that arises when one's field of study is continuously attacked by those who deny evolution altogether.

This discussion of the metaphysics that is closely, sometimes imperceptibly, associated with the evolutionary sciences is not an attempt to refute the sturdy basics of descent with modification. As explained in the introduction, I am not trying to smuggle in a specific spiritual belief system or otherwise advocate unscientific theories such as intelligent design. Rather, my intent is to affirm as much evolutionary science as possible. Yet at the same time, I want to show how the abundant metaphysical assumptions that frame so many features of the evolutionary sciences have become theoretical handcuffs that prevent us from moving to the next phase in our understanding of evolution. For most fields of scientific investigation, metaphysical materialism continues to provide an adequate reality frame for doing science. But in the field of evolution, which has such profound explanatory relevance for human affairs, the metaphysics of strict materialism is now worn out.

Contrary to the assertions of scientific materialists, explanations of evolution that rely exclusively on the mechanisms of chance mutation and environmental selection cannot explain the appearance of self-consciousness and the transcendent powers of human awareness. Moreover, as discussed in chapter 1, materialism's need to assert physical causation as the only possible explanation of the origins of natural phenomena breaks down when confronted with the radical novelty of emergence. As the following discussion will show, the ubiquity of emergent novelty and creativity that can be found throughout the evolutionary process, together with the evident effects of the downward causation produced by emergent systems, points to the influence of both the *formal causation* of information and the *final causation* of an underlying purpose. Yet if we are to come to grips with these evolutionary causes, we need a new kind of categorical framework. This new framework will not be found through a return to the supernatural metaphysics of premodern reality frames; it must retain the spirit of naturalism and be as "minimally metaphysical" as possible. However, while our new framework must keep its metaphysics both transparent and sparingly lean, it must also be willing to recognize the authentic reality of a variety of causal factors that are presently ruled out by materialism.

## Toward a More Adequate Form of Evolutionary Metaphysics

Metaphysical propositions are, by definition, not empirically testable or experimentally falsifiable. But this does not mean that every metaphysical theory used to explain evolution is necessarily just a speculative belief. Metaphysics is a venerable form of philosophy, and philosophy proceeds on the basis of rigorous arguments based on reason, which people then use to form working agreements about what is real and what can be known. If we reject philosophy because it is not empirical, then we have restricted our knowledge to only that which can be disclosed by data derived directly from our senses, and a culture that believes that only empirical observation can deliver truth is one that is destined to be retarded in its evolution.

Karl Popper's well-known test of *falsifiability* (which evaluates knowledge on the basis of whether there is some possible observation that could disprove a given proposition) is only designed to define what constitutes *scientific* knowledge; it is not meant as a test for the truth of all propositions. The examples discussed above show how the neo-Darwinist understanding of evolution includes a number of propositions that are not falsifiable, but this does not mean that Darwin's theory is mere speculation. As I have argued, our current understanding of evolution is an inevitable mix of science and philosophy, and I suspect that this will always be the case. Indeed, it bears repeating that empirical explanations cannot stand alone without some form of accompanying metaphysics. Philip Clayton states this succinctly: "Empirical results raise urgent metaphysical questions and metaphysical positions frame empirical research. These spheres are not autonomous."[15] Thus, our quest for a more adequate form of evolutionary metaphysics is an attempt to improve the philosophical component of the theory, while leaving the empirical science relatively intact. Again, this attempt to improve the philosophy that is inescapably associated with the theory of evolution results from the accumulating empirical facts themselves—the newly emerging scientific picture of the developing universe outlined in the last chapter now calls for an update of evolution's metaphysical frame.

That being said, the first step in the journey toward a more adequate form of evolutionary metaphysics is to distinguish between science, philosophy, and religion (or, if you prefer, spirituality). In my experience, science, philosophy, and religion are like the three legs of a stool supporting humanity's overall quest for truth. These distinct forms of understanding address irreducible aspects of human experience that cannot be erased from consideration. That is, there are three essential kinds of human experience: 1) the direct experience of the natural world as perceived by our senses; 2) the experience of meanings and relationships as understood by our minds; and 3) the experience of values and intrinsic qualities, which are regarded by many as forms of spiritual experience. And as one who has had numerous transcendent experiences of this third kind, I can attest that sensory experience, mental experience, and spiritual experience are distinct and irreducible elements of experiential reality.

As they build on these experiential foundations, the distinct fields of science, philosophy, and religion should ideally inform and support each other; yet their roles are optimized when their relationship retains a degree of separation. Returning to our "stool" analogy, if these "legs" come either too close together, or if they move too far apart, the stool falls over. In other words, philosophy must not be limited to only that which can be proved by science, but nor should philosophy be extended to encompass matters of faith or propositions that must be taken on the authority of a spiritual teacher or religious text. Ideally, philosophy should help balance science and spirituality by both *bridging and separating* these diverse approaches to truth.

Again, science concerns that which can be seen and known with the senses—it compels our agreement through the force of its proofs in the physical realm. Spirituality concerns that which usually cannot be seen— it inspires our hope and faith through its explanations of the meaning of life, the purpose of the self, life after death, and the nature of the ultimate. Philosophy, in contrast, concerns the things of this world that can be detected and known but which are generally beyond the purview of scientific investigation—matters such as our subjective experience, our cultural agreements, and our values. Philosophy makes progress toward truth through reasoned argument leading to cultural agreement about realities that transcend what can be known by science, but which are more certain than the assertions of a specific spiritual belief system. Thus, by limiting our philosophy's metaphysics to the most parsimonious description of the reality it seeks to explain, this helps make it agreeable both to the scientifically minded and to a wide variety of progressive religionists. In other words, if we can explain the extra-physical aspects of evolution by using the most minimal metaphysics possible, we have the best chance of maximizing the value of our philosophy by maximizing its agreement-forming potential.

Our metaphysical explanations must go beyond the empirical facts (by definition), but only far enough beyond so as to tightly contain and frame those facts together with the remaining unanswered questions. And through this method, as our knowledge of evolution develops, our metaphysical frame can also flexibly expand so as to continue to adequately contain our growing knowledge. However, this flexibility is not found in the currently dominant materialistic metaphysics of evolution, which to remain consistent with itself, must posit a causally closed material universe where only physical causation can be recognized.

This metaphysical inflexibility has rendered materialism increasingly inadequate in the face of the mounting evidence for the influence of important extra-physical factors in the evolutionary process. As mentioned, these factors include *information*, which informs the structure and organization of evolving entities, and *value*, which serves to attract and guide the efforts of living things as they strive to survive and reproduce. We examine each of these extra-physical evolutionary influences in the next two sections.

## The Influence of Information on Evolution

The term "information" has a variety of definitions, but here information will be loosely defined as *a pattern that influences the formation or transformation of other patterns*. Every recognizable type of organized entity in the universe is literally "in-formed" by a structuring pattern. This can be clearly recognized in DNA's role in providing the instructions for the formation of living organisms. But information also functions in the pre-biotic domain of evolution as the structural properties of atoms and molecules impact the organization of astrophysical and geological forms. And of course, in the realm of cultural evolution the formative power of information impacts practically every human design. Wherever we find evolutionary "self-organization," we find that information is being used in the process. Although information is embedded in all forms of physical organization and not separated from matter, it is logically distinguishable from mass and energy. To use an analogy, the paper and ink of this book are physical, but the information encoded in the text in the form of words on paper is not identical with, and cannot be reduced to, the physical structure of the book itself. And just as the ideas in this book are "coming from somewhere," the information that is used in the genesis of the organized entities of evolution likewise always comes from somewhere.

As noted, according to cosmologists, the information employed in the organization of the pre-biotic universe has been encoded in matter from the time of the big bang. Then, according to biologists, once life appeared, information gained from interaction with the environment gradually accumulated in the genes and bodily structures of every organism. Over time, the self-organizing propensity of life gathered more and more information into its genomes through selective retention. However, many biologists argue that just as the possibility of planet Earth was present at the beginning of the universe, the possibility of *Homo sapiens* was also present in the self-organizing potentials of the first cells. But is the possibility of all that it means to be human really fully present in a prokaryote? According to environmental philosopher and Templeton prize-winner Holmes Rolston III, such future achievements cannot be found within the possibility space of the first simple life forms. As Rolston points out, this would be tantamount to the claim that Shakespeare's *Hamlet* is in the possibility space of a pile of alphabetical letters. To drive home this point Rolston uses the following analogy:

> By shaking a tray of printer's type, one can get a few short words, which are destroyed as soon as they are composed. If sentences begin to appear (an analogue of the long, symbolically coded DNA molecules and the polypeptide chains) and form into a poem or a short story (an analogue of the organism), one can be quite sure there are some formative, even irreversible, constraints on the sorting and shaking that are catching the upthrusts and directionally organizing them. . . . Something is introducing the order, and, further, something seems to be introducing layer by layer new possibilities of order, new information achieved, not just unfolding the latent order already there from the start in the setup.[16]

As Rolston contends, the facts of emergence and the evident role of information in the entropy-overcoming current of life show that there is more going on than "brute exchanges along the matter-energy continuum." Life is a "river that runs uphill," and an evident causal factor of this directional unfolding is information. Although small gradual changes, such as the changes in the beaks of finches studied by Darwin, may be credibly explained through random mutation and environmental pruning, as mentioned, a growing number of scientists are skeptical that biology's more dramatic examples of emergence can be adequately explained through this process alone. For example, Cambridge paleontologist Simon Conway Morris, author of the influential book, *Life's Solution*, argues that "the uncanny ability of evolution to navigate to the appropriate solution through immense 'hyperspaces' of biological possibility" shows the inadequacy of purely random variation as an exclusive explanation for the source of new forms.[17]

Despite the central dogma that all variation *must be* completely random, the massive amounts of information required for the apparent "evolutionary jumps" that have produced radically new forms of organization remain largely unaccounted for. In his groundbreaking book *Emergence: From Chaos to Order*, University of Michigan scientist John Holland writes: "Despite its ubiquity and importance, emergence is an enigmatic, recondite topic, more wondered at than analyzed."[18] And among the numerous mysteries associated with the phenomenon of evolutionary emergence is the unexplained appearance of novel, measurable information. That is, the emergence of more complex forms of organization necessarily involves what Harold Morowitz calls "information emergences"—along with the appearance of every truly novel evolutionary form, new information comes into the universe. However, the doctrine that the information required for new forms emerges randomly can now be seen to lack credibility—not only because it cannot adequately account for the source of the new information, but also because it transparently serves the philosophical interests of its materialist proponents, whose theories would be invalidated if it could be shown that mutations were not always random.

We have seen how scientific materialists are wedded to the idea that there are no "sources of outside information or preexisting forms" used in the process of biological evolution. But we have also seen how this doctrine of nominalism is actually a philosophical interpretation of evolution that is misleadingly asserted as a scientific fact. Recognizing this, some scientists have rejected the dogma of pure randomness and have attempted to respond to the lack of an adequate theoretical explanation for the source of information in biological evolution. And in the last several decades a number of alternative explanations have been advanced to account for the evident presence of formative patterns.

These theories can be arranged along a continuum with the most reductionistic and physicalist explanations on one end, and the most speculative and supernatural explanations on the other end. So, proceeding from the materialist end of the continuum with the neo-Darwinian theory of "chance mutation and environmental selection," we next find the "self-organization paradigm." Then, moving farther along the continuum we encounter theories of "adaptive mutation," the theory of "morphogenetic fields," and finally on the other extreme end, the theory of "intelligent design." We have already discussed the notion of "chance and environment" as the source of information, so now we will briefly touch on the rough outlines of these alternative theories.

## The Self-Organization Paradigm

The theory that evolutionary entities are "self-organizing" emerged from breakthroughs achieved in systems science in the 1970s. Ilya Prigogine's Nobel Prize-winning explanation of dissipative structures, together with the work Humberto Maturana and Francisco Varela on *autopoiesis* (the process through which organisms "create themselves"), led to the conclusion that order in the universe appears spontaneously as the result of the innate proclivity of natural systems to self-organize. While this theory was enthusiastically received in progressive circles as a more holistic alternative to Darwinian mechanism, it ultimately did not account for the source of the new information involved in the self-organizing process. Rolston offers a pointed criticism of the "self-organization paradigm:"

> An autopoietic process can be just a name . . . used to label the mysterious genesis of more out of less, a seemingly scientific name that is really a sort of mystic chant over a miraculously fertile universe. What is inadequately recognized in the "self-organizing" accounts is that, though no new matter or energy is needed for such spontaneous organization, new information is needed in enormous amounts and that one cannot just let this information float in from nowhere. Over evolutionary history, something is going on "over the heads" of any and all of the local, individual organisms. More comes from less, again and again. A more plausible explanation is that, complementing the self-organizing, there is a Ground of Information, or an Ambience of Information, otherwise known as God.[19]

The discoveries of systems science have enlarged our understanding of evolution and revealed many important connections among the distinct domains of cosmological, biological, and psychosocial evolution. But if Rolston is right, this branch of science has not resolved the problem of the source of information in evolutionary emergence.

## Adaptive Mutation

In the last several years a number of significant discoveries have been made within in the emerging scientific field known as epigenetics. Epigenetics reveals how environmental influences can activate switches in the membranes of cells that turn genes on or off. Among the discoveries of epigenetics, the most significant for evolutionary theory is the finding that the modifications in an organism's genetic read-out that are produced by environmental impacts on its epigenome can actually be passed on to subsequent generations. Yet it remains unclear whether such acquired characteristics eventually disappear after several generations. However, if the science of epigenetics does eventually prove that the characteristics acquired during an organism's lifetime can be permanently passed on to its offspring, this will overthrow one of the central dogmas of neo-Darwinism. That is, the new science of epigenetics shows promise in reviving the long-discarded theory of "Lamarckian evolution," which maintains that the efforts of individual organisms can make a difference in the evolution of their species overall.

A modest and relatively rare example of Lamarckian-type evolution known as the "Baldwin effect" has been recognized by evolutionary science for quite some time. But more recent neo-Lamarckian theories based on epigenetics are far more comprehensive and thus more controversial. Chief among these is the theory of "adaptive mutation," which argues that the "needs" of an organism can actually produce beneficial mutations that permanently alter its genome.[20] While this theory suggests mechanisms whereby the evident "jumps" in the fossil record have been achieved, proponents have thus far limited their speculations to more modest molecular processes. Moreover, although theories of adaptive mutation may help us decipher the riddles of formative causation and the source of emergent information, it will likely be some time before the weight of experimental evidence in this area leads to any significant revision in the standard theories of biological evolution.

## Morphic Resonance

Moving further along the continuum beyond mainstream evolutionary biology, we encounter the theory of "morphogenetic fields" and "morphic resonance." This theory, advanced by a variety of scientists including B. C. Goodwin, Ervin Laszlo, and most notably Rupert Sheldrake, posits the existence of extra-physical influences on evolution, such as subtle energy fields or the causal influence of psychic memory. Evolutionary philosopher Allan Combs explains this concept as follows:

> The essential idea is that when a new form comes into existence for the first time—for example a new snowflake, flower, or animal—a patterning field is created which Sheldrake calls a *morphic field*. This field tends to promote future recurrences of that form. . . . Thus, nature forms habits, and there is a tendency for morphology to become stable with repetition. These morphic fields are not contained within the usual Newtonian restrictions of time and space. Once created, they can exert influence at distant points in space as well as later in time. All this is not to deny the importance of the genetics, but Sheldrake views the physical genes as not the primary factor in defining morphology, but as a kind of antenna that tunes into the morphic fields.[21]

As Combs points out, the metaphysical component of this theory causes it to fall outside the framework of scientific materialism. And because this theoretical account of extra-physical evolutionary influences cannot be connected to the existing body of scientific knowledge, the hypothesis of morphic resonance has been scorned and dismissed as dubious pseudoscience by the scientific establishment.

## Intelligent Design

However, the hostility shown toward the theory of morphic resonance pales in comparison to the intense wrath which the scientific community has directed against the theory of "intelligent design." Proponents of intelligent design argue that many systems of evolution exhibit "irreducible complexity" or "specified complexity" and thus cannot have arisen by chance. These theorists conclude that the indications of design present in evolutionary forms points to the influence of a "supernatural designer" who periodically intervenes or otherwise directs the process. "Intelligent design arguments are formulated in secular terms and intentionally avoid identifying the intelligent agent (or agents) they posit. Although they do not state that God is the designer, the designer is often implicitly hypothesized to have intervened in a way that only a god could intervene."[22]

Now, the theory that intelligent agents are involved in the process of biological emergence is certainly speculative, but not much more so than the assertion that novel designs appear spontaneously from nowhere or that the information used in these processes somehow resides in a subtle energy field. Nor is the notion that outside agents are involved with evolution that far from the alternative theory of "directed panspermia," which proposes that an advanced extraterrestrial civilization spread the seeds of life throughout the universe. In fact, the theory of panspermia has been advanced by a number of prominent scientists, including arch-materialist Francis Crick, and has been favorably received by the scientific community as a genuine possibility. So the problem with intelligent design is not so much its theoretical outlandishness, but rather the fact that it has been formulated and propagated primarily by fundamentalist creationists bent on undermining the credibility of evolution overall. That is, in the eyes of scientists, the real sin of intelligent design theory is that it originates from an authentic "right-wing conspiracy" (supported by the well-funded Discovery Institute) that seeks to change the way evolution is taught in public schools.

After achieving a hard-fought victory over those opposed to the teaching of evolution in the United States, mainstream science has become particularly sensitive to any further creationist meddling in the curricula of public education. So in response to this threat, the scientific establishment enlisted the help of the corporate media, which dutifully condemned intelligent design theorists through thousands of editorials and journalistic exposés. And predictably, the media oversimplified the controversy, characterizing it as requiring the false choice of either mythic creationism or neo-Darwinian orthodoxy as the only options. Thus, ironically, the intelligent design movement has become a boon for scientific materialists, solidifying their control of the subject of evolution and providing a convenient weapon to attack any who question neo-Darwinian dogma by tagging them with the dreaded label of "intelligent design creationist."

Prudence thus requires that I restate the disclaimer offered in the introduction regarding intelligent design theory: I do not advocate an explanation of evolution that requires periodic intervention by supernatural beings, or a preplanned blueprint from which organisms take their form. As previously quoted, I agree with evolutionary philosopher Henri Bergson that "nature is more and better than a plan in the course of realization." Moreover, the philosophical recognition of evolutionary purpose for which I am arguing does not require that one accept a theistic explanation of this purpose to find the arguments plausible. This subject is taken up again in chapters 5, 6 and 7, but for now let me affirm the National Center for Science Education's definitive statement that evolution is a fact: that all living things share a common ancestry and that natural selection is a major mechanism in the occurrence of biological evolution. Although I would like to see a brief discussion of the "philosophy of evolution" added to the curriculum, I do not think intelligent design should be presented as a scientific alternative to natural selection in public education.

Notwithstanding this disclaimer, it is important to reemphasize that the appearance of new, structurally critical information in the emergence of biological forms is still at least partially unexplained. Although Richard Dawkins and others have presented detailed accounts of how complex structures such as eyes and wings may have come about solely through random mutation and environmental filtering, many aspects of biological emergence remain mysterious. And when we examine certain forms of evolutionary organization that have not arisen through the mechanisms of natural selection, purely physicalist explanations are even more inadequate. The classic example of the unexplained influence of information and the role of formative causation in pre-biotic evolution is found in the case of DNA, which emerges prior to the first reproducing living cells. The DNA molecule has the highest information density of any known form of matter. Nothing like it is found anywhere else in pre-biotic physics or chemistry. Each one of these "linguistic molecules" is saturated with information in an amount roughly equivalent to a large set of encyclopedias. And not only does the DNA molecule store massive amounts of data, it also includes the code which governs the retrieval of the information it carries. How this amazing form of molecular organization evolved without the mechanisms of biological natural selection remains a profound mystery. No wonder Francis Crick, the co-discoverer of DNA, suggested that it may have been seeded by extraterrestrials.

In summary, when we frame the facts of evolution, we find that there is something going on here that is currently unexplained. Even if we accept random mutation and environmental selection as the sole source of all innovation in biological evolution, explanations that rely on chance and environment alone cannot account for the original emergence of the universe, the emergence of life, or the emergence of self-conscious humanity. Moreover, none of mainstream science's current theories adequately explain the presence of vast amounts of unaccounted for information that appear in the process of biological emergence. Thus, rather than pretending that natural selection explains everything, we would do well to acknowledge that in order to have a full account of the phenomenon of evolution, some form of minimally metaphysical explanation is required to supplement both what science has succeeded in discovering and what it has failed to explain. So keeping in mind the unexplained influence of information, we now turn to the even thornier metaphysical problem posed by the influence of *value* on evolution.

## The Influence of Value on Evolution

Just as information is evidently employed in the formation of the structures of evolving entities, value or values are similarly required in the evolutionary process to attract and direct the choices of living things. The nature of values will be explored in greater depth in the next two chapters, but here values can be defined simply as "matters of ultimate concern," or as that which "makes a favorable difference in an organism's life." As we will see, values work to pull evolution forward by attracting the attention and fulfilling the purposes of evolving entities. The presence of values thus nourishes both the first-order purposes of life and the second-order purposes of humanity, first discussed in chapter 1.

### *Values and Agency*

In the investigation of the influence of values on the behavior of living things, a key to our understanding can be found in the emergent phenomenon of *agency,* or the faculty of choice. Once we recognize the connection between values and the agency resident in life forms, we can begin to see how values have a definite influence on biological evolution. And this influence becomes even more pronounced with the subsequent appearance of the expanded powers of human agency. Once human will emerges, the influence of values then becomes the primary causal factor in the evolution of human culture.

According to prominent complexity scientist Stuart Kauffman, the capacity of agency—the power of choice—can be found within life's earliest and most primitive forms, which he calls "minimal molecular autonomous agents." To illustrate the function of agency in these simple life forms, Kauffman uses the example of a bacterium swimming up a glucose gradient:

> Without attributing consciousness to the bacterium, we can see in this capacity the evolutionary onset of choice and thus of meaning, value, doing, and purpose. The technical word for meaning is *semiosis,* where a sign means something. Here, the bacterium detects a local glucose gradient, which is a sign of more glucose in some direction. By altering its behavior and swimming up the gradient, the bacterium is *interpreting* the sign. The bacterium may, of course, be *mistaken.* Perhaps there is not much glucose to be found in that direction. Neither "signs," "interpretation," nor "mistakes" are logically possible in physics, where only happenings occur. Thus *meaning* has entered the universe: the local glucose gradient is a *sign* that means glucose is—probably—nearby. Because natural selection has assembled the propagating organization of structures and processes that lead to swimming up the glucose

gradient for good selective reasons, glucose has *value* to the bacterium. And because getting food is the function of organized behavior, as assembled by natural selection acting on fitter variants, getting food is the *purpose* of the activity and is the *doing* or *action* of the bacterium.[23]

As Kauffman explains, agency is a central feature of all living things. Without this radically emergent ability to perceive and to choose, life would not be capable of evolving. As noted in the previous chapter, the impulse to strive to survive and reproduce is inherent in all life forms, and it is this striving that drives biological evolution. Although the choices made by primitive life forms rely on genetically preprogrammed instincts, living agency is *evaluative* nonetheless. This point is brought home by Rolston in his seminal book on environmental ethics:

> Plants and insects have a well-being, and they respond with a (nonfelt) interest in this well-being, as when a tree sends roots down deeper for water or an ant scurries off with a crumb. *Escherichia coli*, a common bacterium, placed in a food supply with both lactose and glucose, prefers glucose over lactose and eats the latter only after the former is gone. The microbe presumably does not have any options in this preference; the preset preference is hardwired into the genes. But this is the way genetic preferences operate, as opposed to the later-evolving neural and consciously expressed preferences. . . . Such organisms, though nerveless, are genuinely autonomous (=self-impelled) evaluative systems, even though it is also true that their behaviors work by genetic programs, biochemistries, instincts, or stimulus response mechanisms. They may have no autonomous options, but they defend a life as a good-of-its-kind. There is an object-with-will, even though there is no subject-with-will. . . . The point is that below the threshold of subjectivity life remains. It can yet flourish or be harmed. Life still has its commitments, something it values, a cybernetic program defended, goods of an objective kind, genetically based preferences.[24]

As Rolston makes clear, life's universal interest in *survival value* can be recognized as a primitive form of value that is actively perceived and pursued by all biological forms. And it bears repeating that if surviving and reproducing were not *values* for living things, there would be no advancing "descent" for natural selection to act upon. Kauffman emphasizes the fundamental function of values within the evolution of life, writing:

> Values are part of the language appropriate to the nonreducible, real, emergent, activities of agents. Thus agency and value bring with them what

philosophers call teleological language, that is, language involving a sense of purpose or "end," as in our common explanations for our actions based on our reasons and intentions. Teleological language has long been a contentious issue among scientists and philosophers, many of whom consider it unscientific. I strongly disagree. Agency is emergent and real, but not reducible to physics, . . . because biology is not reducible to physics. The biosphere . . . is laden with agency, value, and meaning. Human life, which is certainly laden with agency, value, and meaning, inherits these qualities from the biosphere of which it is a part.[25]

We can infer from Kauffman's analysis that, because agency apparently "goes all the way down," the corresponding perception of values goes all the way down as well, influencing all life forms in their ongoing quest to live and thrive. And if the emergence of first-order agency at the level of single-celled life results in the appearance of value-perception, as Kauffman maintains, then it follows that the subsequent emergence of second-order agency in humans results in the appearance of an entirely new level of emergent values. In other words, just as the agency of organisms causes them to strive to survive and reproduce, the emergence of the elevated capacities of human agency results in a new kind of striving—the striving to improve the human condition on every front, which drives the evolution of culture. The first-order agency of animals can be distinguished from the second-order agency of humans because with the advent of "human will" there appears a new level of *freedom*—unlike the more circumscribed will of animals, human will is relatively free will.

## Values and Free Will

The concept of "free" will is a cornerstone of our society. Practically every law is predicated on the proposition that humans are responsible and accountable for their actions. In fact, it is only through the exercise of free will that humans can be considered moral agents; the very idea of morality is meaningless without the underlying concept of truly autonomous agency. Animals have varying degrees of autonomy and spontaneity, but their freedom is constrained by a relative lack of self-consciousness. Animals may have purposes, but as discussed in the last chapter, we humans have purposes for our purposes; we are free to evaluate our evaluations and judge our judgments. And as a result of our self-conscious freedom we are able to recognize complex forms of value that cannot be perceived by beings that lack this freedom.

Yet even though it is central to human life, free will remains a highly metaphysical concept. As noted in the introduction, unlike cognition or emotion, the faculty of volition, or will, has not been fully explained or otherwise specifically located within the neurological structures of the brain.[26] And the idea that something originating in our subjective experience—an uncaused cause—could actually push around the particles in our brains and thus exert efficient causation in the external world cannot be adequately reconciled with a physicalist reality frame.[27] Accordingly, many scientific materialists have gone to great lengths in arguing that human free will is an illusion and that all human choices are actually predetermined by antecedent physical, biological and cultural forces. However, while every human choice is influenced by outside factors, and while many of our actions are coerced by external circumstances, we all *presuppose in practice* that we have relative freedom of choice—just as you are now free to continue reading this page, or to cease. Both direct experience and "hardcore common sense" tells us that our freedom of choice is real, and it is this same reality sense that makes recognition of the metaphysical reality of free will a necessary part of the minimal metaphysics required for an evolutionary worldview.

It then follows that just as values can first be detected with the rise of the most primitive forms of agency, the extraordinary emergence of human free will, with its expanded capacity to recognize quality, inaugurates a new universe of more subtle and complex values. These newly perceived values include sophisticated forms of beauty, truth, compassion, and love. Indeed, as noted above, goodness itself is a value that requires conscious freedom for its very recognition. That is, just as an action cannot be considered truly immoral unless one could have chosen otherwise, ethically commendable actions likewise require relative volitional freedom in order to be recognized as authentically moral. From this perspective we can begin to see how freedom of choice is a necessary component in our ability to perceive higher forms of value—in order to value something, we have to freely agree that it is valuable. Indeed, as explored further in the next chapter, *free will is an organ of perception for values.*

However, the emergence of volitional freedom does not begin and end with the first humans. As human consciousness evolves, it experiences increasing degrees of freedom. The distinguished developmentalist, Abraham Maslow, was perhaps the first psychologist to recognize how the evolution of consciousness results in greater volitional liberty. Maslow's famous "hierarchy of human needs" theory identified a series of stages through which humans pass in their development toward "self-actualization." And according to Maslow, one of the markers of self-actualization is a high degree of personal freedom. Describing this discovery, Maslow wrote:

> Finally I must make a statement even though it will certainly be disturbing to many theologians, philosophers, and scientists: self-actualizing individuals have more "free will" and are less "determined" than average people are. However the words "free will" and "determinism" may come to be operationally defined, in this investigation they are empirical realities. Furthermore, they are degree concepts, varying in amount; they are not all-or-none packages.[28]

The increasing freedom that Maslow detects in the process of personal self-actualization can also be found in the emergence of the major stages of human history. As discussed in chapter 1, the evolution of individual consciousness roughly recapitulates the evolution of human culture. This insight helps us recognize that, like the emergence of higher stages of consciousness, cultural emergence is also driven, at least partially, by the quest for new kinds of freedom. For example, freedom and liberty were central values in the emergence of the modernist worldview during the Enlightenment. And we can see a further dialectical progression in the quest for freedom in the emergence of the postmodern worldview in the 1960s, which originally sought its own kind of liberation from the constraints and conventions of modernist society.

## The Evolution of Values

In our attempt to understand the depths of the evolutionary process, it is important to see how the evolutionary impulse that is felt by all living things is itself connected to the drawing power of values. And by making values central to our inquiry we can achieve a more satisfying account of both the *causes* and the *reasons* that produce cultural evolution. Again, in the standard scientific account, cosmological evolution is caused by the deterministic unfolding of the physical and chemical potentials originally present at the beginning of the universe. And also according to the standard account, biological evolution is primarily caused by random variations in organismal genetics coupled with selection for fitness by the changing natural environment. However, although there have been a variety of attempts to explain the advance of cultural evolution from a purely scientific perspective, there has emerged no "standard account" that has found general acceptance in academia. This is mainly because the forces that drive cultural evolution are neither deterministic nor random. Cultural evolution is the result of *actual selection* rather than natural selection—cultures evolve because people freely choose to make their lives better.

It is worth reemphasizing here that human cultural evolution is a uniquely emergent evolutionary phenomenon—a new type of authentic evolution that has an irreversible impact on the universe. This is demonstrated by the immensity of the global civilization that now encompasses the earth. What drives this unique kind of development is the fact that human needs expand infinitely—humans can almost always imagine how their situation can be improved. Animal needs, by contrast, can be generally satisfied; and this is one reason why animal societies do not show appreciable development independent of their biological evolution. As pioneering sociologist Emile Durkheim realized in the nineteenth century, humans have insatiable desires; as one form of satisfaction is achieved, new possibilities for even greater fulfillment are envisaged. According to Durkheim: "Awakening human consciousness expands the horizon of human desire from the here and now (as with animals) to beyond all limits." This same insight was expressed 1,500 years earlier by Saint Augustine, who wrote: "Our hearts are restless till they rest in God."

However, while the evolution of consciousness and culture is not entirely predictable or algorithmic in its growth, it does exhibit the distinct pattern of dialectical development by stages we have discussed. Using this understanding of cultural evolution's development logic helps us better see the critical role of values in the evolutionary process. As I will argue further in the discussion of cultural progress in chapter 5, human cultures generally exhibit evolution toward increasingly more complex estimates of value over time. Despite the loss of some of the virtues possessed by earlier stages, and despite the persistence of significant pathologies in later stages, cultural evolution has generally led to the improvement of the human condition. For example, when the scope of those worthy of moral consideration expands, when women become the social equals of men, and when individuals achieve increasing liberation from narrow social conventions, we can conclude that authentic evolutionary progress has been achieved.

Recognizing the role of values in cultural evolution also shows how development occurs as a result of the dual influences of dissatisfaction with present circumstances coupled with a vision of an improved future potential—what we might call "a push and a pull." The *push* toward a new stage of cultural development results from the pressure of unsatisfactory life conditions created by the accumulating pathologies of the existing society.

The *pull* arises from the attraction power found in fresh ideals, as individuals begin to glimpse the values of the next emerging stage—the new truth, new beauty, and new ideals of morality that always accompany the birth of a new historical level.

The development of each stage thus takes place within a larger, interrelated systemic pattern that forms a kind of internal cultural ecosystem of values and worldviews. Within this developing cultural ecosystem, the values of each worldview stage are shaped and defined by the problems and deficiencies of its previous stage, with each stage's own accumulating problems in turn shaping the values of the stage that comes after it in time. We can see an example of this in the way that the postmodern value of environmental sustainability arises as a result of the problems created by the modernism's rampant economic development. And we can also see how the modernist value of economic progress was itself shaped by the relative stagnation and lack of social mobility in the traditional cultures that precede the emergence of modernism. Each stage of culture thus develops a discrete set of values that are tailored to its location along the timeline of human history. This is one reason why values are partially "location specific"—as life conditions change with the progress of cultural evolution, that which is most valuable for producing further evolution likewise changes.

In summary, we have seen how values influence evolution through their impact on the agency found in all living things. And as agency evolves and consciousness becomes more active, living things are able to perceive an increasing range of values (such as the value of nurturing offspring). Then as emergent evolution continues, the uniquely human agency of free will appears and inaugurates a new realm of value potentials. In the unfolding course of cultural evolution, humans come to form increasingly complex macro social agreements about what is valuable. These value agreements themselves evolve through a series of emergent stages, which results in the pull of values becoming stronger and stronger due to the increasing freedom of evolving consciousness.

• • •

This chapter has shown how the use of metaphysics is inescapable in our attempts to gain a deeper understanding of evolution. Philosophies such as positivism and scientific materialism, which have been closely associated with the institutional study of evolution from the beginning, have been helpful because they required us to explain as much as possible using material causation alone. However, we are now encountering the limits of physicalism as an exclusive method in our investigation of the phenomenon of evolution. In order to achieve a more comprehensive grasp of this universal process of becoming, we must now confront the evident influences of *formal causation* through information, and what might loosely be termed *final causation* through the influence of values. These extra-physical evolutionary influences may not yet be directly accessible to science, but they are accessible to human knowledge through scientifically informed philosophy. Accordingly, the next chapter takes a closer look at the nature of values and the "gravitational pull" they exert on evolution.

## CHAPTER 3

# Eros—Value Gravity

IN THE PREVIOUS CHAPTER WE EXAMINED the evidence for the extra-physical influences of information and value on evolution. We saw how the process of the emergent development of evolutionary entities is apparently "in-formed" by structural instructions that science cannot yet fully explain. We also saw how living agency, which strives to fulfill matters of ultimate concern (such as survival), is a central factor in the evolutionary process. Evolutionary biologist Lynn Margulis puts it succinctly: "Life is matter that chooses," and every choice can be connected to a value of some kind. Values thus draw evolution forward, pulling it in directions that eventually result in increased powers of choice and emergent volitional freedom.

Recognizing the presence of unaccounted for information, or appreciating evolution's affinity for values, does not negate science or otherwise cause us to regress to premodern or mythic conceptions of our origins. Yet when we face the fact that evolution is indeed influenced by information and value, this does require us to abandon the idea that the products and processes of evolution are nothing but random or otherwise meaningless occurrences.

Values were defined generally in the last chapter using Paul Tillich's phrase: "matters of ultimate concern." Now this chapter expands this conception by examining how the definition of value itself has evolved over time. Further consideration is given to an emerging evolutionary approach to values that recognizes how these fundamental qualities exert a kind of gravity on evolution through their influence on consciousness. This leads to the conclusion that values are neither completely subjective nor wholly objective. As we will see, values are best conceived as *relational structures* that bring subject and object together in the course of seeing and being seen. This is followed by a brief examination of the "gravity of disvalues," which has had an all too evident effect on human history. After that, we explore the idea that among all the potential candidates for the "highest value," the concept of *goodness* best describes the "magnetic center" toward which all values ultimately move. This leads to the final section, which describes evolution's dialectical pattern of development, and which paves the way for chapter 4's discussion of the triad of "primary values" identified as beauty, truth, and goodness. Admittedly, this is the most difficult chapter, but it lays an important foundation for the later discussion of evolutionary progress and purpose in chapters 5, 6, and 7.

## The Reality of Values

Recognizing the evolutionary efficacy of values implies that values are something real, that they have properties which are at least partially independent of our subjective perspectives. The most ancient and famous proponent of this view was Plato in the fourth century B.C., who taught that "the Good" was a perfect and eternal "Idea" or blueprint—a transcendental, preexistent form of perfection from which all particular instances of goodness derived their quality. Correlated with this idea of transcendental goodness as a form of perfection was the *drawing power* of the good, its allure or inherent power of attraction, which Plato described through the concept of *eros*—"the urge toward the realization of ideal perfection." Eros was conceived as a universal force that moves all things towards the transcendental forms of universal value. Although eros was defined as a passionate, intense longing that included erotic sexual desire, the concept was also more broadly associated with the overall impulse for improvement, encompassing the desire for transcendental beauty and its related "Forms" of truth and goodness.

Plato's philosophy of transcendent values was carried forward by Saint Thomas Aquinas in the thirteenth century, who taught the "doctrine of the transcendentals," under which values were conceived as fundamental properties of *being*. Although Aquinas is most often associated with Aristotelian philosophy, he nevertheless advanced this Platonic axiom, describing truth, goodness, and beauty as "transcendentally one" in the sense that each is pure being apprehended via a different modality. According to Aquinas, truth is being rightly known, goodness is being rightly desired, and beauty is being rightly admired. In other words, truth is being's imprint on the mind, goodness is being's imprint on the will, and beauty is being's imprint on the emotions. Through this understanding, value was recognized as the shadow that pure being casts into the phenomena of this world.

This premodern conception of the objective nature of values remains influential among certain groups of contemporary philosophers, who are categorized as "moral realists." But unsurprisingly, the field of contemporary moral philosophy is now characterized by a variety of apparently unreconcilable camps, with moral realists representing just one position among many. In the last chapter we saw how metaphysical theories of reality (such as moral realism) came under attack by the empiricist philosophers of the Enlightenment, who regarded sensory experience as the only basis for knowledge. Staunch empiricists such as David Hume argued that moral beliefs are essentially irrational, but are nevertheless "inevitable and convenient" for the functioning of society.

The empiricists' rejection of values as real entities in the world was carried forward in the twentieth century in analytic philosophy, and especially in the school of analytic philosophy known as logical positivism, which holds that ethical statements or propositions do not have any "truth-value" because they cannot be verified through sensory observation. This position was summed up by Ludwig Wittgenstein, who wrote: "In the world everything is as it is and happens as it does happen. In it there is no value—and if there were it would be of no value. If there is a value which is of value, it must lie outside of all happening and being-so. For all happening and being-so is accidental."[1] Thus, in the view of analytic philosophy, because values are not facts, they are relegated to the status of being "merely subjective" and simply a matter of taste.

The view that values are merely creations or projections of the human will also became a central theme of existentialist philosophy (originally advanced by Friedrich Nietzsche), which took the concept even further. Existentialists maintained that because all values are created by humans, we are thus free to choose our values, and indeed have a responsibility to question every value rather than to passively receive our values from the society in which we live. According to the philosophy of existentialism, the universe is simply absurd and there is no meaning to be found in it beyond what meaning we give to it. The individual is thus seen as tragically and heroically struggling against the abyss of cosmic meaninglessness.

Despite their austerity, the atheistic and pessimistic philosophies of logical positivism and existentialism have been important to the evolution of philosophy overall. Existentialism in particular, which is the most openly nihilistic form of materialist philosophy, explored a reality frame in which every vestige of spirituality was purged. And in so doing it provided a kind of historical punctuation mark, allowing for a new beginning for philosophies that recognize the reality of spirit. Just as empiricism (and later analytic philosophy) helped to create the ideational womb in which science could take form and become established, existentialism helped take materialism to its logical conclusions, and thus showed how this reality frame, when embraced in its fullness, often results in nihilism, ennui, and even despair.

Analytic and existentialist philosophies have always functioned as the handmaidens of the scientific materialist worldview, reinforcing the academic respectability of reductionistic physicalism. These philosophies grew out of the materialist reality frame and have worked diligently to reinforce its conceptions of the universe as a purposeless accident. But now, as I am arguing, it is the scientific data itself—the emerging facts of evolution understood as a unified picture of universal becoming—that demonstrate that this frame of reality is outmoded and needs to be superseded by a new categorical framework that can better account for these new facts by acknowledging the presence of efficacious value and purpose in the evolving universe.

Complexity theorist Stuart Kauffman, who we heard from in the last chapter, is a respected spokesman for this new scientifically grounded evolutionary philosophy of values. In his important book, *Reinventing the Sacred*, Kauffman argues that values naturally emerge with the evolution of the biosphere. Kauffman thus finds evidence for the ontology of values in the emergent behavior of agency exhibited by all forms of life, writing: "We are the products of evolution, and our values are real features of the universe."[2] Kauffman is a credible bridge-builder between materialism and a more spiritual conception of the universe because of his minimalist form of spirituality. He conceives of the "sacred" as simply the "natural behavior of the emergent creativity in the universe." Despite his rejection of traditional theistic notions of Deity, he labels this inherent creativity "God" in an attempt to appropriate the term and use it in a philosophy that regards nature itself with the kind of awe and reverence traditionally found in religious conceptions of the universe. Kauffman states his case as follows:

> If we are members of a universe in which emergence and ceaseless creativity abound, if we take that creativity as a sense of God we can share, the resulting sense of the sacredness of all life and the planet can help orient our lives beyond the consumerism and commodification the industrialized world now lives, heal the split between reason and faith, heal the split between science and the humanities, heal the want of spirituality, heal the wound derived from the false reductionistic belief that we live in a world of fact without values,

and help us jointly build a global ethic. These are what is at stake in finding a new scientific worldview that enables us to reinvent the sacred.[3]

Kauffman's minimal, evolutionary metaphysics of creative emergence provides a good starting point for the rehabilitation of the reality of values, but it still lacks an explanation of how values exert a kind of magnetic or gravitational pull on the evolution of consciousness and culture. As previously described, cultural evolution proceeds according to a developmental logic wherein values-based worldviews emerge through a sequence of stages. And as specifically discussed in the last chapter, new worldviews arise as a result of the *push* of unsatisfactory life conditions and the *pull* of the attraction power of the fresh values of each emerging worldview stage. Although the attracting power of the values of emergent new worldviews is evident in the historical record, the question remains as to the actual source of these higher values.

Most of the values we hold can be traced to one or more of these historically significant worldview structures, and the origin of these macro social agreements themselves can be traced to the leaders and visionaries who initially helped give birth to these worldviews. For example, the values found in the various forms of traditional religious culture were first expressed by the spiritual masters who founded these religions: Moses, Confucius, Gautama, Jesus, and Mohamed, have all provided a source of values for humanity. Similarly, many of the values of the modernist worldview were first pronounced by the philosophers of the Enlightenment, such as Descartes, Locke, Montesquieu, Voltaire, and Kant. And we can likewise see how the founders of progressive postmodern culture have also provided leadership through the articulation of fresh values. For example, Henry David Thoreau, John Muir, Mohandas Gandhi, Martin Luther King, and John Lennon each expressed an aspect of what we can now recognize as the postmodern value system.

However, even if we can trace the source of many of our values to the insights of the great sages of history, the question remains as to whether these expanding conceptions of the beautiful, the true, and the good simply arose in the imaginations of these visionaries, or were somehow *discovered* as part of a universal order or larger source of cosmic value. That is, do we evolve our values by merely bootstrapping new values on top of the deficiencies of existing value systems, making them up as we go along, or do we actually come to find more complex forms of value that are already bound up in the nature of things?

## Moral Realism

This essential question brings us back to the philosophy of moral realism, which contends that our values are not just convenient labels for our personal preferences, but rather extant relational structures "stretched between the truth seeking mind and reality." According to Oxford philosopher and moral realist Iris Murdoch: "The ordinary person does not, unless corrupted by philosophy, believe that he creates values by his choices. He thinks that some things really are better than others and that he is capable of getting it wrong."[4] In her defense of the metaphysical reality of values, Murdoch argues:

> The concept of Good resists collapse into the selfish empirical consciousness. It is not a mere value tag of the choosing will . . . The proper and serious use of the term refers us to a perfection which is perhaps never exemplified in the world we know . . . and which carries with it the ideas of hierarchy and transcendence. How do we know that the very great is not the perfect? We see differences, we sense directions, and we know that the Good is still somewhere beyond. The self, the place where we live, is a place of illusion. Goodness is connected with the attempt to see the unself, to see and respond to the real world in the light of a virtuous consciousness. . . . 'Good is a transcendent reality' means that virtue is the attempt to pierce the veil of selfish consciousness and join the world as it really is.[5]

Murdoch claimed that she did not believe in God, but in this passage she nevertheless equates "the Good" with the idea of perfection, which is "sensed" as a direction "somewhere beyond" any particular instance of goodness. This insight underscores how the gravitational attraction of the most significant forms of value carries with it a sense of the *transcendent*. In defense of this idea, Oxford professor Alister McGrath argues "transcendence continues to be a meaningful concept in contemporary culture. It is a notion that is found in religious and secular literature alike, reflecting what seems to be a common human preoccupation. . . . However these experiences are to be interpreted, there is ample substantiation of their occurrence and perceived importance. . . . While not constituting proof in themselves of an ontologically distinct realm, [these experiences] nevertheless contribute significantly to the persistence of the notion. . . . The stability of the concept of the 'transcendent' is thus partially due to its grounding in human experiences that appear to reinforce it."[6]

Moral realists such as Murdoch and McGrath have used a variety of strategies to overcome arguments advanced by the various philosophical schools that deny the objective reality of values. Some moral realists contend that we can experience and discover transcendent value through the use of our personal intuition about what is right. Another moral realist approach to the ontology of values involves the exercise of "reflexive hermeneutics," wherein one questions their own intuitions of value while comparing their assessments to the estimates of others. Through this approach, one discerns gradations of value by sustained acts of attention or concentrated contemplation. Yet another approach is to locate values, not in the assessment of an individual subject, but rather in the structures of intersubjective agreement that are made between rational persons as they contend with questions of value. And I believe all of these approaches have merit and can be used to find real value within the moral, aesthetic, and scientific/metaphysical issues that confront us.

Because of its emphasis on the transcendent nature of values, the philosophy of moral realism contrasts sharply with the explanations of human values advanced by the branch of social science known as sociobiology. Sociobiology, or evolutionary psychology, claims that human values and behaviors have arisen through natural selection and can be best explained as strategies for gene propagation and evolutionary fitness. Sociobiologists thus locate the source of our values in the adaptations of our prehistoric ancestors. While this approach may be useful for explaining certain human values, such as why so many of us are enamored with celebrities, it is highly reductionistic and does not account for the astounding development of values that has occurred in the last 350 years with the advent of modernism and postmodernism. Sociobiology explains the emergence of human values from a strictly "bottom up" perspective. Conversely, integral philosophy acknowledges that values do arise from "below," through the pressure of unsatisfactory life conditions, but as we explore in the next two sections, the integral perspective goes further by recognizing how values also come from "above," through the magnetic pull of eros that ever kindles our sense of the possibility of a greater good.

## Values as Evolutionary Attractors

Although the "evolutionary" approach to values proposed by sociobiology denies that values are real transcendent entities that exist apart from human preferences or predilections, the moral realist view nevertheless finds support from a different kind of evolutionary approach to values. Research from the fields of chaos theory and the sciences of complexity provides an intriguing analogy of how values may actually act as "evolutionary attractors" in the development of consciousness and culture.

Complexity science has shown how complex adaptive systems evince a tendency to respond to various kinds of *attractors*, which are sometimes described as basins of attraction. An attractor is a mathematical concept that describes the motion of a dynamic system within its "phase space" or bounded area of action. Familiar examples of the effects of an attractor on a dynamic system can be seen in the oscillation of a pendulum or the spiral motion of water swirling down a bathtub drain. Paradoxically, attractors are created by the behavior of a system, and yet they end up governing the very behavior of the system that originally created them. This can be seen in the way a gravitational field originally created by the motion of a planet serves to govern and constrain the ongoing motion of that planet over time. However, the influence of attractors on dynamic systems is often more complex than the simple gravitational effects cited in these examples. In fact, certain attractors actually act to "nudge and urge" dynamic systems into ever more complex and evolved behaviors, such as when a thunderstorm produces a tornado. Applying the analogy of a systemic attractor to the dynamic system of evolution as a whole, we can perhaps envisage how transcendent values such as beauty, truth, and goodness may serve as "perfection attractors" that shape the trajectory of evolutionary development.

This analogy has been previously advanced by University of Texas philosopher of science Frederick Turner, who writes: "The strange attractor of a chaotic system can look very like a Platonic ideal form: though any instance of the outcome of such a system at work is only partial and apparently random, when we see all instances of it, we begin to make out a beautiful, if incomplete and fuzzy shape. Might not virtues, ethics, values, and even in a way spiritual beings, be like those deep and beautiful attractors?"[7] Considering the implications of this analogy, Turner continues:

> If this identification of values as strange attractors can be upheld, the implications for the discipline of history and the human sciences are enormous. In seeking the key principles of historical change, social organization, and economic development in forces or drives that force and push society and individuals, we may have been deeply neglecting these mysterious, yet increasingly intelligible, attractors that invite and draw society and individuals. . . . It may turn out that the real reason why human beings do things is not that they are compelled into them by socioeconomic causes or political and cultural norms, but that they are attracted to them by their goodness and their beauty.[8]

Turner's hypothesis regarding the role of values as strange attractors that influence the evolution of consciousness has also been advanced by other theorists, including Allan Combs and Stanley Krippner, who characterize ordinary waking consciousness as a type of attractor basin. Although the application of chaos theory to the study of consciousness is still in its infancy, this line of investigation promises to be a fruitful field of discovery for the future.

However, we do not need to wait for further research to recognize the attraction power of values from a philosophical perspective. As noted in the last chapter, the historical record which traces the evolution of culture over time reveals how the "magnetic pull" of what might best be termed "value gravity" increases as development unfolds in a way that keeps human needs from ever being completely fulfilled. Humanity's ongoing awakening to new problem situations, together with the intuition of the possibility of ever-greater good, keeps the horizon of potential perfection continually receding. This human intuition that the fullness of goodness always lies "somewhere beyond" gives us a sense of how the eros of goodness works as a gravitational force. And in addition to the pull of goodness, we can also feel the magnetism of the eros of truth as it functions within the institution of science itself, wherein the drawing power of potential new discoveries continually motivates scientists to seek out fresh knowledge. Just as our sense of goodness has evolved by stages into increasingly worldcentric conceptions, our sense of truth has likewise evolved from magical, to mythical, to scientific, and now to increasingly holistic levels of understanding. Thus as I am arguing, humanity's inherent "perfection hunger," our insatiable appetite for the fulfillment of ever higher and deeper needs, is strongly influenced by the presence of transcendent value in the universe.

## Values as Relational Structures

To some, the idea of value gravity may seem supernatural, violating our stated intention to employ only the most minimal metaphysics in our explanation of evolution. Yet the influence of the magnetism of values on consciousness is something we all directly experience on a daily basis, and thus our appetites for higher values are as "natural" as any other kind of experiential reality. We see the actions of exemplary people and recognize goodness, we admire the harmonies of nature and art and recognize beauty, and we feel the power of an accurate account of the way things are and recognize truth. While value judgments always have a relative quality that depends on the "cultural

location" of the observer, the power of inherent quality to attract our attention and desire is nevertheless a universal feature of human awareness. And
although the external presence of existential quality remains relatively
constant, as consciousness evolves and achieves greater degrees of volitional
freedom, it is better able to feel and thus respond to these influences.

Comprehending the nature of values and their influence on evolution is
a subtle and complex task that will likely occupy philosophers for centuries
to come. Although we are still far from a complete understanding of these
qualities, we can perhaps recognize that values such as beauty, truth, and
goodness have what we might call an *objective pole* and a *subjective pole*. On
the one hand, the highest forms of value are not "simply given," waiting for
an outside observer to spot them. But on the other hand, their existence
cannot be located completely within the consciousness of the "perceiver."
For example, it is difficult to imagine that the Grand Canyon of the Colorado River possesses no inherent aesthetic properties, and that its sublime
beauty is merely the projection of the humans who see it. While some may
fail to recognize its beauty, this does not mean that in that situation the
beauty has simply vanished.

The idea that values are *relational structures* is a difficult but important
point, and it requires us to recognize that while values always have a subjective component, the most significant types of value also connect with
external realities. Just as *information* is now recognized as something that
can exist even when there is no one there to receive its message, we can
likewise see how certain types of value have a similar kind of partially free-
standing existence. This claim is well developed in Rolston's *Environmental
Ethics*, where he argues for the existence of *natural values*:

> While it may be true that some ranges of value emerge [only through experi-
> ence], such as the capacity for joy or aesthetic experience, these are capstone
> goods; they are built on valuable substructures. Some values come only with
> consciousness, but it does not follow that consciousness, when it brings its
> new values, confers all value and discovers none. . . . The most satisfactory
> account is an ecocentric model, one that recognizes the emergence of con-
> sciousness as a novel value but also finds this consciousness entering a realm
> of objective natural value. . . . Nature presents us with superposed possibilities
> of valuing, only some of which we realize. It is both provocative source of
> and resource for value. Here fertility is demanded of us as subjects but is also
> found in the objects that fertilize our experience.[9]

In his arguments for relative value realism, Rolston is careful to
acknowledge the difficulties of the myth of the given, writing: "No big

theory, even in science, much less in value theory, is trouble free, and the theory of objective value can be stung by our seeming incapacity to know anything whatsoever in naked objectivity."[10] But his point is nevertheless well taken that evolution generates value in the natural world prior to the arrival of humans.

Thus, after wrestling with the seemingly paradoxical nature of values for quite some time, I have come to see that the most meaningful values— "capstone" values, as Rolston calls them—do have both an objective pole and a subjective pole. As illustrated in figure 3.1, these spiritual forms of value only come fully into existence when the perceiving subject possesses the requisite epistemological capacity to make contact with the ontological presence of existential quality. So it is important to understand that values such as beauty, truth, or goodness are neither entirely objective nor entirely subjective—they are relational structures that bring subject and object together in the course of seeing and being seen. The ability to perceive these higher values is thus tied to the perspective of the observer, and as perspectives develop through the evolution of consciousness, new levels of value become perceptible. In other words, as our awareness expands, we are able to see the quality of the world with increasing depth and clarity.

## Values as Relational Structures

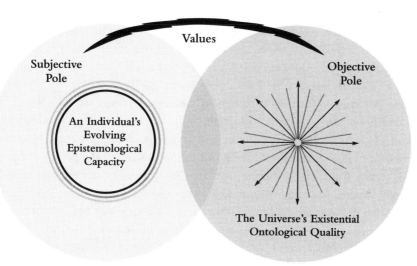

*Figure 3.1*
Objective and subjective poles within the relational structure of values

Here we can see a loose analogy between the behavior of value and the behavior of electricity. An electric current requires both a positive pole and a negative pole for its existence, and the dynamic nature of transcendent value likewise exhibits a similar kind of "circuit phenomenon," requiring both a subjective pole and an objective pole.

Again, because transcendent values are relational structures, because they require both objective quality and subjective appreciation to be brought fully into being, this makes their reality different from physical objects or events. This observation helps overcome the oft-cited objection to value realism raised by "moral skeptics" such as J. L. Mackey, who writes:

> If there were objective values, then they would be entities or qualities or relations of a very strange sort, utterly different from anything else in the universe. Correspondingly, if we were aware of them, it would have to be by some special faculty of . . . perception or intuition, utterly different from our ordinary ways of knowing everything else.[11]

Although it is not apparent to Mackey, as I argued in the last chapter in connection with the discussion of agency, *human free will* is the "special faculty" that serves as an organ of perception for values. We perceive the reality of values by desiring them, or by otherwise agreeing that they are in fact valuable. And as consciousness evolves and one's will becomes increasingly less determined by external constraints, the reality of transcendent values becomes increasingly evident.

While there are certainly aspects of the ontology of value gravity that remain a mystery, we have to say the same thing about physical gravity. Science has yet to explain the causal nexus by which gravitation works or how celestial objects physically interact with each other over vast distances. But as explored further in the next chapter, the eros we feel for better conditions, our natural yearning for the good, the true, and the beautiful, can be explained as part of the natural teleology of evolution as a whole. As process philosopher Alfred North Whitehead understood: "We are attracted to beauty, truth, and goodness because these values are entertained appetitively by the eros of the universe, whose appetites we feel."[12]

Here in the context of this discussion of value gravity, I must acknowledge the possibility that these arguments for the influence of values on evolution might be confused with older, and now discredited explanations of evolution, such as "orthogenesis," or Bergson's concept of the *elan vital* or "vital force" within the evolutionary process. It thus bears repeating that the influence of value gravity can be simply explained as the straightforward phenomenon of consciousness being attracted by, and responding to, value in the world. While the subjective interiors of agency and consciousness may not be accessible to physical science, this does not mean that the philosophical recognition of consciousness' role in the evolutionary process is necessarily supernatural or completely mysterious. Acknowledging the role of value gravity in evolution thus does not require us to recognize anything beyond the directly experiential and basic realities of consciousness and quality.

That being said, although it is readily observable and not supernatural or occult, the drawing power of values on evolutionary entities has until recently gone relatively unnoticed in the science of evolution. Admittedly, as discussed in chapter 1, Darwin's original "principle of fecundity" did acknowledge the proclivity of all life forms to strive to survive, reproduce, and fill every available environmental niche. Moreover, the scientific significance of purpose in living things was recognized by a number of writers prior to Darwin, including the philosopher Gottfried Leibniz in the seventeenth century.[13] But as we come to better understand the gravity of values, we can begin to see that Darwin's fecundity principle is really only half the story. Not only is evolution *driven* by organismal striving, it is also *drawn* by value gravity. That is, the intentionality of agency and consciousness is almost always an intention *for* something valuable, something separate and attractive that all forms of life seek to possess or achieve. And it is this external drawing power of values that animates and directs the intentional dynamics of all living things.

Even though it is not adequately acknowledged by biological science, the influence of value gravity is a real (albeit nonphysical) force that plays a significant role in the evolution of the universe. Our emerging recognition of the gravity of values is thus a kind of "philosophical discovery" that can be loosely compared to the discoveries of physical forces that have been made by scientists throughout the course of history. For example, although it was there all along, the existence of physical gravity as a cosmic force was not recognized until it was pointed out by Isaac Newton and Robert Hooke in the seventeenth century. Similarly, the concept of energy as a basic constituent of the universe was not understood until the laws of thermodynamics were consolidated and explained by Lord Kelvin, Sadi Carnot and others in the nineteenth century. And although the idea of eros has been around since the ancient Greeks (and although it was carried forward in the neo-Platonic philosophy of Whitehead), recognition of the existence of value gravity as an actual force that acts on the evolution of life, and more directly on the evolution of human consciousness and culture, is really only now coming to light. In other words, the connection between evolutionary development and the drawing power of ontological quality on all forms of agency is, in fact, a central aspect of the "physics of the internal universe," which we are only just beginning to understand. And I believe that in the future the role of value gravity in the evolution of life and human civilization will be acknowledged as a fundamental principle of the universe, just as the physical principles of gravitation and energy are recognized today.

## The Gravity of Disvalues

Before going further, this discussion of the ontology and gravity of values must address the issue of what Plato called "tyrannical eros"—the urge toward egocentric gratification. Eros does not always lead us to more moral or otherwise more evolved states. Unrestrained quests for power or selfish desires can produce a decaying effect on cultural evolution. But this "dark side of eros" can be at least partially explained by reference to the stages of development in consciousness and culture we have been exploring. As discussed further in chapter 5, pathologies can be found at every level of cultural development. Nevertheless, we have seen how morality has evolved in the course of cultural evolution from egocentric, to ethnocentric, to worldcentric moral perspectives. So when we look back at earlier stages of history from the perspective of contemporary, worldcentric systems of value, egocentric and ethnocentric estimates of value may appear misguided or even pathological. Yet the urge to improve our conditions must start somewhere.

It is important to remember that the worldcentric conceptions of morality that some of us now enjoy have only been achieved through the long history of human cultural evolution. And as noted, not everyone alive today lives in the "same time in history." Many are stuck in cultural settings wherein access to more evolved forms of morality remain out of reach. For example, putting children to work in fields or factories is a practice that we rightfully condemn in the developed world. But from the perspective of many parents who are struggling for existence in third world conditions, the labor of their children provides much needed food for the family. This need does not make the practice moral, but it does show how the larger perspective that is necessary for one to recognize that child labor is wrong is not always available to those who have yet to reach the level of cultural development required for such a perspective. Consequently, if we want to improve people's morality, we have to work to create the exterior conditions under which higher forms of morality can flourish.

The gravity of disvalues can also have a strong influence on certain people living in developed cultures. As the result of inadequate parental nurture (and in a few cases inadequate cerebral nature), the consciousness of some can become arrested at lower levels of development. And when people whose development remains at an egocentric level operate within more evolved forms of culture, such egocentric individuals can take advantage of the trust and freedom that developed societies have achieved. In such cases it seems that the pull of value gravity can produce responses limited to little more than the animalistic survival value of the self, which is often expressed in egocentric desires and selfish lusts. In other words, the urge to improve one's conditions can be felt at every level of development. Yet that urge is inevitably channeled and conditioned by the values provided by one's worldview. And if one's worldview directs them to "only look out for number one," then the eros of value gravity can result in destructive behavior. An obvious example can be cited in the case of white-collar crime and corporate malfeasance.

A difficult problem for every civilization is thus the ongoing presence of uncivilized individuals who do not share the values of the culture in which they live. It therefore becomes especially important in developed cultures that every effort be made to keep disadvantaged individuals from being "left too far behind" in their personal evolution, lest they be prevented from participating in the value agreements of their larger society. Ultimately, it is only through the co-evolution of consciousness and culture that the powerful eros of value can be harnessed for the benefit of all concerned.

Admittedly, the gravity of disvalues is a difficult and perplexing subject. And its inherent complexities are compounded by its association with psychological shadow issues caused by psychodynamic repression.[14] So this section's exceedingly brief discussion may have raised more questions than it has answered. However, a thorough analysis of this feature of evolution is beyond the scope of the present chapter. Yet hopefully, the further discussion of cultural evolution in chapter 5, and the exploration of "value dynamics" in chapter 9 will shed more light on this difficult topic.

## The Sovereignty of the Good

The discussion so far in this chapter has focused on the reality of values and their influence on evolution. The idea that values are at least partially independent of our perceptions has found support within three distinct approaches to the issue: First, I discussed how the basic biological reality of agency reveals the partial objectivity of values in the way that all life forms strive to survive and reproduce. That is, by striving to achieve a desire (such as a meal or a mate), an agent shows that this desire is beyond current conditions—the agent desires what is not presently possessed and thus demonstrates that the object of desire is at least partially "outside" of it. Second, I showed how values evolve in the course of human cultural development, and how the evolutionary trajectory of values-based worldviews evinces a degree of directionality. This directional development thus reveals the external influence of the eros of values upon the human mind. Third, following the insights of moral realist philosophy, I argued that values transcend the internal estimates of the conscious subject in the way that the very act of evaluation can be recognized as the self's effort to "see and respond to the real world." In other words, moral realists argue that when we evaluate well, we "pierce the veil of selfish consciousness and join the world as it really is." Thus, I have pointed to evidence for the ontology of values in the biosphere, in the noosphere (the realm of cultural evolution), and in the relational structures that are "stretched between the truth seeking mind and reality."

But up to this point we have been looking for evidence of the reality of transcendent values "in the world." What if, instead of "looking out," so to speak, we look in? What if, using the eye of philosophical discernment, we ask ourselves: what is the highest value in our experience; what is the most intrinsic value, or set of values? Contemporary professional philosophers usually shy away from specific appeals to spiritual experience as a result of mainstream academia's aversion to spirituality in general. But for those who have transcended the modernist worldview and are thus able to recognize authentic spirituality from a post-traditional and postmodern perspective, reflective introspection can serve as a valuable supplement to a strictly reason-based approach. Integral philosophy thus finds room for considerations of spiritual experience, even as it subjects such considerations to the rigors of close philosophical examination.

In contemplating what our inward experience reveals about the highest form of value, many of us may conclude that *love* is the greatest or most intrinsic value. Other candidates may be considered, such as *freedom* or *happiness*. But as Iris Murdoch observed, love is certainly "the most ancient and traditional claimant, though one which is rarely mentioned by our contemporary philosophers." Yet is love really the highest value? "Love can name something bad." Love can be the source of our greatest errors, and false love can lead to false good. So although love names an element of the highest form of value, there is another term that comes even closer to the center of things. When we consider our most direct intuition of transcendent perfection in light of these philosophical considerations, we may discover that the most appropriate overall term for this fleeting experience of ideal quality can be found in the word *good*.

In her famous essay, *The Sovereignty of the Good Over Other Concepts*, Murdoch contends that the concept of good surpasses love by serving as its aim, arguing that "Good is the magnetic center toward which love naturally moves." Murdoch then adds that love "is the energy and passion of the soul in its search for the Good, the force that joins us to Good and joins us to the world through Good. Its existence is the unmistakable sign that we are spiritual creatures, attracted by excellence and made for the Good."[15] Put another way, "love is the desire to do good to others."

Perhaps this is just a matter of semantics. But words do matter in philosophy. Distinguishing between love and goodness may seem overly abstract, yet the more precise we can be in our identification of the essence of value, the more we can understand how value in general, and transcendent values in particular, serve as attractors of evolutionary development. And a greater understanding of evolution leads directly to a more evolved world. So as I am arguing, something "out there" is valuable; we are in the constant presence of the real potential of a better state of affairs, both personally and globally. We feel the potential for improvement, we sense the eros of higher goodness yet to be reached, and we should not be surprised if this yearning for greater perfection carries with it a sense of the sacred. Freeing the world from war and poverty, protecting our fragile environment, creating social justice, reaching our personal potential and giving our gift to others—these aspirations *are* sacred.

Admittedly, this sacred attractor of eros is partially beyond language. In fact, some philosophers maintain that the good cannot be isolated or clearly identified, that it is the actual *source* of vision and thus not ordinarily seen in itself. Even if we attempt to name it, one could argue that the nature of transcendent value is so diverse and ineffable that trying to fit our description into a single word, or group of words, we will quickly find that our terms overflow with more meaning than they can hold. However, in order to make progress in our knowledge of intrinsic quality, we must come to agreement about the viability of certain value terms, such as "goodness." Indeed, intellectual history has placed us in the position wherein we can now rehabilitate and reinforce the language of transcendent value, even while we are careful to remember the constructivist lessons of postmodernity. That is, we can talk about transcendent goodness even as we steer between the myth of the given and the myth of the framework—recognizing that the highest forms of value have both an objective pole and a subjective pole. We can thus speak of transcendent value without rendering it either completely absolute or completely relative.

In our attempt to move forward in our philosophical understanding of this evolving universe, I therefore propose that we make use of the term "good" as the label for the "true north" of eros's pull toward increasingly higher states of evolution. Good and goodness are worthy terms because they are closely related to their sister concepts of "improvement" and "better." Let the word good thus stand for *perfection's plumb line*, the most reliable indicator of the directional pull of value gravity.

Yet as soon as we settle on the term "goodness," we find that this concept is intimately connected to a dynamic structure of meaning that contains two additional and indispensably related concepts. These are the related ideas and ideals that have been repeatedly mentioned in the discussion so far—the beautiful, the true, and the good. The next chapter is devoted to a thorough discussion of this ancient and venerable triad of values, including the difficulties involved in trying to define these qualities. But before concluding the present chapter, we consider the underlying dynamic pattern from which this three-fold structure of value arises.

## Evolution's Dialectical Pattern

The motion of evolution is not linear or unidirectional. In some instances it regresses, in other cases it stagnates, and sometimes it merely expands horizontally without an appreciable increase in complexity or noticeable improvement. Moreover, we can identify multiple lines of development that evolve at different rates. So in our consideration of the influence of values on evolution, one thing we can say with confidence is that evolution does not exhibit a straightforward progression toward the good, or a steady march to utopia, despite the incessant influence of value gravity. Understanding evolution's directionality is a matter of perspective, and if we narrow our perspective sufficiently, it is easy to conclude that conditions are actually deteriorating over time. For example, arguments for positive cultural evolution are difficult to make if one's frame of reference focuses primarily on the first half of the twentieth century.

Despite the fact that humanity has largely recovered from the setbacks of the twentieth century, new threats have arisen and pessimism about our future evolutionary prospects remains widespread. In fact, at the time of this writing the marketplace of ideas is flooded with predictions of modernity's imminent collapse. And I suspect some postmodernists secretly relish the prospect. But despite our growing global problems I believe that assumptions regarding humanity's inevitable decline are not well founded. There will always be competition between the forces of growth and decay, but this should not cause us to lose faith in our evolutionary potentials. I will save my main arguments for net progress in evolution until chapters 5 and 6. The point for now is that although the motion of evolution is complicated and even messy, it nevertheless evinces certain trends that are unmistakably good. This is especially evident in the case of cultural evolution, which results from our collective efforts to make things better. So I think the most likely future scenario is that we will continue to achieve genuine improvements on multiple fronts, despite inevitable setbacks and the ongoing corrosive effects of error, ignorance, and "tyrannical eros."

In the preceding examination of value gravity, we saw how the basic values of surviving and reproducing influence even the most primitive forms of biological agency and thus achieve initial traction on evolution's earliest organisms. Then as life forms develop, consciousness becomes more active and the values of biological well-being become better articulated and defined. The subsequent emergence of human consciousness then reveals a new universe of values previously imperceptible to animal consciousness.[16] And as human consciousness develops alongside evolving human culture, values continue to evolve through a series of worldview systems that embrace successively wider conceptions of value. But again, even though there are certainly many ways that human cultural evolution has made things better, like evolution as a whole, the trajectory of human history cannot be accurately characterized as an "upward escalator toward the good."

Within the motion of evolution, including both its progression and occasional regression, we can recognize a distinct developmental pattern that guides and shapes the process. This is the well-known pattern of dialectical development, through which overall constructive results are achieved partially through the process of creative destruction. Hegel originally described this dialectical process as: affirmation, negation, and then negation of the negation. This process has also been described as "differentiation and integration," or perhaps most recognizably as "thesis, antithesis, and synthesis."[17] Most of us are familiar with this so-called "law of change." We start with an existing condition—the thesis. As time passes, the thesis decays and becomes increasingly inadequate. This is initially remedied by the appearance of an antithesis—a condition or thing that is defined through its opposition to the problems or inadequacies of the original thesis. In the formation of this opposition or polarity, it is important to emphasize that this tension is inherent within the original conditions and is not produced by the influence of outside factors. Then, out of the energy of tension produced by the polarity of thesis and antithesis, a creative emergence occurs—a novel event or new condition that synthesizes the best qualities of the thesis and antithesis into a transcendent new whole. As illustrated in figure 3.2 the synthesis transcends the opposition between thesis and antithesis by creating a way to include the best of both within the new condition. Through this technique of dialectical development, evolution is able to solve problems and achieve progress. Eventually, however, any improved synthetic condition becomes a new kind of thesis through which the process continues.

Examples of this dialectical system in action can be seen throughout the evolutionary process. Sometimes these dialectical dynamics are extremely evident, but at other times the process is more subtle. Moreover, dialectical polarity does not always lead to synthetic resolution. In some cases, tension between lower and higher levels of evolution is apparently continuous, with each level shaping the development of its opposition in an ongoing process that may never be resolved. Nevertheless, as abundant examples of evolutionary development demonstrate, where there is an energetic polarity, there can often be found a transcendent synthesis waiting to be achieved.

As philosopher Michael Corey observes: "The natural world is full of opposing forces which, by virtue of their tension with one another, produce a desirable result. The dialectical process appears to permeate the whole of physical reality, down to subatomic particles themselves, which exist in balance with one another through a variety of electromagnetic and nuclear forces."[18] Additional examples of dialectical relationships in pre-biotic evolution can be seen in the network of "self-activating loops" involved in the

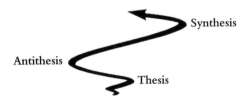

*Figure 3.2*
The spiral structure of the dialectical system

organization of self-replicating, "autocatalytic" molecules.[19] In biological evolution, the most obvious example of dialectical growth can be seen in the technique of sexual reproduction—the structure of male, female, and offspring is a perfect model of the action of the dialectical system. Dialectical relationships are also evident in biology in the formative process of competition and cooperation. In their influential book, *The Dialectical Biologist*, Richard Levins and Richard Lewontin describe an approach to biology that focuses on the feedback systems existing between individual organisms and their larger environment at every level of life.[20]

The idea that dialectical patterns of development exist in nature has been criticized by certain philosophers, including Sartre, who objected that "using dialectic in nature would reduce people to products of physical laws." But this can be understood as more of an objection to the deterministic conclusions of the Marxist philosophy of dialectical materialism than to the existence of the dialectical system itself. Although recognition of the dialectical pattern of development was a central theme of communist philosophy, this should not deter us from seeing its validity within a philosophy that is not deterministic nor otherwise constrained by physicalist limitations.

Although the operation of the dialectical system of development can be readily detected in nature, when we examine the historical record of human cultural evolution the pattern becomes even more evident. Dialectical development is especially apparent in the historical unfolding of the worldview structures we have been discussing. For instance, we can see in history how the thesis of the traditional worldview is partially negated by its modernist antithesis—the truths of science become antithetical to the earlier forms of truth found in scripture. Then as modernism's "season of synthesis" begins to come to an end, it increasingly matures into a stale thesis of itself wherein its mounting shortcomings become ripe for the subsequent postmodern antithesis. In fact, the postmodern worldview defines itself largely in antithetical opposition to modernism. We can see this in the way that modernism's core value of objective scientific truth is replaced by postmodernism's more subjective, constructivist understanding of truth. The postmodern antithesis also rejects the overriding value of economic progress, replacing it with a preference for environmental sustainability.

In the last fifty years or so, postmodernism has served to help correct and remedy many of the excesses of modernism, and there is obviously much work still to be done. But even now we can detect how the postmodern season of synthesis will also eventually evolve into a more static thesis which will in turn make way for a new level of antithesis. And the postmodern worldview's staunch anti-modernist stance is already beginning to supply the problematic conditions that are calling forth a new movement along the dialectical spiral of development, one that seeks a grand synthesis of the pre-traditional, traditional, modernist, and postmodern value systems within a transcendent yet inclusive new whole.

This idea of transcendence and inclusion is actually another way to describe the dialectical process of development. The antithesis transcends and the synthesis includes. This technique, whereby evolution unfolds from within itself, always building on what has come before, can be observed in myriad examples throughout evolution, as noted above. Thus, in our attempts to work for a better world through the evolution of consciousness and culture, we do well to use evolution's own method of growing up while simultaneously reaching down. And it is through this appreciation of evolution's ubiquitous dialectic technique that we come to realize that *the degree of our transcendence is ultimately determined by the scope of our inclusion.*

Some readers may ask: is recognition of the ubiquitous evolutionary pattern of dialectical development a kind of metaphysics? In answer to this I can say that while dialectic relationships can be observed in both physical and metaphysical contexts, I do not think that the dialectic itself is necessarily metaphysical. Although this dynamic relationship is not a material entity, it is clearly observable in the material interactions of abundant natural forms. And thus the recognition of this relationship is no more metaphysical than the recognition of an ecosystem, or similar kinds of formative dynamic system of relationships found in nature.

So if we are willing to accept, even if just for the sake of argument, that the motion of evolution reveals a dialectical pattern of development, then we might suspect that the contours of this development are themselves shaped by the structure of that which is drawing them forward. In other words, if the dynamic motion of evolution is indeed responding to an attractor, if values really do exert a gravitational pull on evolutionary development, then perhaps the structure of evolution's trajectory can tell us something about the structure of intrinsic value itself. That is, if evolution's advance reveals the motion of a three-fold synthetic process, or system of development, we might expect to find that the nature of intrinsic value similarly consists of a dynamic system comprised by three essential parts.

In the previous section I explored the idea that the magnetic center of intrinsic value can best be conceived through the idea of goodness. But no matter how broadly we may conceive of the good, it remains a unitary concept that implies a unilinear direction of advance. Although one could argue that biological evolution generally responds to the unitary value direction of "survival value," cultural evolution is clearly more complex in its responsiveness to value gravity. And as will be explored further in the chapters ahead, it appears that cultural evolution roughly unfolds according to three distinct yet complementary directions, which reveal the underlying influence of evolution's dialectical pattern. So although the good may name one of these directions, our analysis suggests that the value of goodness participates in a structure containing two additional elements. Goodness can accordingly be understood as the "true north" of value only by virtue of its interaction with other related values from which it derives its essentially synthetic and emergent quality.

This leads to the conclusion that the emergent, synthetic, dialectical nature of humanity's cultural evolution is itself a response to the underlying dialectical structure of value gravity, which is attracting cultural development and pulling it forward. And from this perspective, the value of goodness can be recognized as only part of this magnetic attractor—the pull of goodness arises out of and relies on the prior dialectical tension of two other deeply intrinsic qualities. While there are many forms of this polarity, and many labels which we could apply to name its various manifestations, when we look for the most intrinsic concepts that are bound up within the dialectic of goodness, the words that come the closest to the essence of the matter are the terms *beauty* and *truth*.

Following this insight, the next chapter continues this discussion of values by examining the ancient and venerable triad formed by the concept of synthetic goodness, and its dialectically related values of beauty, and truth.

## CHAPTER 4

# Primary Values—Beauty, Truth, and Goodness

As I will now argue, the values of beauty, truth, and goodness, taken together and understood as an integrated system of *primary values*, represent a kind of "great attractor" of evolutionary development. When we take the philosophical perspective on evolution originally articulated by Whitehead, that evolutionary development is essentially "an increase in the capacity to experience what is intrinsically valuable," we can begin to sense how these *most intrinsic* values are an indelible part of the evolutionary process. By way of orientation, the following philosophical analysis of value is intended to help us better recognize the value of evolution overall. And as explored further in chapter 9, an enlarged appreciation of the meaning and value of evolution can actually help us overcome many of the global challenges that now confront us.

The conclusion that beauty, truth, and goodness are the primary values toward which evolution moves is based on several factors which we examine in this chapter: The first is the remarkable degree of "consensus evidence" regarding the special significance of these three values. Agreement that beauty, truth, and goodness are the most intrinsic values can be found among thinkers and visionaries from the West and East, and in both ancient and modern contexts. The second factor is the way these three distinct yet related qualities work together as a dialectical system, containing and disclosing each other in the process of their recognition. The third factor is found in the observation that the teleology of evolution is directed toward beauty, and thus ultimately toward goodness and truth as well. And the fourth factor that leads to this conclusion about the special significance of these three values is the way they provide a form of perfectly minimal metaphysics that can help establish a new evolutionary worldview that harmonizes science and spirituality. Each of these factors will be examined in turn.

## The Philosophical Pedigree of the Primary Values

The idea that beauty, truth, and goodness are the primary or most intrinsic forms of quality is an ancient idea first described by Plato. But the consensus evidence for the primacy of this triad far exceeds the bounds of Platonic and neo-Platonic philosophy. As noted, the neo-Aristotelian philosophy of Saint Thomas Aquinas proclaimed the centrality of beauty, truth, and goodness. These three values were also considered to be primary by a variety of Enlightenment philosophers, the most notable being Immanuel Kant. Kant recognized the beautiful, the true, and the good as the three essential categories of *a priori* understanding. He used these modes of understanding to organize the subject matter of his three great philosophical works: *The Critique of Pure Reason* (which is about truth), *The Critique of Practical Reason* (which is about morality or goodness), and *The Critique of Judgment* (which is about aesthetics or beauty). Moreover, the values of goodness, beauty, and truth serve as the focus for the major branches of philosophy identified as ethics, aesthetics, and metaphysics.

In his recent book, *The Open Secret: A New Vision for Natural Theology*, Alister McGrath adopts the traditional framework of truth, beauty, and goodness as a means of unfolding the potential of a renewed natural theology. McGrath describes the ancient origins of this philosophical triad and goes on to trace the perennial reappearance of this value structure in history. Focusing on the Enlightenment period, McGrath writes:

> The linking together of truth, beauty, and goodness during the eighteenth century was associated with the rise of Romanticism, helping to articulate its dissatisfaction with severely rationalist approaches to nature. Often referred to as the "Platonic triad," these concepts played an important role in providing intellectual underpinnings for the Romantic exploration of the human encounter with nature. Thus Johann Gottfried Herder (1744–1803) regularly appealed to this natural triad—which he unashamedly referred to as his "holy trinity"—as something approaching a self-evident truth. Similarly, Johann Wolfgang von Goethe (1749–1832) claimed that all of Plato's ideas related to an eternal whole, consisting of truth, goodness, and beauty.[1]

Despite the fragmentation of philosophy over the last two hundred years, prior to the rise of postmodernism one could still find wide academic support for the theory of "primary values." For example, in the 1950s the University of Chicago, in association with the Encyclopedia Britannica, sought to codify the "Western canon" through the publication of an ambitious, multi-volume text entitled: *The Great Ideas, A Syntopicon of*

*Great Books of the Western World.* This publication included an entry on the topic of the primary values:

> Truth, goodness, and beauty form a triad of terms which have been discussed together throughout the tradition of Western thought. They have been called "transcendental" on the ground that everything which is, is in some measure or manner subject to denomination as true or false, good or evil, beautiful, or ugly. But they have also been assigned to special spheres of being or subject matter—the true to thought and logic, the good to action and morals, the beautiful to enjoyment and aesthetics. They have been called "the three fundamental values" with the implication that the worth of anything can be exhaustively judged by reference to these three standards—and no others.[2]

However, beginning in the 1960s, the credibility of the "Western canon" was called into severe question by a generation of academics who sought to critique and deconstruct what they saw as the failed ideas of the bankrupt culture of modernism. Drawing from the earlier critiques of Nietzsche and Heidegger, some postmodern philosophers argued that "values" are just arbitrary interpretations imposed by establishment power structures. And accordingly, the notion that there are certain "primary values" was roundly dismissed as the height of idealistic pretense. Yet as discussed in chapter 2, these postmodern philosophers had great difficulty getting away from metaphysical conceptions of value, and this was especially the case when it came to notions of truth.

Although deconstructive postmodernists have not achieved majority positions within the faculties of most universities, they have come to dominate in some departments, and the rise of this intensely critical form of scholarship has served to further fragment academia and to call into question almost every established convention. Yet the current lack of academic consensus about anything having to do with values actually provides an opportunity for the presentation of a new perspective on the significance of values within evolution. Critical academia has shown both the problems of the "received wisdom" about values, as well as the opposite absurdity of completely denying the reality of values (despite their best arguments). And this creates the need for some fresh thinking on the subject, which integral philosophy is attempting to supply. Some of this "fresh thinking," however, has been around for quite a while. An evolutionary understanding of values was advanced by a variety of respected twentieth century philosophers, including Pierre Teilhard de Chardin, Alfred North Whitehead, and Michael Polanyi. And today, recognition of the role of values in evolution continues to be advanced by noted thinkers such as Holmes Rolston, Philip Clayton, Charles Taylor, John Haught, Frederick Turner, and Ken Wilber. Indeed, all of these philosophers acknowledge the central significance of beauty, truth, and goodness in one way or another.

It is also worth mentioning that the specific triad of beauty, truth, and goodness has found a prominent place in the teaching of a variety of Eastern spiritual luminaries, including Mahatma Gandhi, Sri Aurobindo, and Thich Nhat Hanh. For example, Sri Aurobindo writes that there are three essential "spiritual paths" open before the seeker: the path of the heart (the way of beauty), the path of the intellect (the way of truth), and the path of the will or action (the way of goodness). Aurobindo adds that "these three ways, combined and followed together, have a most powerful effect."[3]

Notwithstanding the distinguished heritage of this value triad, our analysis so far has not fully answered the central question: why these three specific values? Why not exalt "wisdom, compassion, and humility," or any other group of lofty ideals? The case for goodness as the "magnetic center" was examined in the last chapter, but so far the reasons why beauty and truth are considered to be part of the same structure have not been addressed. While philosophical propositions are not subject to "proof," I can say that after working with these concepts for many years, I have come to see that beauty, truth, and goodness are actually woven into the fabric of being. In other words, the aesthetic, the rational, and the moral, constitute essential, irreducible dimensions of human experience that continually come to the forefront whenever we think about the world from philosophical and spiritual perspectives. Thus it is no accident that many of the sensitive thinkers who have sought to understand the nature of things have reached similar conclusions about the way the universe works. That is, the fact that these three specific values have been independently discovered again and again down through the ages by some of the best human minds provides strong evidence that these essential dimensions of quality are authentic aspects of reality. And if the primary values of beauty, truth, and goodness really are "in the nature of things," then we would expect them to play a central role in the evolution of the universe.

## The Dialectical Relationship of the Beautiful, the True, and the Good

In my reflection on the directions and methods of evolution, I have come to see how the three-fold pattern of synthetic development known as the dialectic is an indelible part of the developmental logic through which the universe comes to be. As described at the end of the previous chapter, at the very least the dialectic is a well-established universal habit, and perhaps some will allow that it is more than this—that it is the essential creative technique through which evolution unfolds self-similarly from within itself. My sense is that the phenomenon of evolutionary emergence is closely linked with the process of dialectical synthesis, although a thorough exploration of this idea is beyond the scope of our current inquiry. But regardless of its ultimate cosmic significance, a dialectical pattern can definitely be recognized within the relational structure of the primary values of beauty, truth, and goodness.

This relational structure is not fixed or static; it is fluid and dynamic, and always in motion. This can be seen in the way that each of these value concepts can occupy different positions in the dialectical system at different times and in different situations. For example, sometimes a synthetic transcendence is achieved through beauty, such as when a blighted neighborhood is restored through the refurbishment of its buildings. And at other times the most direct path to goodness is found by reference to the truth, such as when scientists discover the cure for a disease. According to Harvard sociologist Pitirim Sorokin, in the purest forms of beauty, truth, or goodness, we can recognize how each value subtly contains and discloses the others.

> Though each member of this supreme [value] Trinity has a distinct individuality, all three are inseparable from one another. . . . The genuine Truth is always good and beautiful. ... Goodness is always true and beautiful; and the pure Beauty is invariably true and good, These greatest values are not only inseparable from one another, but they are transformable into one another, like one form of physical energy, say, heat, is transformable into other kinds of energy, electricity or light or mechanical motion.[4]

Sorokin's thinking echoes the ideas of Saint Thomas Aquinas, who taught that beauty, truth, and goodness were transcendentally one, but that each discloses "pure being" through a different modality. However, while I do not think that these distinct values can be easily conflated, Sorokin's analysis suggests that there are instances when each member of the triad can be somewhat interchangeable. But as a starting point for our understanding of the dialectical relationship of these values, as illustrated in figure 4.1, we can observe that beauty most frequently occupies the position of the thesis—an intrinsic value at relative rest. That is, the extent to which something is beautiful is the extent to which it is relatively complete; its evolution can apparently proceed no further. Even though it is often possible to make something more beautiful, our perception of the beauty itself arises from our intuition of the way that something exhibits the faint traces

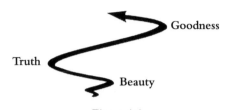

*Figure 4.1*
The dialectical relationship of the primary values

of perfection. Yet even the most exquisite beauty cannot permanently satisfy our yearnings in an evolving universe wherein improvement always remains a possibility, and wherein the desire for beauty can never be completely fulfilled. Thus, the thesis of beauty is not complete; additional fundamental values are also needed in our philosophical attempt to understand the essence of dynamic quality.

And as we look for another aspect of essential value—a complementary yet distinct companion to the value of beauty—we find the concept of truth. Truth is not the diametrical opposite of beauty, yet it does point in a different direction. In the dialectical structure of the primary values, truth serves as the antithesis of beauty in the way that truth points the way forward into a larger reality. Just as beauty signifies the presence of relative perfection in the present, truth can be contrastingly associated with the good that has yet to come. Hegel understood the antithetical role of truth within the larger structure of the dialectic, writing that "the truth is merely the dialectical movement."

Beauty and truth also reveal their dialectical polarity in the way that beauty signifies subjective satisfaction and truth signifies objective description. In other words, assessments of beauty are inevitably bound up with personal tastes, whereas assertions of truth are purportedly beyond mere opinion. Yet conversely and paradoxically, beauty is usually associated with external conditions in the world, whereas truth can be said to have been attained when one's internal thoughts and beliefs become consistent with reality. Again, although the relation of beauty and truth reveals a polar tension, which can also be recognized in the related polarity of art and science, these values are not opposites—they are ultimately both forms of goodness. Beauty and truth thus complement each other in describing different types of essential and intrinsic value. However, neither beauty nor truth are complete in themselves, and their inherent dialectical dynamism points to the synthetic nature of transcendent goodness.

Goodness most often occupies the position of the synthesis because of the way in which it defines the useful limits of beauty and truth. As noted, the dialectical motion of evolution precedes though an interplay of polarities, and when either element of an authentic polarity is privileged or extended too far, the result is pathology. The avoidance of such pathology in any developmental situation is thus achieved by finding the dynamic equilibrium, the right relation, which brings these dialectical forces together in progressive, synthetic harmony. Goodness is thus revealed as it contrasts with the pathology it seeks to avoid.

The synthetic role of goodness within the dialectical trajectory of evolution can be illustrated with the analogy of a sailboat tacking against the wind. A sailboat cannot sail directly into the wind; it has to advance obliquely, tacking back and forth to make progress. And we can see a similar kind of advance in the evolution of human values. Each historically significant worldview—each octave of beauty, truth, and goodness—strives for a new and better way; yet each emergent value system is situated in history and must work to overcome the preexisting pathologies of the previously dominant worldview. The burden of historically received pathologies inevitably shapes the character of emergent value systems as they seek to become what the previous worldview was not. And this attempt to "get away" from preexisting pathologies usually causes value systems to "go too far" in the opposite direction in their quest to avoid the excesses of their historical predecessor. The evolution of values in general, and worldviews in particular, thus "tacks back and forth" toward the improvement of the human condition, thereby producing the structure of a dialectical spiral of development within history.

This description of the dialectical dynamism of goodness, and its sister values of beauty and truth, helps explain why none of these concepts can be satisfactorily defined. As discussed in the last chapter, the most intrinsic forms of value are relational structures—dynamic systems or processes that encompass both subject and object, and which resist being completely reduced to either of these two poles. In other words, to insist on a general or universal definition of goodness, truth, or beauty, is to misunderstand the nature of these realities. Although we are surrounded by abundant particular instances of quality that can be defined as good, it is a mistake to insist on a formal definition of goodness itself because our understanding of goodness is continually evolving. Any such definition would only be relative and temporary, and would tend to give the false impression that goodness was simply an objective quality. Again, the evolving reality of goodness is a direction of improvement that expands infinitely—there is no practical end to improvement and thus no final definition of goodness. This is why values cannot be understood as definable entities or objective facts. Because values are evolutionary gravitational forces subject to ever-deepening discovery, we must understand them through a dialectical epistemology that does not require them to stand still and behave like objects. Ultimately, we cannot define values; it is our values that define us.

## The Teleology of Beauty, Truth, and Goodness

The very idea of teleology in evolution is anathema to most scientific materialists. The notion that evolution is somehow directed toward a goal or final end has been widely criticized as being naive and unscientific. But much of this criticism has been directed toward the most primitive versions of teleological explanation, such as the idea that all events are predetermined by a Deity, or that God is personally directing all developmental details. These notions of the direct intervention of divinity, or the strict unfolding of a preexisting cosmic blueprint, bring with them the inevitable "philosophical problem of evil," which raises questions about how a "divine plan" or "designed universe" could allow for persistent human suffering in the world. Teleology is thus a complex and easily misunderstood subject and I want to be very careful so as not to let this discussion, here or in chapter 6, be confused with cruder forms of teleological explanation that are either overly deterministic or excessively supernatural.

The concept of teleology is closely related to the idea of purpose, which is the primary focus of the upcoming discussion in chapters 7 and 8. But even though the main arguments for purpose in evolution will be saved until then, I can nevertheless point to the obvious and uncontroversial fact that purpose is *in* the universe. As we saw in chapters 1 and 2, all forms of life have a purpose—unlike non-living things, even the simplest organisms strive to survive and reproduce. Then as life evolves, the semi-automatic purposes of primitive organisms develop into more conscious and powerful forms of purpose that can make complex choices and solve problems creatively. We also saw that with the appearance of self-conscious humans comes the dramatic emergence of a wholly new level of purpose. This unique form of emergent purpose possessed by humans is a kind of "second-order purpose"—a self-reflective type of purpose that includes rational, moral, and aesthetic aspirations. And we also observed that human purpose has continued to evolve over the course of history through the emergence of new levels of volitional liberty and increasing degrees of personal freedom.

Thus, given the abundant presence of emergent purpose on earth, the only way to deny the presence of a larger purpose within evolution overall is to make a strict dualistic distinction between "purposeless nature" and "purposeful humanity" (ignoring the significance of purpose in animals). And this has been the exact route taken by analytic philosophers, existentialists, and scientific materialists in general, who see humanity as somehow out of place in the universe, struggling against a meaningless and absurd cosmos. But ironically, this dualistic understanding of humanity's duty to fight against the amoral cosmic process contradicts the reductionistic materialism out of which it arose because the proposition that humans have somehow transcended nature is itself a metaphysical theory that transcends physicalism.

Yet even if we set aside the biological and cultural purposes of individual agents, we can nonetheless observe a directionality in emergent evolution that can, at the very least, be modestly interpreted as trending toward increasing beauty. John Haught, a respected evolutionary theologian at Georgetown University (who testified against the teaching of intelligent design in the internationally publicized Dover School District trial in 2005), recognizes an "aesthetic cosmological principle" under which there is a strong impetus toward beauty in evolution. Articulating what he calls a "loose teleology" inspired by process philosophy, Haught writes:

> Science itself has given us reasons for suspecting that our universe has at the very least a general kind of directionality. Nature abandoned the monotony of its earliest moments and blossomed over the course of billions of years into an astounding display of diversity and beauty. By any standards there is an enormous difference in aesthetic intensity between the nearly homogenous sea of radiation present at the time of cosmic beginnings and the biological and cultural complexity that prevails on our planet (and perhaps elsewhere) today. It seems to me that there is an obvious directionality here—as we survey the cosmic process over its fourteen-billion-year history. And, although the directionality constitutes no proof of an intentional cosmic director, it does suggest strongly that something momentous is going on in the universe.[5]

Process philosophy's most well-recognized proponent is Alfred North Whitehead, whose work appeared in the first half of the twentieth century, and has since been expanded and developed by a wide variety of talented philosophers and theologians. Process philosophers argue that beauty, or the "perfection of harmony," is the ultimate satisfaction of the teleological aims of universal development. According to Whitehead, beauty is "the one aim which by its very nature is self-justifying." In his depiction of beauty as the highest goal of universal becoming, Whitehead included truth and goodness as part of this goal by identifying the true and the good as ultimately forms of beauty. Whitehead regarded truth, or intellectual distinction, which he described as the "delicate adjustment of thought to thought," as a type of "intellectual beauty." He thus equated sensible beauty with truth by "stretch of metaphor." Whitehead also characterized our desire for goodness and our sense of duty to others as a kind of "moral beauty," remarking that: "All three types of character [aesthetic, intellectual, and moral] partake in the highest ideal of satisfaction possible for actual realization, and in this sense can be termed that beauty which provides the final contentment of the Eros of Universe."[6]

I find Whitehead's arguments attractive and fairly satisfying, but I do not mean to rest my case in process philosophy. Process philosophy provides an important contribution to the evolutionary perspective being articulated here, but it has its limitations and is not offered as a final and authoritative explanation of the meaning and value of evolution. Although process philosophy is a kind of integral, evolutionary philosophy, its metaphysics is highly complex and somewhat counterintuitive, and its arguments that "occasions of experience" can be found at every level of universe organization are difficult for many to accept. The conclusions of process philosophy are thus described in connection with our discussion of beauty, truth, and goodness to illustrate how the teleology of these values has been associated with evolution's directionality in previous philosophies.

However, even if we remain skeptical regarding the idea that cosmological and biological evolution exhibit a trend toward the beautiful, if we look for teleology in evolution beyond the confines of isolated and impersonal "nature," and include cultural evolution within our purview, teleological goals and purposes can be seen as unmistakable aspects of the evolutionary process. The primary institutions of cultural evolution all exhibit strong teleological goals. For example, the teleological goal of our legal system, as well as many other social organizations, is fairness, justice, and morality. The clear teleological goal of science is truth. And the teleological goal of art certainly includes beauty and truth in at least some of its expressions. If we allow ourselves to imagine a future and more completed state of social evolution, our aspirations will almost certainly include more accomplished science and medicine, more beautiful surroundings in greater harmony with nature, and a more moral social order where fairness, freedom, and opportunity are in abundant supply. Thus, even the most casual consideration of cultural evolution reveals the evident teleological pull of beauty, truth, and goodness upon human society.

We will return to the exploration of teleology in connection with our discussion of progress in nature in chapter 6. But before we complete this introductory discussion of the role of beauty, truth, and goodness in the evolutionary process, I want to show how this conception of the primary values can be very useful in the forging of a scientifically grounded understanding of evolution that transcends the limitations of reductionistic materialism.

(Parenthetically, here and in the chapters that follow, I will continue using the value triad of beauty, truth, and goodness as a short description or rubric for values in general. Limiting our terminology to the use of a single word, such as "goodness" or "values," would miss an opportunity to describe this "great attractor of evolutionary development" as a *system*. That is, unlike any individual word by itself, the phrase "beauty, truth, and goodness" helps to convey the depth, complexity, and subtlety that are essential to our understanding of dynamic quality.)

## Beauty, Truth, and Goodness—Perfectly Minimal Evolutionary Metaphysics

Previously, we heard Stuart Kauffman call for a "reinvention of the sacred"—a new agreement about what is real that will help us better acknowledge the awesome significance of the universe's boundless creativity and the unmistakable influence of values within the evolutionary process. Traditional worldviews recognize the sacred but are often at odds with science. The modernist worldview has fought the good fight against myth and superstition and has brought us the power of science, yet in doing so it has lost touch with the immanent and transcendent presence of the sacred, which our spiritual traditions understood. So just as traditional religious conceptions of reality have become outmoded in the course of history, we are now witnessing the relative exhaustion of modernist scientific conceptions of reality. Of course, this does not mean that we must completely discard the enduring truths of either traditionalism or modernism. We need to evolve beyond these previous value systems by using evolution's own technique of including the best aspects of these worldviews in a new conception that simultaneously transcends their limitations.

Although I am in general agreement with Kauffman's program, I do not think we need to "reinvent" the sacred because we did not invent it in the first place. The sacred nature of our beautiful universe has been there all along—it is a fact that we have been coming to know gradually by stages throughout humanity's history. And we are now entering a new phase of history wherein participants in the leading edge of intellectual and cultural development are beginning to recognize that the impulse that compels them to develop their potential and work for a better world is the very same evolutionary impulse that originally gave birth to the universe. We are coming to see that the values found within the heart of our conscious lives can also be found within the cosmos as a whole. Thus as I am arguing, we need a new frame of reality that can accommodate both the facts of science and our strong sense of the sacred nature of the universe.

Yet if we simply proclaim a spiritual belief system—if we declare for example that all can be explained through God, or that the material universe is an illusion and nondual oneness is the only reality—we will have essentially fallen back on a contemporary version of a traditional explanation. On the other hand, if we do not discard the materialistic philosophies which maintain that the universe is meaningless and that the advent of humanity is a purposeless accident, we will remain stuck in an outmoded worldview that cannot connect with the intrinsic values we know are really there. So if we are going to adequately reframe our conceptions of the real in a way that both transcends and includes the best of what has come before, we will need a new set of metaphysical premises—premises that are rational and closely tied to scientific facts, yet simultaneously in touch with the trans-rational nature of the sacred. And if these metaphysical premises are anything less than minimal and relatively self-evident, they will end up being just another speculative belief system.

However, our new frame of reality need not banish or replace robust spiritual beliefs. As we will discuss in chapter 9, a wide variety of contemporary spiritual paths are already consistent with an evolutionary worldview. Our new evolutionary metaphysics can thus supplement and complement a culture of spiritual pluralism by remaining strictly philosophical. As noted, philosophy functions best when it works to bridge and separate science and spirituality; the best philosophy thus resists being either reduced to science or expanded into a form of spiritual belief system. And the minimally metaphysical philosophy that can best accomplish the task of providing a reality frame that is friendly to both science and spirituality is one that acknowledges the central role of beauty, truth, and goodness, together with the free will required to recognize these values, in the evolution of our universe. That is, the insight that evolution demonstrates a creative advance toward the beautiful, the true, and the good allows us to acknowledge the evident influence of spirit that can be found within the facts of science without relying on the authority of spiritual teachers or texts. This conception can help us craft a philosophy that is metaphysically flexible and open to a variety of interpretations, but which allows for a natural teleology that includes a flourishing humanity. In the next two chapters we will see how the minimal metaphysics of beauty, truth, and goodness can be used as a criterion for assessing ongoing evolutionary progress. And once we can clearly see how evolution progresses, this can help us discern evolution's overall purpose.

The values of beauty, truth, and goodness provide a useful yet minimal metaphysics of evolution because they are not a belief system—they are evident, ubiquitous, and directly experiential. Even though each worldview stage has its own version of these values, and even though the conception of these values itself evolves through the dialectical process of cultural evolution, these basic value categories nevertheless recur within every stage of development. Even though exactly what is beautiful, true, or good can be defined differently, and even conflictingly, by each successive worldview stage, some version of these values can always be found. Regardless of a person's location within the scale of cultural evolution, we can find something that is true, something that is good, and something that is beautiful for them.

A philosophy that recognizes the ontological reality and causal efficacy of beauty, truth, and goodness in evolution does not require the idea of God to find these influences plausible, but neither does it require that a theistic conception of Deity be rejected or ruled out. The source and destiny of the universe's motion toward the beautiful, the true, and the good can be explained differently by the various forms of spirituality that will find a welcome home within our expanded evolutionary worldview. By remaining open in this way, our new reality-framing agreement can make real progress by transcending scientific materialism without becoming a religion. In other words, if our new understanding of evolution is informed by both science and spirituality, without becoming identical with either of these institutions, we will be able to establish an inclusive evolutionary worldview that can accommodate both minimalistic forms of spirituality (such as that articulated by Kauffman) as well as robust conceptions of a loving Creator. Thus, even as we hold different and even conflicting convictions about the true nature of spirit, we can nevertheless find cultural unity within a philosophically sophisticated evolutionary worldview that can come to terms with a universe of purpose and progress—a universe whose purpose is growth toward beauty, truth, and goodness, and whose progress is measured thereby.

# CHAPTER 5

# Evolutionary Progress
# in Human History

EVOLUTIONARY PROGRESS IS A surprisingly difficult concept. On the one hand, our basic intuition tells us that we live in a marvelous creation, that the formation of our planet and the appearance of life are astounding accomplishments, and that we should be deeply grateful. Most of us can't help but sense that the emergence of our life-giving home in the cosmos is a momentous achievement representing unmistakable *progress* beyond the previous conditions of empty space or a lifeless solar system. And in addition to progress in cosmological and biological development, many of us also sense that progress has been achieved through the growth of our civilization. When those of us who live in the developed world reflect on the twenty-first century society we enjoy, we often marvel at its technological sophistication, its global connectivity, and its well-established political and social freedoms. If we are pressed, most of us will admit that despite the problems, there are many features of modern life which represent distinct *improvements* over the conditions endured by our ancestors.

Yet on the other hand, the majority of both physical and social scientists are very uncomfortable with the idea of evolutionary progress. While this preference for "value neutrality" is perhaps understandable within the context of experimental investigation, the unwillingness to recognize relative value has been extended beyond the methodology of scientific analysis. The denial of progress has now become a central feature of the *philosophical interpretations of evolution* which inevitably accompany the many popular accounts of evolutionary science written by scientists for the general public. And beyond the popular scientific literature on biology and physics, the idea of progress in cultural evolution has also been rejected by many social scientists for whom cultural relativism is the prevailing norm and attempts to rank societies are viewed as inevitably biased and hopelessly misguided.

Even within popular culture, concern for the ongoing degradation of the environment has given many the sense that the developed world is caught in a downward spiral, that the advent of modernity has on balance made things worse, and that our best hope is to replace the idea of progress with the more modest goal of sustainability.

Thus, at this moment in history, evolutionary progress is a decidedly unpopular idea. While there may be broad agreement regarding the desirability of specific kinds of social progress, such as progress in education or progress in technology, the idea of general evolutionary "Progress" (with a capital P) is seen by many as a fallen and discredited myth. And it is ironic that those who refer to themselves as "progressives" are often the most suspicious of theories that offer grand narratives of progress.

Notwithstanding the many good reasons to be skeptical about the notion of evolutionary progress, in this chapter and the next I will undertake the culturally dangerous task of arguing that all forms of evolution are progressive in the long run, that evolution is an unmistakable generator of value, and that we all have a duty to affirm both the actual progress made thus far and the potential progress that is within our power to achieve. Ultimately, evolution is a "grand narrative"; we cannot deny this reality, and thus we cannot escape our responsibility to interpret and evaluate it. Despite the ongoing presence of tremendous trouble and suffering in our world, and despite the inevitable setbacks and crises that lay ahead, integral philosophy's understanding of evolutionary progress in both history and nature can renew our confidence that the human condition can be, and most likely will be, gradually improved over time.

Although I hold that all forms of evolution are generally progressive, the discussion in this chapter begins by considering cultural evolution, where the case for progress can be most readily made. Once progress in human history has been shown, in the next chapter it will be easier to recognize similar kinds of progress in the domains of biological and cosmological evolution as well.

## The Idea of Progress

Progress in the development of civilization is essentially an Enlightenment idea. Although some scholars trace the concept to the ancient Greeks or the medieval Christians, the full realization of the real possibility that the human condition can be dramatically and increasingly improved began with the emergence of modernist values. The values of early modernism included a new approach to truth, which led to the worldview-shattering discoveries of the seventeenth century. The breakthroughs of Galileo and Newton revealed the seemingly unlimited potential of the human mind to unlock the mysteries of nature. Progress in truth through science was so stunning that it made the potential for progress in every area of society seem not only likely, but inevitable. And progress in truth did indeed lead to progress in goodness. As the Enlightenment unfolded, the resulting emergence of democratic forms of government and inalienable human rights represented an authentic moral advance over feudalism. So it is no wonder that by the early nineteenth century, progress had become a kind of modernist religion.

Then came the discovery of evolution—Hegel and other Idealist philosophers described the evolution of human history, and then Darwin and other scientists explained the evolution of life. The new science of evolution fortified the arguments of those who saw human social progress as natural and even predestined. As noted, this led to the regrettable philosophy of social Darwinism and the concept of the survival of the fittest, which was used to justify European imperialism and colonialism. The Victorian ideology of "progressionism" was also used to justify the industrial degradation of nature, with pollution being seen as merely an inconvenient byproduct of an otherwise exalted betterment for humanity. The Victorian commitment to progress reached its apogee in Karl Marx, who saw progress as an inevitable "law of history." Marx's unshakable belief in progress resulted in the idea of social progress becoming imbedded in communism, which claimed to be the true bearer of the progressive goal of humanity. Yet ironically, the rise of communism in the twentieth century would ultimately make a mockery of the idea of progress, exposing the dangers inherent in the immature implementation of "progressive" ideologies.

Progress was one of modernism's most powerful ideas, yet its power also served as a corrupting influence on modernist institutions as a result of the hubris that it spawned. The triumphalism with which progress was embraced made its downfall as an idea all the more dramatic. Beginning with the carnage of World War I, intellectuals started to question and then to reject the notion that modernism was inevitably progressive. Growing disbelief in modernism's promises of unending progress eventually became a significant contributing factor in the rise of modernism's antithesis, the critical worldview we can now identify as postmodernism. And because the idea of progress was so quintessentially modernist, its rejection became an essential feature of postmodernism. Postmodern thinkers focused on the failures and crimes of modernism, emphasizing its regressive and corrosive effects on society and nature. By the middle of the twentieth century, deconstruction of the idea of inevitable social progress had become widely accepted in intellectual circles, as the recent horrors of World War II and the beginning of the nuclear arms race seemed to confirm the worst predictions of a host of pessimistic philosophies. Yet even as postmodern values were adopted by many academics and intellectuals, the modernist worldview remained the cultural center of gravity of the majority of those living in the developed world, and progress in science, technology, and material standards of living continued unabated.

Now in the early twenty-first century, as modernism continues to gain ground through the globalization of its economic system, the perils of progress are ever more starkly revealed. The progress of modernism is resulting in global warming and destruction of the natural environment; it is causing waves of migration that bring poor and desperate people to the developed world where most become part of a semi-permanent underclass; unregulated global competition is undermining social welfare systems and living standards for workers in developed nations; and globalization is resulting in the vast accumulation of wealth and power by transnational corporations and economic elites. The global spread of modernism is also exacerbating religious fundamentalism, as traditional cultures are pushed into defensive postures that often lead to terrorism and social repression. Moreover, the worldwide use of scientific agricultural practices and the adoption of scientific medicine have resulted in the unintended consequence of severe overpopulation in many developing countries. This in turn has led to increasing poverty and fueled the growth of the other problems listed above.

But despite the indisputable pathologies and global threats produced by 350 years of modernism, the balance sheet of "progress" is not unequivocally negative. Modernism has brought unprecedented material prosperity and longevity to the broad masses living in the developed world, and now the prospect of a middleclass lifestyle is becoming an achievable dream for millions in China and India. The continuing advance of globalized modernism has resulted in the end of colonialism and the expansion of democratic freedoms. And the spread of modernist values has also done much to diminish sexism and racism, as societies that were once closed and cut off from global currents can no longer resist the penetration of Western media and the globalized Internet.

## The Dialectic of Progress and Pathology

Thus, like previous stages of cultural evolution, modernism has brought humanity both incredible gifts and horrific disasters. Retro-romantic post-modernists, who often reject the benefits of progress and yearn for a return to a simpler time in history, have only been able to justify their vilification of modernism by comparing its worst pathologies with the best achievements of the premodern stages of cultural development. Yet this is how the dialectic of development unfolds. Once the postmodern antithesis started out to correct the problems of the modernist thesis, postmodernism's more ardent adherents ended up taking their antithetical views to the extreme, thereby exposing the latent pathologies of their own worldview. But as we now attempt to move beyond postmodernism toward an integral perspective, we can more clearly see how each stage of cultural evolution brings new powers for both good and bad. Social philosopher Jürgen Habermas explains these dialectical dynamics as follows:

> Evolutionarily important innovations mean not only a new level of learning but a new problem situation as well, that is, a new category of burdens that accompany the new social formation. The dialectic of progress can be seen in the fact that with the acquisition of problem-solving abilities new problem situations come to consciousness. A higher stage of development of productive forces and of social integration does bring relief from the problems of the superseded social formation. But the problems that arise at the new stage of development can—insofar as they are at all comparable with the old ones—increase in intensity.[1]

In other words, as cultural evolution achieves new depths of understanding and new powers over the material world, these very advances carry with them corresponding problems and pathologies that can only be solved by still further evolution. Whitehead stated the problem succinctly: "Error is the price we pay for progress." It thus appears that progress and pathology are linked in a kind of indestructible polarity, wherein every step forward results in new categories of problems that are intimately related to the positive features of that same developmental advance. Perhaps equally important is the fact that, although emergent stages of cultural evolution result in improvements, some of the benefits conferred by previous stages are often lost in the process. And this leads to the question of whether the inevitable co-evolution of progress and pathology means that *net progress* is an illusion. Could it be true that the more we try to make things better the more we make things worse? Given the severity of our world's problems, this is a conclusion that can certainly be reached by people of good sense and good faith. However, I believe such pessimistic assessments of cultural development can be overcome through the understanding of evolution provided by integral philosophy. When we come to appreciate how consciousness evolves, when we see how synthetic transcendence emerges through the dialectical tension of thesis and antithesis, we can then better detect authentic progress in cultural evolution, despite the appearance of new problems and setbacks that inevitably accompany the process.

## Elements of Progress

Estimates of progress are inevitably evaluative. From an analytic perspective, in order to be able to say that something has progressed we must have two elements: directional change, and a criterion for judging whether the change constitutes relative improvement. Considering the first element, there has certainly been abundant directional change in the state of human culture since the advent of modernism, and this is especially true in the developed world. Since the Enlightenment we have witnessed both exterior social changes as well as interior changes in values and worldviews. Externally, of course, we now have a globally connected technological civilization that would have been unimaginable to our premodern ancestors. And internally, the ongoing movement from premodern to modernist and postmodern worldviews is resulting in greater knowledge and education, expanded cultural literacy, and a larger sense of acceptance and even sympathy for perspectives and beliefs that differ from our own. But as we have discussed, not everyone living in the developed world holds modernist or postmodern values. Approximately thirty percent of Americans, for example, are culturally premodern, remaining within traditional religious worldviews. However, even though development has been uneven, the first element of progress—directional change—can now be recognized as a self-evident fact of human cultural history that has been accelerating for the last 350 years.

Turning now to the second element of progress—a criterion for improvement—we can again observe that some of the changes brought about by modernism have been unambiguously good. Although the polarity of progress and pathology can always be detected, few will argue, for instance, that the advent of scientific medicine, the end of slavery, or the appearance of the Internet, are not real improvements of the human condition. On the other end of the spectrum, there have been changes that are unambiguously bad, such as environmental degradation or the ongoing

threat of nuclear war. But beyond these relatively easy cases for evaluation, we are still faced with the question of whether there has been net
progress overall. For how can we make such an assessment in a non-biased
way? Are not all criteria by which we might judge improvement hopelessly
anthropocentric? Indeed, from the perspective of most other species of life,
the growth of human culture has been an unmitigated disaster. So in our
assessment of cultural development, how can we overcome the fact that all
values, and thus all evaluations of improvement, are at least partially relative
to the interests of the observer?

These are important questions that must be addressed by anyone arguing for progress in the evolution of human history. And in order to address
concerns that there can be no valid criteria for improvement, we must deal
with two related problems that impact our analysis: the first is the problem
of the relativity of all values, and the second is the problem of anthropocentrism. The challenge of anthropocentrism is described in the next chapter's
discussion of the biological progress of life. Now, in the next section, we
focus specifically on the problem created by the fact that most values are
situated within, and specific to, established human worldview structures.

## Value Relativism

As noted in chapter 4, it is a mistake to try to concretely define values
such as goodness, because there is no single objective standard by which
one can assess the truth of a moral proposition. Recognizing this conundrum, postmodern relativists have argued that there are no "morals," there
are only "customs," and thus no group has the right to force its customs
on others. Such a claim, however, is pregnant with its own contradiction.
The recognition of the relativity of values is itself situated within the postmodern worldview, and is thus colored by postmodernism's own interests
in correcting the pathologies of modernism and traditionalism. Although
modernism had originally arisen in a dialectical move away from the
traditional Christian worldview, by the mid-twentieth century, the "establishment" of the developed world was characterized by a cultural alliance
between modernism and traditionalism. Despite the moderating influence
of modernism, during the time that the social structures of postmodernism
began to emerge, the moral absolutism of the traditional worldview was
continuing to exert a strong influence on the culture of the developed
world. Combating this moral absolutism thus became a defining feature
of the postmodern worldview. And emerging postmodernism did make

authentic moral progress by condemning the racism, sexism, homophobia, ethnocentrism, and authoritarianism that remained within the dominant culture of the time. By showing the relativity of values, postmodernists diminished traditionalism's moral hegemony over modernism and reduced its overall influence on the culture of the developed world.

However, it is philosophically incoherent to maintain that because we have come to see how values are relative, this somehow delegitimizes all further value judgments. In order to recognize the relativity of values we actually have to make a value judgment in the first place, so we cannot then claim that such a critical value judgment invalidates all further value judgments. Taken too far, the progressive thinking that sees how no value system is final or absolute can fall into a kind of value paralysis, becoming blind to comparative excellence. While values will always be relative where human will is free, if we embrace relativity without restraint we end up with the rather absurd result of having no ground to stand on when it comes to our values. Values are not absolutely relative, they are only partially relative.

As discussed in chapter 3, the most intrinsic forms of value are neither entirely objective nor completely subjective; values have both an objective pole and a subjective pole. The subjective pole always renders values partially relative because intrinsic values only fully exist where there is consciousness to recognize them. And it is this subjective aspect of values that accounts for the differences between worldviews—as consciousness evolves, values change. However, a constant pitfall in the practice of evaluation is to allow evolution's strong dialectical currents to push us into one extreme or another. For example, seeing the subjective element, some conclude that values are absolutely subjective, and thus merely customs. But this, of course, is a reaction against the opposite extreme, seen in many traditional perspectives, where the objective pole of values is mistaken for confirmation of the absolute objectivity and final authority of a given value system. Yet once we come to see that values are deeply dialectical, both in themselves, and in the trajectory of their evolutionary development, we can see that extreme value relativism is just another form of absolutism.

The way forward beyond the potentially debilitating critiques of postmodern value relativists can be found in a dialectical understanding of cultural evolution that synthesizes the thesis of objective value with the antithesis that holds that all values are merely subjective. A dialectical, evolutionary perspective can see how both of these positions are partially right, but it can also see how privileging one perspective over the other leads to pathology. Recognizing the dialectical nature of values keeps us from making the mistake of either flattening and discounting all value judgments as equally relative, or exalting some value judgments as absolutely better in all circumstances. The very nature of values causes them to resist being completely collapsed into either the subjective or objective category.

Because this subtle dialectical understanding is often missing from the perspectives of the existing worldviews we have discussed, none of these worldviews can accurately assess the relative development of different value systems. Therefore, resting in nonjudgmental cultural relativism may seem a safer bet than risking a regression to older ethnocentric notions of cultural superiority. But once we come to see that consciousness and culture do actually evolve, and that this development produces a dialectically structured internal cultural ecosystem, we can begin to value the evolution of culture more accurately and more compassionately. The dialectical epistemology provided by the emerging evolutionary worldview can champion and promote cultural development while simultaneously recognizing the intrinsic value of each stage of development as it is.

Stated differently, an evolutionary perspective can value the relativistic truth that all worldviews deserve respect ("people have a right to be who they are"), that each worldview is evolutionarily appropriate for its given life conditions, and that the accomplishments of earlier levels are prerequisite for the achievements of later appearing levels. Yet this perspective can also value the developmental truth that sees how the scope of those worthy of moral consideration expands as worldviews evolve over time, how our grasp of truth is enlarged through cultural evolution, and thus why some perspectives are more advanced than others. Again, "more advanced" worldviews are not better in every way, they are always subject to the ever-present dialectic of progress and pathology, but they are nevertheless more inclusive and mature.

Another important benefit of the evolutionary approach's understanding of the dialectical dynamics of cultural evolution is that this also keeps us mindful of the relativity of our own value system, and of the fact that even this evolutionary perspective will itself be eventually transcended in the ongoing course of evolution. Yet even as we remain circumspect, we nevertheless have a duty to use the power of this emerging perspective to help solve our global problems by working to bring about further cultural evolution. Once we recognize how values themselves evolve, we can take postmodernism's valid critiques in our stride without becoming paralyzed in our ongoing duty to evaluate. Acknowledging that values always have a partially relative quality does not mean that we can make no valid judgments. Rather, this postmodern insight requires not that we judge less, but that we judge more—that we judge our judgments and always keep in mind that the highest values and the fairest judgments are the ones that consider the interests of the largest wholes, while also preserving the relative sovereignty of each individual.

## Sources of Moral Authority

So where can we find our collective moral authority? As is the case with all worldviews, most of our values are related to the problems we face. As we have seen, each value system is tailored to the specific problems that it encounters along the timeline of history during which it originally arose. And it is the inherent immorality of problematic life conditions—the suffering and injustice that these negative conditions represent—that provides the duty and the corresponding moral authority for the value solutions that connect to these problems. In other words, when we can agree about a problem such as environmental degradation, this creates the potential for valid value agreements about the solutions, such as better protections and more investment in alternative energy. Thus, the moral authority that justifies acting on our values is derived from our duty to address the concrete problems that plague us.

Ultimately, all values are justified by agreement; so working to improve the human condition inevitably involves persuading others regarding which problems are most important and thus which value-solutions we should focus on. If we really care about what we value, eventually we have to put a stake in the ground and make the arguments that justify these values. And this is exactly how some of the most momentous accomplishments in cultural evolution have been achieved. The founders of the United States did just this when they declared the "self-evident truths" that all men are created equal and have the inalienable right to life, liberty, and the pursuit of happiness. The modernist value agreements embodied in the Declaration of Independence and the Constitution were seminal factors in the evolutionary emergence of the developed world. And to this day, these ideals remain a guiding light of progress, not only for Americans, but for billions of people throughout the world. However, although healthy forms of homegrown modernism remain the best hope for evolution for the majority of the world's premodern population, those of us in the developed world who have already received the full benefits of the progress offered by modernism are seeking to make progress in new directions.

Although the postmodern worldview, as I am defining it, remains mostly countercultural, although its adherents make up only about twenty to thirty percent of the population of the developed world, it has nevertheless been extremely influential. Even though the term "progress" is rarely used due to its close association with modernism, postmodernists continue to champion their own versions of progress, such as progress in our compassion for oppressed or disadvantaged peoples, progress in our concern for the environment, and progress in our tolerance and commitment to cultural pluralism. Moreover, postmodernists have achieved real progress through their attempts to moderate and correct the pathologies of modernism. The culture of the developed world has indeed been improved by those who have questioned the values of materialism, consumerism, and unrestrained economic development. But these examples of postmodern progress have come at a price. Like the earlier worldviews of modernism and traditionalism, postmodernism has its own pathologies, including the frequent denial of overall progress in the state of the human condition. As noted, the idea that no form of culture can be said to be superior to any other originally arose as a corrective to the Eurocentric hubris that was embedded in the immature ideals of progress envisioned by modernism. Yet this form of staunch value relativism can hold us back in our attempts to make the world a better place. If many of our best and brightest thinkers are ambivalent or even hostile toward the idea of cultural evolution, our ability to form the kind of broad based agreements that will be necessary to achieve further cultural evolution will clearly be diminished.

## A New Definition of Social and Cultural Progress

How a culture defines progress is crucial to its ability to solve problems and improve conditions for its members. And as we now attempt to remedy both the problems created by the rise of modernism, and the preexisting problems that modernism has been unable to resolve, our philosophical understanding of progress becomes very important. In order to achieve the further cultural evolution that is urgently needed, our civilization requires a new definition of progress that transcends the limitations of both modernism and postmodernism. As we will discuss in this section, this new definition of social and cultural progress includes the incremental advance into the emerging evolutionary worldview (for those who are ready and able), as well as ongoing progress across the entire existing spectrum of cultural development. Again, describing and defining progress is a philosophical exercise in evaluation, and our ability to evaluate well is greatly facilitated when we are not limited to the values of a single worldview or ideology. Thus, the strength of the evolutionary perspective is found in its ability to make use of the positive and enduring values of every historically significant worldview in its estimates of overall progress.

As previously described, despite the ongoing impact of globalization, the state of evolution of human consciousness and culture is spread out over several thousand years of historical development, with the majority of humanity remaining centered within premodern value systems. Progress in cultural evolution is thus occurring on multiple fronts: In much of Africa we are witnessing progress from pre-traditional tribal worldviews into traditional religious worldviews; in most of Asia culture is progressing from traditional worldviews into the modernist worldview; and in the developed world we are witnessing ongoing progress from modernism into the postmodern value system. And now we can even begin to see a "post-postmodern" or "evolutionary" worldview appearing on the horizon of history beyond postmodernism.

Each of these fulcrums or crucibles of development provides distinct criteria with which to evaluate whether cultural circumstances have been improved and progress has thus been achieved. For example, the traditional worldview's criteria for progress include such things as the reduction of hunger and crime, growth in church attendance, and decline in the number of children born out of wedlock. Progress is assessed by modernism as increased wealth and material standards of living, growth in democratic freedoms, and reduction of disease. For postmodernists, progress includes the movement toward environmentally sustainable economies, growth in social justice and equality, and the rejection of material acquisition as a measure of happiness.

Recognizing this ongoing progress across multiple fronts of development, the evolutionary perspective defines progress broadly as the overall development of consciousness and culture. And according to this definition, upward movement into each of these previous worldviews can be recognized as authentic progress. Thus, the evolutionary criteria for progress includes the criteria of every historically significant worldview to the extent that a given worldview's values serve to improve the human condition by attracting people to a relatively more evolved form of culture than that in which they find themselves. In other words, rather than viewing humanity as a homogenous whole with only one edge of development, the evolutionary perspective recognizes that the progressive improvement of the human condition is occurring simultaneously on many levels, with each level of evolution experiencing continuous growth and development within the confines of its worldview structure.

However, in addition to recognizing progress across multiple fronts of development, the evolutionary worldview also seeks to make progress by better integrating and harmonizing the developed world's three major competing worldviews. The evolutionary perspective thus seeks to reduce the staunch anti-modernist bias of postmodernism by showing how our culture depends on the ongoing success of healthy modernist values. And this perspective also seeks to make progress by persuading modernists that postmodern values can be safely employed to improve modernism's errors, such as the frequent elevation of economic interests as the highest value.

In short, the integral, evolutionary worldview provides an opening for further progress through a new synthesis of values that brings together the best of traditionalism, modernism, and postmodernism into a more unified culture that can achieve the requisite political will necessary to tackle our global problems more effectively. In pursuit of this synthesis "evolutionaries" seek to recruit people to the emerging evolutionary worldview itself. And in chapter 9 we will further examine the evolutionary worldview's specific proposals for political and social evolution. Although it will likely be generations before integral values provide the cultural center of gravity for the developed world, the adoption of this evolutionary perspective by a significant minority can prevent the inevitable expansion of the postmodern worldview from destabilizing the healthy forms of traditionalism and modernism which serve as an ongoing foundation of our civilization.

The evolutionary perspective shows us how to preserve the core values of older worldviews while simultaneously pruning away their pathologies and removing the "evolutionary scaffolding" that prevents them from serving us into the future. For example, pre-traditional indigenous worldviews can continue to serve us by reminding us of our deep connection to nature. Traditional worldviews can keep us in touch with the wisdom of our ancestors; by changing very slowly and cautiously, traditionalism provides a degree of long-term cultural continuity. Modernism can continue to serve us as a source of entrepreneurial vitality and economic growth, and through scientific discovery. While modernism cannot continue to expand in unsustainable directions, such as suburban sprawl or extraction of fossil fuels, its growth can continue indefinitely in economic sectors such as technology and information. And postmodernism too can serve us by continuing to act as a moderating influence on modernism, and by returning spirituality to its place as a central feature of our culture. Not a monolithic kind of spirituality that takes the form of a single religion or official belief system, but a culture of spiritual pluralism, diverse in its beliefs but unified in its commitment to the myriad forms of beauty, truth, and goodness that each of us can experience and create. Progress according to the emerging evolutionary worldview is thus progress in all worldviews in the service of evolution.

## Justifying Claims for Cultural Evolution

Yet if values are inevitably situated within worldview structures, on what basis can the evolutionary worldview claim to be more evolved? Indeed, how can it claim that postmodernism is more evolved than modernism, or that modernism represents progress over traditionalism? The answer to this crucial question is found in history, which provides a large-scale record of how people have solved problems and improved their conditions over time. We have seen how the values of each historically significant worldview are related to the specific set of problems that prevailed during the time in history when that worldview first appeared. And we have also seen that because the conditions of practically every period of human history continue to exist in varying degrees in different parts of the world today, each of these historical worldviews has an ongoing role to play in ameliorating its specific problem set.

For instance, where pre-traditional social and cultural conditions exist, traditional values and institutions are often most effective at ameliorating problems. Examples of this can be found in contemporary sub-Saharan Africa, where many pre-traditional groups are choosing to improve their conditions by adopting various forms of Protestant Christianity. The effectiveness of traditional values for solving pre-traditional problems can also be seen in the developed world, where gang members and troubled youth seem to respond best to the structure and discipline offered by tradition-based, conformist approaches.

Following this pattern, in established traditional societies, many (especially the young) are attracted to the personal freedom and economic prosperity offered by modernity. Some postmodern writers have tried to deny this by contending that traditionalists only aspire to modernism because of "false consciousness," having been duped by advertising and seduced by the insidious culture of consumerism into embracing values that will only make them unhappy in the end. While this may be true in some cases, it is condescending for postmodernists to judge traditionalists this way.

Traditionalists may sometimes be mistaken about what is real or what is valuable, but these people are nonetheless capable of determining what is truly in their self-interest in the long run. And for the last 350 years, traditionalist populations worldwide have been evolving toward modernism, but generally not vice versa. Indeed, modernism has produced more cultural evolution than any worldview before or since.

This pattern of ongoing growth through the established stages of history can also be seen in the continuing movement from modernism into postmodernism. For at least the last fifty years, where the social and cultural conditions of successful modernism have prevailed, the sensitive, pluralistic values of postmodernism have offered a path toward further evolution. As we will explore further in chapter 9, the emergence of postmodern values has helped moderate the excesses of modernism and has offered an alternative to the traditional forms of morality that previously held sway over the modernist mainstream. Postmodernism has also provided a wide variety of lifestyle alternatives for those living in the developed world, including alternative forms of politics, medicine, and spirituality. Although the postmodern worldview has become the majority demographic in only a very few places, it is nevertheless a vibrant and growing countercultural segment that can be found within most modernist societies.

But here I must state a caveat. As described in connection with our discussion of the evolution of consciousness and culture in chapters 1 and 3, the evolution of human history cannot be smoothly conceived as developing along a unidirectional course of advance. As with the consciousness of individuals, collective culture evolves along multiple lines of development. Yet also like consciousness, we can nevertheless generally locate a culture's "evolutionary center of gravity" along the continuum formed by these "major stages" of worldview development we have discussed. An accurate assessment of cultural evolution accordingly lies somewhere in between a strict multicultural view that sees every culture evolving along its own unique historical trajectory on the one hand, and a simplistic, unilinear conception of absolute development on the other hand. Therefore, our understanding of the evolution of human history needs to be nuanced by incorporating perspectives such as that articulated by development scholar Thomas McCarthy, who advocates replacing "the idea of a single path to a single modernity with that of a multiplicity of hybrid forms of modernization."[2] And I have attempted to convey such a nuanced view by emphasizing that, to be sustainable, modernist social structures must grow largely out of the soil of their own native traditional cultures.

That said, only the most staunch value relativists will deny that human worldviews have demonstrated evolution over time. This is not just my value judgment. The historical record clearly reveals the emergence of successive worldview stages, and these stages have arisen from the collective agreements that have been repeatedly made by billions of people over the last several thousand years. While this structure of worldview development has been documented by social science research in psychology, sociology, and anthropology, the best evidence for this recurring pattern of cultural evolution continues to be found in the events of history. As illustrated in figure 5.1 the history of worldview development reveals a dialectical trajectory of evolving value agreements that form the steps of consensus that humans continue to reach regarding the direction of relative improvement for their social and cultural conditions. And this distinct pattern of development arises within human history because cultural evolution is not only being driven by free human choices, it is also being drawn by the gravitational pull of values. Thus, just as the shape of a spiral galaxy reveals the gravitational forces through which it is formed, the dialectical spiral of human historical development similarly reveals the gravitational influence of values on the evolution of consciousness and culture.

As the world becomes increasingly connected through globalization, ongoing evolution into each of these existing worldviews is exacerbating the inherent dialectical conflicts that naturally occur between these stages. And the growing pressures of this culture war, both domestically and internationally, are creating the need for a transcendent yet inclusive new worldview that can help harmonize and integrate all the various worldviews that will continue to exist within our larger cultural ecosystem throughout the remainder of this century and beyond. This new evolutionary worldview's definition of progress thus includes ongoing worldwide

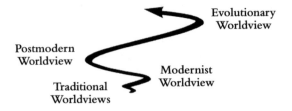

*Figure 5.1*
Dialectical development of values-based worldview stages

growth along the entire existing spectrum of cultural evolution, as well as incremental cultural progress in the developed world beyond the anti-modernist limitations of postmodernism.

• • •

In conclusion, as a result of our world's currently unsustainable conditions, we are under mounting pressure to help bring about cultural evolution on every front of its development. As we pursue this important mission, our efforts to achieve further progress can be greatly facilitated by integral philosophy's enlarged understanding of how relative and partial progress has been achieved in the past. This expanded perspective reveals how the evolution of values has been a primary driver of cultural evolution overall. So even though assessing the relative evolution of values is fraught with pitfalls and paradoxes, in order to meet the challenges of the twenty-first century, we must be willing and able to recognize the evolution of values within culture. And once we distinguish the evolutionary worldview's concept of progress in cultural evolution from the immature beginnings of this concept in nineteenth century modernism, this more nuanced and sophisticated understanding of the historical progress of humanity can rehabilitate our aspirations for further progress into the future by showing how progress itself is a deep feature of evolution as a whole.

This chapter has built on the discussion of worldview development first broached in the introduction. However, these arguments for the evolution of values are extended further in chapter 9. So if my analysis so far has not yet been completely persuasive, I invite you to skip ahead to chapter 9 where this discussion will be brought to its full conclusion through additional arguments and examples. But if you are still with me at this point, then please carry on to the next chapter. Although I believe progress in history is well established by the accumulating record of human choices for improvement, the present chapter's discussion of cultural progress is only the beginning of our larger investigation of evolutionary progress overall. Next in chapter 6 we turn to an examination of progress in nature to see how the development of human culture is only the latest phase of an overarching trajectory of progress that has been unfolding for billions of years.

## CHAPTER 6

# Evolutionary Progress in Nature

Although there are a variety of ways to measure or otherwise justify progress in the evolution of human culture, as we analyze evolution philosophically, we find that progressive growth is actually a deep feature of evolution overall, which can be traced all the way back to its primordial beginnings with the big bang. In order to more clearly discover and more fully understand this profound characteristic of evolutionary development, we must look beyond the evolution of human history and into the underlying evolution of matter and life. As explored in this chapter, evidence for both cosmological and biological evolutionary progress can be found in the structural sequence of emergence, which grows in value by continuously building on itself.

First, our discussion of progress in biological evolution examines the various objections to the notion of natural progress that have been raised by scientists and philosophers. Then I explain how integral philosophy overcomes these objections by recognizing multiple dimensions of emergent quality that increase in opposing yet complementary directions as evolution unfolds. Then, once we have established how the development of life makes progress, we then investigate how the same structural pattern of transcendence and inclusion that reveals the growth in value in biological evolution also demonstrates progress in cosmological evolution as well. Finally, once we have established how the unfolding of evolutionary emergence in all of its domains is unmistakably progressive, this leads to the last section's consideration of the relationship between progress and teleology. There we will see how the nature of evolutionary progress reveals a nondeterministic, participatory kind of teleology, through which the creatures of evolution themselves help decide where evolution is heading. After completing the overall argument for evolutionary progress in this chapter, this enlarged understanding of progress will then be used to illuminate the investigation of evolution's purpose in the next chapter.

## Progress in Biological Evolution Overall

At the time of this writing, biological progress remains a vexed subject. A large number of biologists deny it outright, others admit to it, but in narrow and circumscribed ways, and only a very few are willing to embrace it as a beautiful expression of the blossoming of life's potential. The concept of progress in the evolution of life has been renounced or evaded for a variety of reasons. First, it is difficult to measure; second, it has unmistakably spiritual implications which trouble many scientific materialists; and third, it has been subject to historical abuses, which now taint the concept in the eyes of many as being either regressively religious or outright racist.

Prominent biologist Stephen Jay Gould has been the most vocal opponent of biological progress. As noted in chapter 2, Gould famously wrote that "progress is a noxious, culturally embedded, untestable, nonoperational, intractable idea that must be replaced if we wish to understand evolutionary history."[1] Following Gould's lead, many writers in the scientific community repeatedly emphasize that progress in biological evolution is an outmoded concept that has been thoroughly refuted. Characterizations that recognize some organisms as "higher" than others have now been largely purged from the evolutionary literature. However, some of the more thoughtful commentators have been careful to qualify their rejection of progress as being limited only to the scientific analysis of evolution, leaving questions about the larger philosophical significance of life explicitly open.

Yet when we examine the many popular science books, magazines and websites that discuss the subject of evolution, the vast majority ignore the subtle differences between science and philosophy and give the impression that evolution has been shown to be nonprogressive as a matter of scientific fact. For example, the popular website *TalkOrigins.org*, which authoritatively claims to represent "mainstream" evolutionary science, under the heading "Common Misconceptions about Evolution," definitively states: "Evolution is not progress. Populations simply adapt to their current surroundings. They do not necessarily become better in any absolute sense over time."[2]

Many in the scientific community reject the notion of progress in biological evolution because they feel that the concept of progress involves an unscientific value judgment. Indeed, value neutrality is a basic feature of the scientific method. Scientists avoid making value judgments so as to remain objective, to discover how the world actually is, for better or worse. Science accordingly tries to limit itself to facts, remaining silent regarding matters of intrinsic value. Intrinsic values are qualities that are valuable in and for themselves, such as human life or the beauty of nature. A value can be said to be intrinsic if it is not "for the purpose of" something else. However, while science usually leaves questions of *intrinsic* value to philosophy or religion, scientists deal with questions of *instrumental* value on a regular basis. In contrast with intrinsic values, which are ends in themselves, instrumental values are qualities which are good for the achievement of a particular goal. For example, a polar bear's thick coat is instrumentally valuable for surviving and reproducing in the arctic. Unlike intrinsic values, instrumental values can be empirically tested. Once a criterion for evaluation has been established, such as reproductive fecundity, the instrumental value of a given adaptation can be measured scientifically. Scientists can thus determine the relative instrumental value of evolutionary developments for the purposes of surviving and reproducing. But scientists usually stop short of saying whether surviving and reproducing are goods in themselves.

In keeping with this reasoning, some argue that from a scientific perspective, the only kind of evolutionary development which is "better" is evolutionary development which is instrumentally better at achieving the goal of surviving and reproducing. And by this criterion, the life forms that have shown themselves to be the most "progressive" are bacteria, which have survived longer and in greater numbers than any other kind of organism. Yet this reductionistic conclusion has not satisfied all biologists, with some continuing to have a nagging intuition that there has been an increase in more than just the individual fitness of specific species.

Given the "anti-progress" climate of our time, it bears repeating here that the concept of progress contains two elements: the first is that directional change has occurred over time, and the second is that this change represents improvement or betterment. While the presence of the first element of directional change may appear obvious in the growth of traits such as organismal complexity or intelligence, even this seemingly straightforward concept has been disputed or problemitized. So before we can address the more central issue of intrinsic improvement, we first have to establish biological evolution's directional advance.

## Measuring Directionality in Biological Evolution

In order to establish a comprehensive directional movement in the unfolding of biological evolution we need to find large-scale trends that involve multiple species. Developmental tendencies within individual species, such as growth in the brain size of hominids, cannot be used to establish directionality in evolution overall. In their search for trends that extend beyond the growth of individual species, biologists have proposed a variety of criteria by which to measure directional development across species, such as the use of energy, or the ability to obtain and process information about the environment. But these criteria have been criticized as lacking clarity or not being measurable. The most popular candidate for overall directionality in evolutionary development has been the growth of complexity in organisms. Yet even this seemingly obvious trend has been shown to be problematic. Philosopher of biology Daniel McShea explains:

> Complexity is probably the answer most biologists would give if asked what sort of trend characterizes evolution as a whole, or what characterizes progress. However, most would also agree that this assessment is mostly, if not entirely, impressionistic. The difficulty is that complexity—in the colloquial sense, at least—has no operational definition. . . . We might call a car complex on account of its many parts, but we might also call a device with few parts such as a violin complex if its manufacture involves lots of steps, or if its few parts are machined very precisely, or if those parts are made from some high-tech material. In biology, colloquial complexity connotes an uncertain mix of organismal features, such as number of part types, degree of hierarchical structure, adaptedness, sophistication, and so on. This richness makes the word useful in many contexts, but it also makes it difficult to apply in any precise way. Suppose we wanted to compare a human with our fish ancestors hundreds of millions of years ago. As the eminent paleontologist George Gaylord Simpson put it, "It would be a brave anatomist who would attempt to prove that recent man is more complicated that a Devonian ostracoderm." So if the claim is that progress is complexity, the skeptic reasonably wants to know: complexity in what sense, measured how? In the absence of a clear answer, the term complexity in discussions of progress looks like a code word for proximity to humans, and a devious way to make the ordering in the Great Chain of Being sound more scientific.[3]

We can see from this passage how attempts to establish criteria with which to measure directional trends in evolutionary development are resisted by scientific materialists such as McShea. Even though growth in complexity seems like an apparent feature of biological evolution, it is nevertheless denied by many in the scientific community because of its close association with the larger philosophical concept of progress overall. As McShea's disparaging reference to the "Great Chain of Being" at the end of the quote inadvertently reveals, many scientists have their own "devious" philosophical reasons for objecting to the recognition of directionality in evolutionary development. That is, if directionality could be shown scientifically, such a finding would come very close to establishing progress in evolution overall. And because of evolution's powerful cultural significance, if scientists were able to definitively establish that evolution progresses, this would have profoundly negative consequences for the metaphysics of materialism; because if we can establish progress, then *purpose* cannot be far behind. As ardent materialist William Provine candidly admits, "The difficult trick is to have the progress without the purpose."[4]

Reading the literature, one gets the distinct impression that the question of directional development in evolution as measured by science has become a battleground on which larger philosophical conflicts are waged by stealth. Scientists offering criteria with which to measure large-scale directional growth are criticized for "rigging" their analysis to make humans come out on top of the evolutionary hierarchy. McShea states this objection as follows: "This notion of humans as the most dominant, intelligent, or complex seems to some biologists to be transparent anthropocentrism, an attempt to flatter ourselves, to feed human vanity, or to put a scientific gloss on the Christian notion of humans as central in the universe, and since Darwin, as central to the evolutionary process."[5] Yet, ironically the clear implication of this statement is that even if humans were, as a matter of scientific fact, found to be more intelligent or dominant, we would have to reject such science as being too Christian.

Recall that according to the standard neo-Darwinian explanation of evolution, changes can occur only by random variations in the genetic code produced by individual mutations or genetic drift. Selection for fitness by the environment can only occur after random changes have produced slight differences between organisms. So because all initial changes are said to be random, neo-Darwinian theory cannot satisfactorily explain the presence of overall directional change, even if the fact of this kind of development can be established scientifically. In other words, it is hard to see how these genetic changes could be both random and progressive at the same time. Thus, the staunch defenders of neo-Darwinian orthodoxy have reason to object to progress, not only because progressive directional development is difficult to measure, but also because their theory cannot account for it.

And this perhaps explains why even the rather clear-cut measurement of life's directional advance has been disputed or explained away by many in the scientific community. Nevertheless, it can in fact be shown scientifically that long-term, large-scale directional change is an empirical feature of biological development. After devoting a substantial part of his academic career to the subject, professor of biology Jeffrey Schloss has effectively refuted the conclusions of Gould and others who deny directional development, making clear that directionality can be found, even from the "biocentric" perspective of a scientific materialist. Schloss writes:

> It turns out empirically that a constellation of taxonomic and life history traits has increased over evolutionary time: species diversity, trophic depth, homeostatic control, sensory acuity, behavioral and locomotive freedom, various measures of complexity at cellular, organismal, and social levels, body mass and lifespan, per capita parental investment, and capacity for intersubjective awareness and inter-organismal attachment.[6]

The analysis of Schloss and others clearly establishes that directional change over time is an empirical fact of biological evolution. Although this trend is not evident in every lineage, and although some trends lead in opposite directions, there is nevertheless an arrow in evolutionary time that points toward generally greater complexity, diversity, and the other traits identified in the quote above.[7] While these findings have not been widely disseminated in the scientific literature due to their unpopular implications, the empirical validity of the underlying research has not been disputed. And this evident directionality has in fact been acknowledged (sometimes grudgingly) by a number of prominent evolutionary biologists, including John Maynard Smith, Ernst Mayr, and Edward O. Wilson. Thus, despite the objections and attempted refutations, the first element of progress is actually well established. And this brings us back to the second element of progress, which requires that this directional change has been for the better.

## Progress and Prejudice

Perhaps objections to the concept of overall progress in biological evolution can be overcome by simply distinguishing between science and philosophy. Perhaps we can conclude that overall progress is difficult to measure, that it is essentially a question of intrinsic value, and that it is best to move on to a purely philosophical treatment of the subject. The problem with this is that most of the scientific luminaries responsible for educating the public about evolution make no distinction between science and philosophy. The important difference between instrumental value and intrinsic value is rarely acknowledged. So because many in the scientific community continue to argue that the concept of progress is problematic and unscientific, and because it is assumed that only science can deliver truth, evolution is said to be simply nonprogressive, and in fact meaningless.

Indeed, neo-Darwinian experts seem to place special emphasis on the meaninglessness of evolution. In his book *The Progress Paradox, New Republic* editor Gregg Easterbrook comments on the popularity of existential despair among cultural elites, writing:

> Modern thought evinces a strange homage to meaninglessness, as if the absence of significance were a welcome reading of the human prospect. . . . Contemporary thinkers have spoken almost as if enraptured by pointlessness. Richard Dawkins, who holds a chair in the public understanding of science at Oxford University, in 1995 said [evolution] is "neither good nor evil, neither kind nor cruel, but simply callous: indifferent to all suffering, lacking all purpose." In 1996 Jessica Mathews, president of the Carnegie Endowment for International Peace, declared [in a *Washington Post* editorial] that "human life is a cosmic accident with no purpose." Page upon page of similar statements can be found from contemporary writers, artists, professors, and intellectuals. . . . And one can marvel why some of Western society's most privileged individuals—the holder of an endowed chair at Oxford, the president of an important foundation charged to seek world peace—are so eager to decree humanity pointless.[8]

Although Easterbrook's point is well taken, from an integral perspective this penchant for pointlessness is not a mystery; it is actually an expression of the dialectic of progress manifesting itself within the evolution of culture. As we have discussed, the theory of evolution has been used not only for scientific purposes, but also for the cultural purposes of establishing the power of the modernist worldview over its original historical rival, the traditional religious worldview. So to assure the supremacy and finality of the modernist account of our origins, it is seen as necessary to purge evolution of every vestige of meaning so as to counter the excessive religiosity of traditionalism.

And beyond its aversion to myth, modernism has also sought to dispel notions of progress for other reasons. Two of the pathologies of the traditional worldview that some modernists (as well as most postmodernists) have fought hard to overcome are racism and a general disregard for the welfare of animals and the larger natural environment. In his book on evolution, *Out of Control, Wired Magazine* founder Kevin Kelly, states this case emphatically:

> Progress smells of human-centeredness. To some it stinks of religiosity. Among the earliest and most fervent supporters of Darwin's scandalous theories were Protestant theologians and seminarians. Here was scientific proof of the dominant status of mankind. Darwinism offered a beautiful model for the orderly march of insentient life toward the peak of known perfection: the human male. The continuing abuse of Darwin's theories to bolster racism

didn't help the notion of evolutionary "progress" either. More important in the story of progress's demise has been the wholesale downshift of human position from the center of the cosmos to an insignificant wisp on the edge of an insignificant spiral in a dusty corner of the universe. If we are marginal, then what progress can evolution have? Progress is dead, and there is nothing to replace it. The death of progress is nearly official in the study of evolution, as well in postmodern history, economics, and sociology. Change without progress is how we moderns see our destiny. . . . all progress seen in life and society is a human-induced illusion. The prevalent notion of a "ladder of progress" or a "great chain of being" in biology doesn't hold up under the facts of geological history. . . . All creatures on the globe at any one time are equally evolved, having engaged in evolution for an equal amount of time. To put it bluntly, humans are no more evolved than most bacteria.[9]

This passage by Kelly brings out some additional objections to the recognition of biological progress. Beyond the objection of some scientists that there is no measurable criteria for improvement, and beyond the objection of the philosophy of scientism that recognizing progress causes metaphysical trouble, we can also find additional cultural objections to theories of biological hierarchy. These cultural objections stem from historical abuses of the theory of biological progress. The first such abuse arose from the traditional teaching of "man's dominion over nature," which was used to justify the worst kinds of exploitation and degradation of animals and the natural environment. However, as a result of the evolution of consciousness we can now see that treating nature as having only instrumental value for use by humans is immoral, a pathology of traditional values that we must overcome. The second form of abuse was even more insidious, and this was the use of the theory of progress to justify racism. The theory that some animals were higher than others was extended to humans, resulting in whites being classified as more biologically evolved than nonwhites. Scientific theories that recognized progress in the development of life were thus subverted into the service of oppression. And obviously, this false and morally repugnant hijacking of science has given biological progress a bad name.

These historical abuses demonstrate that hierarchical evaluations are powerful and even dangerous. This is why it is so important to evaluate accurately and appropriately, especially when it comes to appraising the intrinsic value of humans. The abuse of the concept of progress and the subsequent rejection of the idea shows how the evolutionary currents of thesis and antithesis can result in one faulty evaluation giving rise to an opposite form of faulty evaluation. Do only humans count? Of course not.

But are humans no more valuable than plants or insects? For most of us, this proposition violates both our hard-core common sense and our basic moral intuitions. If we analyze the reasons behind these intuitions we may come to see that the critique of all human evaluations of progress as inevitably anthropocentric is itself situated within the larger stance of value relativism that is a cornerstone of the postmodern worldview. And in the discussion of value relativism in the previous chapter on cultural evolution, we concluded that the partial relativity of values is a fact, but this should not be used as an excuse to avoid our duty to evaluate. Thus, in response to this dilemma, we are here exploring a new worldview, one which seeks to transcend postmodernism's attempts to flatten all hierarchy. This new evolutionary perspective agrees with many of postmodernism's valid critiques of previous theories of progress, but this new perspective nevertheless recognizes how evolution builds on itself and moves in directions of increasing quality.

## The Value of Wholes and Parts

As we are coming to see, one of the primary catalysts that is causing the emergence of this new evolutionary worldview is a deeper understanding of evolution itself. And at the heart of this deeper understanding is a recognition of how the process of evolution generates value naturally and prolifically as it unfolds. To demonstrate this point, this section examines evolution's trend toward increasing quality using two crucial concepts that are central to integral philosophy. The first concept focuses on the structural pattern produced by evolutionary emergence, and the second concept reveals how this expanding structure of emergence produces complementary forms of intrinsic and instrumental value.

The analysis begins by reexamining evolution's natural hierarchy of developmental levels. Chapter 1 explained how the process of evolution as a whole has manifested itself through three major domains or primary levels of emergence (physical, biological, and cultural), with each domain itself unfolding through a nested sequence of emerging levels. This hierarchical structure is formed by evolution's basic technique of building increasingly more complex systems upon simpler foundational systems. Although science did not begin to study the processes or structures of emergence until the twentieth century, the deeper meaning of this hierarchical ordering pattern has intrigued philosophers throughout history. Venerable thinkers such as Leibniz and Hegel spent significant time contemplating this structural feature of the natural world.

Then beginning in the 1960s philosopher Arthur Koestler advanced the theory of "holons" and "holarchy," which described the pattern created by emergence wherein each evolutionary entity is a whole in one context and a part in another. Koestler pointed out that in the sequence of emergent evolutionary levels, every *whole entity* is composed of parts, but is also itself "a part" that is included in larger wholes. For example, in the sequence of biological emergence, a cell is simultaneously a whole that contains organelles and molecules, and also a part that is contained by living tissue. Every form of evolutionary organization consists neither of simple wholes nor simple parts; in the organization of evolution there are only "whole/parts," or what Koestler called "holons." Moreover, the development of holons does not result in a simple hierarchy, like geological strata stacked on top of each other. Rather, the pattern resembles the structure of an onion or a nested series of concentric spheres that are interdependent and complexly interactive—this structure of evolutionary systems is thus itself a system. Koestler also coined the term "holarchy" to refer to the natural hierarchy formed by evolution's construction of holons within holons. Figure 6.1 illustrates two complementary views of this developmental pattern: The top graphic illustrates the nested structure of a holarchy's "development by envelopment," as well as how each holarchic level "transcends and includes" its predecessors. The bottom graphic illustrates the holarchic principle of "more depth less span." That is, as emergence builds on itself, higher levels of development are generally less physically numerous than lower levels. This naturally occurring form of organization can be found in practically all forms of evolutionary development.

Koestler's important insight about the underlying structure of evolution has since been adopted by a number of prominent writers on evolution, including Lynn Margulis and Ken Wilber. Recognizing the evident growth in value demonstrated by this pattern, Wilber writes:

> In any developmental or growth sequence, as a more encompassing stage or holon emerges, it *includes* the capacities and patterns and functions of the previous stage (i.e., of the previous holons), and then adds its own unique (and more encompassing) capacities. In that sense, and that sense only, can the new and more encompassing holon be said to be "higher" or "deeper." . . . Organisms *include* cells, which *include* molecules, which *include* atoms (but not vice a versa). Thus, whatever the important value of the previous stage, the new stage has that enfolded in its own makeup, plus something extra (more integrative capacity, for example), and that "something extra" means "extra value" relative to the previous (and less encompassing) stage. This crucial

## Two Views of the Holarchic Structure Produced by Evolutionary Emergence

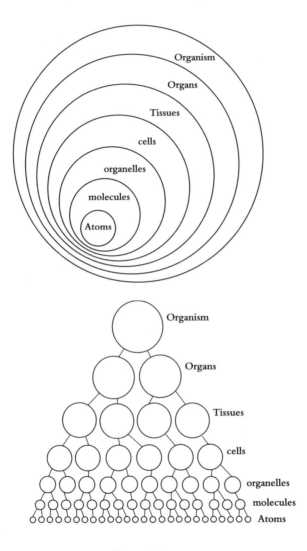

*Figure 6.1*
Different graphical representations of the same structure of interdependent hierarchy produced by the emergence of holons, known as a "holarchy"

definition of a "higher stage" was first introduced in the West by Aristotle and in the East by Shankara and Lieh-tzu; it has been central to developmental studies ever since.[10]

Wilber's explanation of the growth of value through holarchical development begins to reveal the connection between the theory of holons and the theory of intrinsic and instrumental value introduced above. Recall that intrinsic value is a good in itself, and instrumental value is a good for something other. Applying the recognition of these complementary categories of value to evolution's whole/part pattern, we find that holons exhibit both kinds of value as a result of their participation within this structural sequence. That is, in their function as parts, holons are instrumentally valuable to the larger wholes that embrace them. And in their role as whole entities, holons possess intrinsic value *in themselves*. This recognition of the simultaneous existence of both instrumental and intrinsic value within evolutionary forms provides the basis of Holmes Rolston's influential environmental ethics. Rolston explains:

> Organisms value other organisms and earthen resources instrumentally. . . . Plants make resourceful use of water and sunshine. Insects value the energy that plants have fixed by photosynthesis; warblers value insect protein; falcons value warblers. . . . Organisms value these resources instrumentally because they value something intrinsically: their selves, their form of life. No warbler eats insects in order to become food for a falcon; the warbler defends her own life as an end in itself and makes more warblers as she can. From the perspective of a warbler, being a warbler is a good thing. . . . A life is defended intrinsically, without further contributory reference—unless to defend the species and that still is to defend a form of life as an end in itself. Such defenses go on before humans are present; and thus both instrumental and intrinsic values are objectively present in ecosystems. The system is a web where loci of intrinsic value are meshed in a network of instrumental value.[11]

Rolston's description of the presence of both intrinsic value and instrumental value within biological systems has been extended by Wilber, who describes how these different forms of value increase in opposing yet complementary directions as evolutionary holarchies build over time. In other words, as evolution unfolds it results in both increasing intrinsic value and increasing instrumental value.

Beginning with intrinsic value, Wilber observes that as evolution produces larger and larger encompassing holonic levels, each new level contains more and more parts and thus more and more whole entities. And as holons come to embrace more whole/parts within themselves,

**Emergent levels of evolution**
**grow in complementary directions of value**

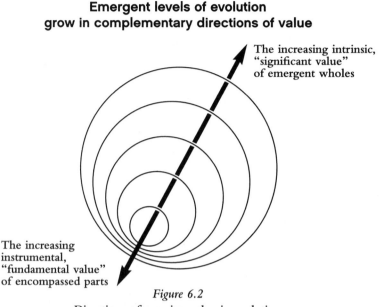

The increasing intrinsic,
"significant value"
of emergent wholes

The increasing
instrumental,
"fundamental value"
of encompassed parts

*Figure 6.2*
Directions of growing value in evolution

this increases their intrinsic value, or what he calls their "evolutionary significance." Wilber thus concludes that "cells are more significant than molecules, because cells contain molecules . . . An ape is more significant than a cell, and so on."[12]

Yet according to this theory of "holonic ecology," as evolutionary levels grow in wholeness or intrinsic value by embracing more parts, the parts themselves simultaneously become more and more instrumentally valuable. For example, in the scheme of evolution, as atoms are encompassed by molecules, and as molecules are in turn encompassed by cells, and then cells by organs, the underlying atomic level is taken up and used by more and more evolutionary entities. And as a given holonic level becomes increasingly more useful in this way, it becomes more instrumentally valuable to the successively larger wholes that embrace it. As Wilber explains, "the more partness-value a holon has—that is, the greater number of wholes of which that holon is a part—the more *fundamental* that holon is . . . An atom is more fundamental than an ape."[13] This conclusion is supported by the fact that atoms can exist without apes, but not vice versa. (Note that Wilber uses the terms "fundamental" and "significant" as synonyms for instrumental and intrinsic value respectively; and we will continue to use these synonyms interchangeably as our discussion continues.) Using the structure of emergence first shown in figure 6.1, figure 6.2 illustrates the key theoretical insight that shows how evolution generates value in opposite yet complementary directions as it unfolds.

The philosophical perspective that can recognize growth in both fundamental value and significant value helps us overcome both extremes in our interpretation of progress—the view that flattens all hierarchy and recognizes no progress, as well as the view that values only humans and is blind to the intrinsic value of nature. This philosophy affirms that all life has intrinsic value while also recognizing that some forms of life are more significant than others. And this theoretical approach provides a way to validate our moral intuition that the evolution of life has indeed progressed from its simple beginnings, and that humans are "higher" than other forms of life. What makes humans more evolved is our embodiment of a level of emergence that transcends biology. The physical bodies of humans may not be that different from the bodies of other complex mammals, but our minds, elevated by cultural evolution, constitute a level of emergence that distinguishes us from our animal cousins.

## Biocentric Egalitarianism

However, before we rest in this conclusion, we must address counterarguments raised by the principle of "biocentric egalitarianism," also known as "bioequality." This is the position articulated by Kevin Kelly in the quote above, which holds that all life forms have equal value and equal worth. Although as Wilber points out, bioequality is a "qualitative distinction that denies all qualitative distinctions," it arises from a valid concern about fidelity to science, as well as from an ethical commitment to the sanctity of life and the natural environment. This philosophical position thus deserves fair consideration within the context of our discussion of biological evolutionary progress.

The biocentric view of evolution has both modernist and postmodern versions. The postmodern version is most often articulated by those who ascribe to the philosophy of "deep ecology," which emphasizes that nonhuman life has intrinsic value beyond its instrumental value to humans. According to this egalitarian perspective, all beings are "aspects of a single unfolding reality," with humans being viewed as simply "plain members of the biotic community,"[14] like any other species of animal. And because deep ecologists classify humans as merely one species among many, they believe that we are not superior to other species in any kind of moral sense. Therefore, according to this view, humans cannot ethically justify their ongoing destruction of the environment because human needs are no more important than the needs of other species.

Deep ecologists thus reject any kind of hierarchy or ranking in evolution on the basis of their spiritual commitment to the essential unity of the universe and the "oneness" of all beings. In response to this, Wilber has sought to honor this spiritual commitment while also showing how it is possible to nevertheless recognize the growth of value in evolution. He accomplishes this by positing an additional type of value in his theory of holonic ecology. According to Wilber, every entity of evolution possesses three types of basic value—intrinsic value, instrumental value, and what he calls "Ground-value." As discussed, life forms have intrinsic value in themselves and for themselves, as well as instrumental value for use by others in their ecosystem. But in addition to these developing forms of value, evolutionary entities also have a kind of changeless, existential value by virtue of their participation in the underlying unity of the universe. Wilber writes, "All things and events, of whatever nature, are perfect manifestations of Spirit. No holon, whether conventionally considered high or low, sacred or profane, simple or complex, primitive or advanced, is closer or farther from Ground, and thus all holons have equal ultimate value or equal Ground-value." After explaining these three types of value, Wilber then distinguishes the changeless nature of Ground-value from the evolving nature of intrinsic value, writing: "The fact that all holons have *equal Ground-value* is often confused with the notion that they must therefore all have *equal intrinsic value* ("bioequality"), and this paralyzes any sort of pragmatic action at all."[15]

To this I can add that although deep ecologists are certainly right that humans depend on the environment and have a duty to protect and preserve other species as ends in themselves, we need not discount or ignore the unique and highly valuable aspects of human life in order to conserve the wellbeing of nature. In fact, as discussed further in the next section, the evolutionary perspectives of integral philosophy can actually increase our appreciation of nature's value overall and amplify our power to protect and preserve the environment.

Like the postmodern version of bioequality found in philosophies such as deep ecology, the modernist or, more specifically, the scientific materialist version of this position also holds that humans are no more evolved than other species. However, under the materialist version of this position, humans are not seen as equal to other species because we are all "aspects of a single unfolding reality," but rather because all lines of evolution have been evolving for the same length of time. This position is articulated by biologist Lynn Margulis, who writes: ". . . all extant species are equally evolved. All living beings, from bacterial speck to congressional committee member, evolved from the ancient common ancestor which evolved autopoiesis and thus became the first living cell. The fact of survival itself proves superiority, as all are descended from the same metabolizing Ur-form."[16] Notwithstanding the numerous and otherwise brilliant writers who have articulated this argument for bioequality, this reasoning is highly fallacious. It is like saying that if two musicians practice an equal amount of time, the quality of their music must be identical. However, although scientism's argument for bioequality is weak on its face, it is based on two underlying assumptions that need to be addressed: the first is that fidelity to science requires that we eschew value judgments in our analysis of evolution, and the second is that because changes in life forms occur randomly, such changes cannot be progressive. I will address this latter assumption first.

The idea that the role of randomness in the process of biological development somehow excludes the possibility of improvement rests on a conception of evolution which ignores its cosmological and cultural domains of development, and which defines the process narrowly as changes occurring among biological organisms. So again, because these changes are said to result from purely random genetic mutations or genetic drift, it is argued that such changes cannot lead to a progressive increase in value, and that evolution is merely a "random walk." By this reasoning, the concept of "more evolved" is thus decoupled from the concept of "more valuable."

In response to this first assumption, I can reaffirm that the apparent randomness of the genetic mutations that produce variations in organisms (which the environment then selects for fitness) is an essential mechanism of biological development, and a significant element of Darwin's theory of evolution. But it is nevertheless possible to honor Darwin's important discovery of the role of random mutation without concluding that the process is incapable of producing improvement. As Rolston observes: "randomness is an advancement generator . . . Randomness guarantees the trial-and-error exploration of the potentialities of the system. . . . What systemic nature achieves over evolutionary time is made possible by randomness, but the headings are shown by the statistical results—not the lack of heading shown by randomness in the innovative process."[17]

We turn now to the second assumption behind scientific materialism's bio-egalitarian philosophy, namely, that an understanding of evolution that is appropriately informed by science is one which makes no distinctions of value among evolutionary entities. In other words, making value judgments about evolution is out of step with a scientific worldview. In answer to this, I can again point out that while value neutrality is important to the experimental method of science, we cannot accurately apprehend the natural world unless we have an ability to evaluate it. In short, evaluation is essential to perception. As an analogy, consider Yosemite Valley—could one possibly understand it without recognizing its sublime beauty? Is Yosemite's priceless value equivalent to the dusty plains of Fresno that lie only a few miles away? Such a conclusion seems absurd.

Among all the things that humans can seek to know, evolution is one of the most significant. And something this significant cannot be accurately understood unless it is appropriately valued. Thus as I am arguing, we cannot comprehend or even really see the realities of evolution without the use of a philosophy that can recognize evolution's multiple dimensions of emergent value. Indeed, it is only through this kind of "depth perception" that we can begin to understand evolution in its fullness.

## Anthropocentrism and the Value of the Noosphere

We have been examining how evolution unfolds through a series of major and minor levels of emergence, with each new level generally including and depending on the level from which it arose. When we now combine this understanding of evolution's structure with the value insights of "holonic ecology" described above, this shows how the emergence of life transcends and includes the realm of matter and energy, hence matter and energy are more fundamental and life is more significant. The same can be said about the emergent domain in which human consciousness and culture evolve. The psychosocial layer of evolution, also known as the *noosphere*, transcends the biosphere in the way that it inaugurates a new kind of evolution, which moves at a faster pace and is partially independent of the underlying biological evolution from which it emerged. With the emergence of the noosphere, a new universe of values appears; values that can only be experienced by humans. Although animals experience values through their striving to survive and reproduce, humans are able to experience depths of beauty, truth, and goodness that are clearly beyond the capacities of animal consciousness. And this ability to experience values itself evolves through the ongoing emergence of the stages of consciousness and culture we have discussed.

We need not conceive of biological progress simplistically as a continuous line of development culminating in humans. Higher intelligence develops in a variety of different biological lines besides mammals, such as birds, and even cephalopods. But even if we acknowledge that complex forms of consciousness are widely distributed in the animal kingdom, this does not negate the evolutionary uniqueness of human consciousness. The consciousness possessed by humans displays a level of emergence found nowhere else in life. Yet the fact that humanity exhibits an entirely new level of evolutionary development is somehow lost on the scientific experts who deny progress. These writers treat the evolution of human consciousness and culture as if it were simply a strange case of biological evolution involving more developed tools.

However, when we look for progress in life beyond the current constraints of physical science, when we allow ourselves to recognize more than mere instrumental value, the uniquely intrinsic value of human life becomes evident. The emergence of humans actually brings beauty, truth, and goodness into the world, because prior to our appearance these values were only faintly recognized at best. And as we have seen, transcendent values have both an objective pole and a subjective pole—they are brought into being partially through their recognition. So how could we fail to see that this dramatic emergence of values represents a progressive increase in intrinsic value? If value itself is not valuable, what is?

Here it is important to reemphasize that integral philosophy's attempt to rehabilitate the idea of evolutionary progress not only transcends postmodernism's value relativism, it also includes postmodernism's egalitarian sensibilities. In its quest to find intrinsic value in evolution, the integral perspective affirms the biological equality of all human groups, renouncing racism, and also affirms the intrinsic value of all life, and indeed all "holons." Integral philosophy's environmental ethics acknowledge that the biosphere is more *fundamentally* valuable than humanity, while simultaneously recognizing that the appearance of humanity has added *significant* value to the evolution of life. As discussed in the previous chapter, the moral immaturity of modernist values resulted in the idea of progress being abused, which subsequently caused postmodernism to reject the idea entirely. But now, the emerging evolutionary worldview can safely reclaim the power that comes from the recognition of progress by taking the concept to a higher level—a new philosophical synthesis that transcends and includes the values of traditionalism, modernism, and postmodernism.

Once we acknowledge that the emergence of humanity constitutes authentic and undeniable evolutionary progress, we can use this understanding to establish the progress of intrinsic value across the entire spectrum of biological development. One of the ways this can be accomplished is by charting the steps of emergence that form a nested structure of successive enveloping developments along the evolutionary timeline (as shown in figures 6.1 and 6.2). The phylogenetic tree of life may have the apparent structure of a "sprawling bush," with no main trunk or obvious tip, but when we focus on the key innovations of emergence, rather than on the sequence of speciation, a somewhat different structure appears. We can see how certain innovations of emergence, such as the vertebrae or the neuron, are built upon by latter occurring instances of emergence. In his book *The Emergence of Everything*, Harold Morowitz charts fifteen levels of biological emergence between prokaryotes and primates, with each level building on and including the successful adaptations of the preceding level. Although the image of a "ladder of emergence" may be too linear, there clearly exists a structural sequence of encompassing levels that demonstrates a progression.[18] When we add to this the philosophical insight that the emergence of human consciousness and culture represents something more than just another incremental level of biological emergence—that the appearance of the evolving noosphere on planet Earth is a cosmic event equivalent in significance to the original emergence of life from inanimate matter—we can see how the sequence of emergence presents a clear trajectory of progress.

So despite the obvious problems created by the rise of our globalized civilization, I hope our discussion so far has provided some reasons to conclude that the emergence of humanity represents a kind of *success*—that the biosphere giving rise to the noosphere is a sign that the biosphere has succeeded in producing its own transcendence. Thus, if we use the emergence of humanity as a value anchor for our conclusions about progress, we can then begin to properly value the levels of emergence within the evolutionary history of the biosphere that continue to be contained within, and used by, the line of development that led to humans. In other words, looking down the fossil record at the series of biological ancestors whom we now embody in our own bodies, we can perhaps better appreciate the progressive steps of biological emergence that led to the transcendence of the biosphere itself.

Ultimately, the value of humanity cannot be separated from the process that has led to human life. We carry our origins with us in our very being. And we demonstrate the value of these origins as we continue to carry forward the evolutionary process by appreciating and creating value of every kind. Simply stated, we become more evolved, and the world becomes more evolved, as we create value. And as evolution continues to work through us as we strive to make the world a better place, we come to see how the concept of "more evolved" cannot be disconnected from the concept of "more valuable." As Rolston writes: "There is value wherever there is positive creativity."

This philosophical analysis of biological progress takes concerns of anthropocentrism in its stride, giving full credit to the intrinsic value of every biological line of development and indeed every form of life. Yet even as we value life in all its fullness, our philosophy should not neglect to value the evolutionary achievement that has produced humanity. Using the sequence of emergence as a gauge of progress necessarily involves the interests of humans, but this is justified by the fact that the very structure of emergence itself demonstrates that humans are an expression of the interests of evolution.

In summary, because of its immense cultural and symbolic significance, the evolutionary story of our origins is too important to be left to the interpretation of science alone. If our culture does not develop a more adequate philosophy of evolution that can come to terms with both the fact and the value of evolution, this important subject will remain mired within the impoverished philosophy of scientism. However, if we are not constrained to force our analysis of progress into value neutral, instrumental criteria—if our philosophy liberates us from both the modernist metaphysics of scientific materialism and the postmodern metaphysics of value relativism—we can begin to value the lives of humans and all living things more appropriately. Once we reject the often tacit proposition that only science can deliver truth, we can reclaim the criterion of intrinsic value as a valid basis for inquiry into the meaning of evolution. And once we acknowledge that evolution is an enormous generator of value, we can find justification for our moral intuitions, which tell us that the emergence of life does constitute progress beyond the pre-biotic realm of matter, that the evolution of life itself does progress through emergent steps resulting in increasing levels of consciousness, and that the unprecedented emergence of human consciousness and culture does constitute significant progress beyond the biological realm of pre-human life.

Progress in culture and progress in life suggest that progress itself is a deep feature of the larger movement of evolution as a whole. And this points to the presence of progress in the domain of cosmological evolution, which we now consider.

## Progress in Cosmological Evolution

The previous chapter provided a detailed description of how the evolution of human history has progressed through a series of values-based stages of consciousness and culture. And now in this chapter we have seen how the evolution of life has progressed through a series of nested levels of emergence that eventually led to the ultimate transcendence of the biosphere itself. So what can we conclude about the underlying evolution of the universe prior to life? Does it evince progress?

When we recount the history of billions of years of development from the isolated atoms of hydrogen and helium, through the formation of stars and galaxies, the forging of the heavy elements, and eventually to the emergence of solar systems capable of sustaining life, it seems that progress has indeed been achieved. But we can now go beyond an impressionistic understanding of cosmic progress by using the criteria for improvement we developed for assessing biological progress.

In our examination of biological development above, we saw how the accumulating character of evolutionary emergence creates a holarchic pattern of interdependent layers, with each layer transcending and including its predecessor, building on what has come before. Although this nested chain of emergence is more pronounced in biological evolution, we can see this structural pattern partially functioning in cosmological evolution as well. Moreover, we saw how biological evolution eventually succeeded in producing its own transcendence through the emergence of the noosphere, which inaugurated an entirely new kind of evolution. And this same pattern can be seen in cosmological evolution which, on this planet and most likely elsewhere, has succeeded in producing its own transcendence through the emergence of the biosphere.

Although every emergent step in the evolution of the cosmos adds another level of wholeness, and thus another level of intrinsic value, it is these major steps of emergence—events that produce new categories of evolution—that provide the foundations of our understanding of progress. Once we recognize that the transcendent emergence of a new category of evolution represents a kind of *success* for the underlying evolutionary domain out of which it arose, we can see how such an emergent new category comes to function, at least partially, as a goal or end for its underlying domains.

In our analysis of evolution's value generating activity above, we saw how progress in value runs in two directions. As evolution unfolds through emergent steps, every new step becomes *more significant* to the extent that it includes previous steps and thus previous wholes—the more wholes a given whole encompasses, the more significant it is. Yet each new layer of significance also *increases the fundamental value* of the parts it embraces.

Applying this same analysis to pre-biotic evolution shows that when the domain of cosmological evolution is transcended by, but also included within, the emergent domain of biological evolution, life becomes an end or goal of the underlying domain of evolving matter. As the biosphere builds on the underlying "physiosphere"—as life uses matter as its fundamental foundation—life becomes a *purpose* of matter in this instrumental sense. Rolston states this with elegant simplicity: "Life makes matter count."

Cosmological evolution literally becomes *a part* of biological evolution as atoms and molecules become parts of cells. However, the transcendence and inclusion of the physiosphere by the biosphere is not always a volumetric envelopment or physical containment. Obviously, the physical universe is much larger than the biological universe. But the biosphere encompasses the physiosphere in a more meaningful way. Life contributes something new to the realm of matter and energy. Living things are made out of matter and energy, yet they are more than this; they cannot be completely reduced to the realm which they have surpassed. The intrinsic value of the domain of cosmological evolution is thus partially captured and taken up by this new level of biological emergence. In this way, the emerging biosphere uses the underlying physiosphere as its fundamental foundation, just as the noosphere in turn uses the biosphere as its fundamental foundation.

Figure 6.3 illustrates two contrasting views of the structural relationship formed by the three major domains of evolution. The figure on the left shows how the biological realm of evolution transcends and includes the previous domain of cosmological evolution, and in turn, how the domain of human consciousness and culture transcends and includes the realm of biology, as described above. Yet simultaneously and conversely, the figure on the right shows how the biosphere and noosphere can also be alternatively conceived as "arising from within" their antecedent evolutionary domains—life emerges *within* the larger physical cosmos, and subjective consciousness and intersubjective culture likewise emerge *within* a biological context. These opposite, but mutually reinforcing conceptions of the structural relationship of emergence result from the multidimensional character of evolutionary development.

However, even as we recognize how, in the course of evolution, the biosphere makes instrumental use of the physiosphere, and then the noosphere

## Opposite, yet mutually reinforcing conceptions of the structural relationship of evolutionary emergence

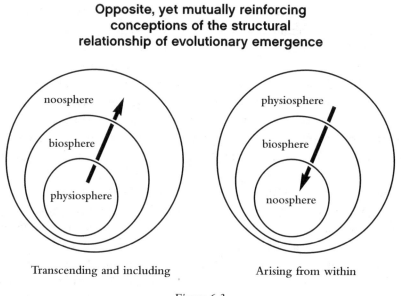

Transcending and including          Arising from within

*Figure 6.3*
Alternative conceptions of the structure of emergence

makes instrumental use of the biosphere, this does not erase the value of these underlying transcended domains. Because practically every holon is simultaneously both a part and a whole, the persisting wholeness of every holon ensures that a degree of intrinsic value is always preserved. Nevertheless, through the process of advancing holarchic development, transcended levels contribute a portion of their wholeness by becoming parts.

Newly emerging levels of evolution are thus able to bring forth some of their fresh value by taking up and using a portion of the intrinsic value of underlying antecedent levels. And it is in this sense that a new level of emergence becomes an *instrumental purpose* for all the levels it transcends and includes. In other words, whenever a holon is put to use within a larger encompassing system, this use endows the encompassed holon with a new form of instrumental purpose. Thus, just as there are two kinds of evolutionary progress—fundamental and significant—there are also two kinds of evolutionary purpose—instrumental and intrinsic.

This philosophical analysis reveals how the concepts of progress and purpose work together. Progress illuminates purpose, and purpose, once established, gives us a basis with which to further evaluate progress. From this perspective, the progress of cosmological evolution can be assessed by virtue of its foundational contribution to the subsequent appearance of life—the emergence of life can be recognized as an instrumental purpose of the evolving, pre-biotic cosmos. Following this reasoning, at the micro level of cosmological evolution, the emergence of carbon and oxygen atoms (both crucial for life) can be seen as progressive steps beyond a universe of hydrogen and helium. Similarly, the subsequent emergence of heavier elements such as iron constituted progressive steps beyond that. Likewise, at the macro level, the emergence of the first generation of stars constituted progress beyond the previous era of nucleosynthesis, and the subsequent emergence of second generation stars and their accompanying planets was a further progressive step beyond that.

But again, isn't this analysis gravely distorted by anthropocentric conceit? How can we claim that life's appearance in a tiny corner of this vast universe represents the aim of billions of years of cosmological development without appearing self-servingly suspect? In response to this concern we can find additional support for the conclusion that the emergence of life is at least one of the purposes of cosmological evolution in the record of what science has discovered. That is, beyond the holarchic structure formed by the emergence of transcendent evolutionary levels, we can find additional evidence for the claim that cosmological evolution progresses toward life in the well-established physics of the so-called "anthropic principle," which could be more accurately called the "life principle." This principle is founded on numerous observations of apparently coincidental "fine-tuning for life" that exists within the fundamental constants of physics.

As examples, the mass of a proton relative to an electron, the strength of electromagnetism relative to gravity, the strength of the force binding nucleons to nuclei, and the size of the electron's charge, all appear to be infinitesimally adjusted to make possible the subsequent development of living systems.[19] In fact, if these physical relationships had not been exactly as they were from the beginning, the resulting universe would have been incapable of supporting life. And beyond the "exceedingly delicate tuning of values" found in the set-up at the very beginning, physicists have also discovered a variety of later appearing physical processes and constants, at both micro and macro levels, that exhibit similar kinds of exacting adjustment.[20] Prominent theoretical physicist Paul Davies writes: "There is now broad agreement among physicists and cosmologists that the universe is in several respects 'fine-tuned' for life."[21] After surveying the recent findings of astrophysics, which reveal the astounding ubiquity of these "cosmic coincidences," Rolston observes that this science reveals a universe that is "open but pregnant for life, one that is perhaps not predictable but one that portends storied development. In the plasma we begin to see a plan, or, better, a plot."[22]

Some scientific materialists have attempted to dispute the significance of these findings, arguing that it is not surprising that we observers find ourselves in a universe that makes observation possible. These skeptics thus argue that it is a mistake to make too much of this "principle" because it is essentially tautological or vacuous. Yet this argument fails to acknowledge that these findings are not obvious or expected; rather, they *are* surprising (and to many scientists unsettling) empirical discoveries that have been uncovered by the sustained labors and impressive successes of quantum physics, relativity physics, and astrophysics. As physicists have plumbed the depths of the structures of cosmological evolution they have consistently discovered uncanny instances of infinitesimally intricate adjustment, wherein only the slightest difference would have made impossible the subsequent appearance of life. As Davies concludes, we have hit the "cosmic jackpot." "Extraordinary physical coincidences and apparently accidental cooperation . . . offer compelling evidence that something is 'going on.' . . . A hidden principle seems to be at work, organizing the universe in a coherent way."[23]

Thus, when we combine the evidence that our universe is fine-tuned for life with the evidence of the nested levels of emergence that form the chain of dependent transcendence that we now literally embody, we find strong support for the conclusion that the generation of life is an instrumental purpose of cosmological evolution. But again, recognizing life as an instrumental purpose of pre-biotic evolution does not mean that life is the cosmos's *only* purpose. The evolving cosmos retains part of its pre-transcended intrinsic value as an end in itself. And this can be seen in its astounding beauty, which has been dramatically and increasingly revealed by the recent images from the Hubble telescope. The amazing aesthetic properties of the starry heavens provide proof that this domain of evolution has tremendous significance and wholeness-value apart from life or human culture. Because as Whitehead realized, "beauty is the final contentment of the Eros of the universe."

## Progress and Teleology

The next chapter considers what our growing understanding of the evolving universe reveals about evolution's overall purpose or purposes. But before concluding this discussion of evolutionary progress, it is worth examining how evolutionary progress reveals a kind of *relative teleology*. Progress in the evolution of the physiosphere, the biosphere, and the noosphere, does not necessarily point to a clear final goal or absolute end of the evolutionary process, but progress in these realms *does* indicate relative movement in the direction of increasing value (by definition). We do not need a fixed pole star or definitive omega point to determine whether progress has been made. For instance, on the question of cultural progress, we merely need to inquire whether the human condition has been improved relative to its previous state. We can simply ask: Has suffering been lessened? Are people more free? Where this is the case, we can say that progress has been achieved. Yet in the assessment of progress, we must also remain mindful that cultural progress can only be judged from within an agreement-based value frame, and our value frame itself is evolving and progressing. So here we are not only working to discern whether conditions have improved, we are also working to improve our concept of improvement itself.

The discussion of "value gravity" in chapter 4 touched on the evident teleology of beauty, truth, and goodness, noting how these values (and their related sub-values) exert a drawing power on consciousness. So now that we have seen how evolution results in authentic progress in the realms of matter, life, and culture, we can revisit the evolutionary influence of value gravity in light of this clarified understanding of progress.

The philosophical proposition being here advanced is, of course, that evolution is actually progressing in the directions of beauty, truth, and goodness. But again, recognition of this directional movement does not lead to the conclusion that evolution is completely preplanned or specifically designed in advance. Our enlarged understanding of the nature of values and their gravitational influence on evolution shows that the process is more than the straightforward execution of a plan. Evolution's *telos*, its movement toward increasing realizations of the beautiful, the true, and the good, is partially self-generating—evolution increasingly creates its own teleology as it unfolds. This is because values need agency to bring them completely into being—transcendent values have an objective pole and a subjective pole—so creature recognition and choice is required as a necessary element for values to come fully into existence. And this means that exactly what is valuable is not completely predetermined; our choices help decide what is relatively more perfect. In other words, in the case of humans at least, value gravity is participatory in that it requires the assent of subjective awareness in order for its power to take hold—the teleological pull of the potential for improvement works by persuading interior consciousness to take action and bring about the exterior changes which result in a more evolved world.

It is in this way that the *products* of evolution are recruited to the task of determining the direction of the *process* of evolution. This partially self-generating or *autopoietic* teleology is particularly evident in the dialectical dynamics of human cultural evolution, wherein the winding path of development requires constant correction. In the struggle to improve our conditions, humans must continuously steer evolution's dialectical course back to the heading of goodness, which can often only be seen in contrast with the pathology that we seek to avoid. Some may object that this kind of participatory teleology only functions at the human level of evolution. But as I am arguing, although cultural evolution is a distinct form of evolutionary development, its essential connection to other forms of evolution points to the universal quality of its features. In other words, much of what is true for cultural evolution is at least partially true for evolution overall. And as we have seen, the evolution of life is predicated on the striving of organisms to survive and reproduce. All forms of life thus affirm the value of both individual and intergenerational survival and thus participate in evolution's ongoing teleology.

Still, recognizing that the teleology of evolution is participatory and not completely predetermined does not conclude the argument. We must also defend this teleological proposition from some of the remaining philosophical objections which continue to apply.

The first objection to teleology is that it implies that the future is somehow influencing the present. Although recognition of creature participation through the subjective pole of values takes care of part of this objection, there remains the question of the objective pole of values: does this posit a mysterious influence from the future? Well, only insofar as we can imagine the future potential of a more perfect state. And our present sense of the potential for further improvement, our hope for a better future, is itself kindled and nurtured by the nature of beauty, truth, and goodness. That is, the direct experience of these intrinsic values often carries with it a sense of connection to a larger whole. For instance, when we discover truth, part of the excitement we feel comes from our sense that there is much more truth yet to be discovered. We can never know truth in its fullness, and the same can be said about goodness and beauty. Part of what makes the experience of truth, beauty, or goodness so special is the way these values provide a kind of self-similar connection to a greater, transcendent reality. As Murdoch wrote, "How do we know that the very great is not the perfect? We see differences, we sense directions, and we know that the Good is still somewhere beyond." Ultimately, the authentic experience of goodness, truth, or beauty is a spiritual experience, which gives us a taste of unity. And this fleeting glimpse of unity includes the unity of time in the present moment, wherein future potentials can be palpably felt.

But despite the mystical overtones of this description, the teleological pull of beauty, truth, and goodness is not entirely mysterious. Our imagination is part of our inherent creative freedom, and the influence of future potentials is something we all feel regularly. As discussed in chapter 4, we feel the pull of beauty through our desire for the pleasure and satisfaction provided by nature and art. We feel the pull of truth through our curiosity and thirst for knowledge. And we feel the pull of goodness through our sense of duty to live up to our potential and do the right thing. As we have seen, value gravity exerts its influence on the *interiors* of evolution; values attract the choices of living agency and consciousness, and this is how the future potential of greater value influences changes in the present.

This explanation also takes care of another objection to teleology, which contends that its causality is undemonstrable, or supernatural. This objection is satisfied when we realize that the causality of the potential for greater perfection manifests through the power of creature choices. All living things exhibit agency, and all living things thus participate in evolution's teleology as they continuously choose to survive and reproduce. And this purposeful participation in evolution becomes even more pronounced with the advent of humans. Human agents can recognize values with an expanded scope and depth and can thus feel the pull of value gravity more strongly, and reveal its direction more fully through the accumulation of their choices. Indeed, an external record of these internal influences can be found in the patterns of human history, which clearly reveal the dialectical trajectory of progress we have discussed.

The presence of beauty, truth, and goodness—both actual and potential—is something we can all sense to a greater or lesser degree. And it is the ubiquitous reality of these values that serve as the "final cause" of the motion of evolution. Thus, we can perhaps sense how sublime beauty, profound truth, and loving kindness partake of the lingering memory of eternity that remains within the finite universe of time, calling us forward into the future.

• • •

In conclusion, our instinctual duty to make things better is guided and clarified when we see that this impulse is part of the larger overall movement of universal development we now call "evolution." Connecting our values to this large-scale cosmological process amplifies the significance of our values—it increases their "mass" and hence their gravitation. We can thus achieve progress more effectively when we understand progress more fully.

## CHAPTER 7

# Purpose in Evolution

Now we come to the heart of our inquiry. As a result of the stupendous accomplishments of physical science, we have before us a broad understanding of the origins of the universe. We now know that evolution is a universal process that encompasses and unites the domains of cosmological, biological, and cultural development through a nested sequence of radically novel emergences. Although most of the scientific facts that make up this new picture of evolution have been around for decades, we have really only just begun to appreciate how evolution is a universal process of becoming that affects everything.

Alongside the scientific discoveries of our evolutionary origins, some philosophers and social scientists have found that this universal process is not merely physical and external; these scholars have shown how evolution is unfolding within us as our values and perspectives develop on the inside. While it has been over a century since psychologists first recognized that human consciousness evolves, our culture has yet to adequately connect this insight with our growing scientific understanding of evolution overall. However, when we realize that the force of evolution is pervasive and ubiquitous, when we observe how it influences our thoughts and desires, and how it shapes our cultural landscapes, we can begin to appreciate how this comprehensive new picture of evolution represents a breakthrough in understanding. And so at this point in history we are faced with the task of fully acknowledging and digesting the meaning of this breakthrough and coming to terms with its implications for our civilization.

The meaning and value of evolution—the purpose of evolution—is something that perhaps no human can know in its fullness. Yet like most forms of truth, the significance of evolution is something we can come to discover incrementally through sustained philosophical reflection. Little by little we can discern the meaning of why we are here. We have seen how certain writers have beheld the facts of evolution and concluded that they are meaningless; but this seems unwarranted. While we may never know the ultimate cosmic impetus for the initial big bang and the evolutionary unfolding that has followed, this does not mean that our reflection on the subject can amount to nothing more than idle speculation.

The discussion in chapter 2 showed how important it is to distinguish between science and philosophy. And this is especially important within the subject of evolution, where science and philosophy are often intertwined. While the empirical facts of evolutionary science cannot stand alone without some kind of philosophical frame, we do not have to accept materialism as the only philosophy compatible with these facts. The discussion in chapter 2 thus attempted to tease apart the empirical and the metaphysical in an effort to reconstruct a philosophy of evolution that can provide a more adequate interpretation of this primary activity of our universe. Some distinguished philosophers have argued that only our physical senses can provide valid knowledge, and that any explanations that go beyond science are purely speculative, and thus relatively meaningless. But I obviously reject this conclusion. "The human hand has evolved to grasp things, and so has the human mind." That is, it is possible to gain valid knowledge about this universe through philosophical inquiry which transcends the bounds of science but which does not become pure speculation in the process.

And just as it is crucial to distinguish science and philosophy, it is also just as crucial to distinguish philosophical knowledge from propositions that are essentially matters of spiritual conviction or belief. Philosophy can be distinguished from theology or spirituality in the way that philosophy concerns what can be *known* in our world and in our lives. Philosophical observations may not be empirical sensory perceptions, but such observations can nevertheless be pointed out and confirmed by others. Although it is often difficult to draw hard lines between philosophy and spirituality, we can perhaps agree that philosophy functions best when it concerns matters that are subject to human examination—events of "this world" that are perhaps not physical, but that can nevertheless be apprehended and even demonstrated. As an illustration, the proposition that Mozart was a great musician is not a scientific fact that can be "proved," but it can be demonstrated by pointing to worldwide agreement on the matter. While it is certainly possible to disagree that Mozart is "great," this does not diminish the general truth of this point.

As I also argued in chapter 2, science, philosophy, and spirituality serve as the "three legs of the stool" of human understanding, and all three are needed for an adequate approach to truth. Yet for each of these approaches to truth to function best, they need to be afforded a degree of separation from one another. Within this understanding, spirituality and theology are indispensible; yet this field of human inquiry should not be conflated with philosophy, because philosophy has a distinct and very important role to play in the development of our culture. So in this chapter we will examine the purpose or purposes that philosophy can "observe" within the enlarged picture of evolution that is now before us. I will argue that the dynamic patterns of evolution reveal the presence of meaning, value, and purpose, and that purpose is actually an unmistakable message carried by the evolutionary process itself.

Then, once we have gone as far as we can go within the bounds of philosophy (as I am defining it) in this chapter, in the next chapter I will use these philosophical insights about evolution's purpose to reflect on the larger theological implications of this theme.

## The Experience of Purpose

Purpose is *in* the universe. We all have it and experience it directly and regularly. And as we have seen, all forms of life also have purpose. Although the purposes of simple life forms may be genetically instinctual and apparently mechanical, these creatures' interactions with the world are nevertheless *non-computational*—even with exhaustive knowledge of their present state, the exact future state that will result from their choices cannot be calculated with any possible computer.[1] Indeed, it is this purposiveness in living things (or at least quasi-purposiveness) that actually distinguishes life from non-living matter. This unique ability of living things to strive and choose is the primary reason why biology cannot be reduced to physics. And to choose is to evaluate—every choice, no matter how instinctual, constitutes an evaluation. Therefore, because life forms are "spontaneous evaluative systems," their ability to strive and choose allows them to evolve non-deterministically in ways that matter alone cannot—it is the inherent striving of life forms which enables them to fill every available ecosystemic niche, and which results in the increasingly complex phenomenon of the evolving biosphere. Moreover, it is this spontaneous creativity inherent in biological evolution that allows life to evolve at a much faster rate (once it gains momentum) than the glacial pace of deterministic geological evolution.

Just as the first-order purpose (or quasi-purpose) possessed in increasing measure by all life forms is the primary factor that distinguishes them from matter, the second-order purpose (self-reflective purpose) that emerges in humans is similarly the primary factor that distinguishes us from other forms of life. Our human sense of purpose is an aspect of our free will, and as discussed in chapters 2 and 3, it is the freedom of our will that gives us the ability to perceive and thus pursue higher values. And it is this emergent capacity to discern truth and make moral distinctions that gives us the ability to evolve our culture. Because of our sense of higher purpose—because we can feel the ever-widening potential of a better way—humans are continuously driven and drawn toward more complex forms of social organization. By benefiting from, and participating in, humanity's unique form of cultural evolution, human consciousness is able to evolve beyond its biological origins. Moreover, humanity's expanded capacity for purposiveness allows cultural evolution to unfold at a faster pace (once it gains momentum) than biological evolution, due to the superior power of "actual selection" over natural selection. And as human cultural evolution accelerates, our purposes and values become more refined and are gradually transformed from the negative motivations of fear and the avoidance of pain, to more positive motivations toward our expanding conceptions of beauty, truth, and goodness.

Thus, in the scheme of evolution, creature purpose is far more than a "trace element," it is not merely epiphenomenal; it is actually a major feature of the development of the universe. Emergent purpose within life forms is a primary driver of the evolutionary process and a seminal factor that distinguishes evolution's major levels. Again, life's inherent purpose differentiates it from matter, and humanity's transcendent purpose differentiates us from other forms of life.

The fact that we all have a direct experience of purpose—that we know what it is like from the inside—gives us a sense of the kinship between our human awareness of purpose and the purpose experienced by all forms of life. That is, the purpose of almost all living things is to survive and reproduce—to keep from becoming food, to find food, and to find a mate (in roughly that order). Like animals and even plants, we can feel these biological purposes in our own experience. The feeling of fear, the feeling of hunger, and the feeling of sexual desire are all accompanied by a sense of urgency, and their relief or satisfaction provides a feeling of pleasure or even ecstasy. Among these biological influences, the evolutionary impulse of purpose is particularly acute in the case of our sex drive, wherein the eros of value attraction becomes fully embodied. But as we discussed in chapter 3, this same sense of eros that can be felt in our bodies can also be felt in our minds as we are attracted to the deeper reaches of eros, which Plato described as the "passion for intellectual beauty and wisdom, [that] culminates in the mystical vision of the eternal, the ultimate source of all beauty."[2]

The way purpose is distributed across the evolutionary spectrum lends itself to a comparison with other universal forces. For example, one of the most significant aspects of Newton's theory of gravity was his revelation that the force that moves the planets is the same force that causes apples to fall from trees. And the fact that this gravitational force is consistent across scale gives us a sense of its lawful and universal nature. Thus as we now consider purpose as a similar (albeit non-physical) kind of universal force, we can perhaps sense that the purpose which causes plants to grow and birds to build nests is, in some ways at least, the same purpose that drives us to seek our own self-actualization and to give our gift to the world. Moreover, by contemplating the "phenomenology of purpose," we can begin to sense how our individual, micro-purposes are related to the macro-purposes which we are attempting to discover within evolution as a whole.

Although the major events of emergence found within human cultural evolution clearly result from the purposes of individual humans, the causes of specific forms of emergence in biological evolution cannot be directly tied to the individual purposes of organisms. At least not according to standard Darwinian theory. However, we can perhaps sense that there is nevertheless a connection between the micro-purposes of individual life forms and the macro-purposes exhibited by biological evolution's generation of value over time. And the nascent sciences of epigenetics and adaptive mutation (discussed in chapter 2) may soon be able to demonstrate this connection explicitly.

## Evidence for Purpose in Evolution

Some philosophers have argued that claims for purpose in evolution are completely devoid of evidence, and that the triumph of the Darwinian account is that it shows how evolution functions through blind mutation and environmental selection, without the need of any purpose whatsoever. In response to this I can begin by observing that "purpose" is not a material entity subject to investigation by science. Scientists cannot even measure or prove purpose in humans, so we certainly cannot expect their instruments to detect purpose in evolution as a whole. As noted, scientists have not been able to fully explain how purpose or will functions within the neurological structures of the human brain, and many scientists go so far as to argue that free will is an illusion. So the only evidence for purpose in humans is their apparently purposeful behavior. And as further explored in this chapter, it is the apparently purposeful, emergent behavior of evolution that provides similar evidence for its purpose.

As discussed in the previous chapter, scientific examination of the physical features of cosmological evolution reveals compelling evidence that the universe is organized for life. Yet the fine-tuning of the pre-biotic physical universe only reveals an apparent purpose *for* evolution. If we want to find direct evidence of purpose *in* evolution, we must look to the presence of life and its inherent agency. And if we want to discover the comprehensive purpose *of* evolution as a universal process, our investigation must be broadened beyond matter and life so as to include the psychosocial evolution of humanity. Evidence for evolution's purpose is thus found in a set of interconnected observations about the behavior and character of evolution overall. As a preview of the forthcoming discussion, these observations can be summarized as follows:

1. Evolution generates value—it progresses by emergent steps that result in an increase in both instrumental value and intrinsic value. The nested structure of development that results from evolution's 13.7 billion year trajectory of growth has achieved unfathomable value, and it is in this relatively consistent movement toward value that we can recognize purpose.

2. Evolution exhibits a rising flow of creativity that consistently overcomes entropy, ingeniously solves difficult problems by navigating through immense hyperspaces of possibility, produces astonishing diversity and originality, and continually transcends itself through the emergence of radically novel forms and new levels of organization.

3. Evolution's purpose can be directly felt within us across a spectrum of experience that includes biological, personal, social, and spiritual impulses for improvement. The kinship between our individual purposes and the overall purpose of evolution is found in the way our personal purposes mirror and connect with the larger interdependent structure of wholes and parts that orders the unfolding of evolution throughout the course of its development.

These observations regarding the evidence for purpose in evolution are interrelated, and their individual evidential strength is mutually reinforced by combination. So as we now consider these elements of purpose in sequence, please keep in mind that these arguments are not presented as a "chain," wherein the weakness of any link undermines the strength of the whole, but rather as a "braided cable," wherein the otherwise thin strands reinforce each other.

## Purpose in the Pattern—Evolution's Generation of Value

In the last chapter we explored two crucial concepts that underpin the argument for progress in biological and cosmological development: 1) the whole/part holarchy of emergent levels that forms evolution's structural pattern; and 2) the complementary growth in intrinsic and instrumental value that arises from this dynamic structure of successively emerging levels. We will now revisit these concepts and use them again here in our analysis of evolution's purpose.

Recall that in the course of evolution, as more complex and encompassing levels of emergence appear, each new level becomes *more significant* to the extent that it includes previous levels and thus previous wholes—the more holonic levels of organization encompassed by a given instance of emergence, the greater its *intrinsic or significant value*. And with each new layer of emerging significance we also find complementary growth in value in the opposite direction. As new levels of evolution emerge, they impart *instrumental or fundamental value* to the stages they have encompassed as parts. That is, as a given holonic level is taken up and *used* by a higher, emergent level, this gives the lower level a "service opportunity"—an increase in "partness value"—which in a way, contributes to the underlying level's "self-actualization."

Although instrumental value is often thought to be less important than intrinsic value, both kinds of value are indispensible to the evolutionary growth of value overall. The importance of instrumental/fundamental value is well articulated by Rolston, who writes:

> There is nothing secondary about instrumental value. . . . We think that a person is narrow and selfish who cultivates intrinsic worth and withdraws from seeking any instrumental value in the community. A person's intrinsic worth—for example, creative ability—is not separable from the power to confer a benefit on others. Excellence does not consist in what a thing is merely for itself, but in what it is for others. This is true of persons, animals, and plants [and indeed all holons]. Excellence is not a matter of encapsulated being, but of fitness in a pervasive whole.[3]

When we come to appreciate how the growth of instrumental/fundamental value and intrinsic/significant value reinforce each other and contribute to their mutual manifestation, the fact that evolution is a prolific generator of value becomes indisputable. And this perspective on evolution's natural value-creating behavior sheds light on evolution's underlying aim, which can be seen in the existential connection between value-creation and purpose.

The words "purpose," "values," "needs," and "aims" are all part of the same family of meaning. Although we can make fine distinctions between them, we can also see how these concepts are intimately related. And here we can refer to our direct experience of the phenomenology of purpose discussed above. Most of us have a sense of how our purposes are animated and directed by our values and how our values are confirmed by our purposes. This direct connection between purpose and value is well understood by evolutionary theologian John Haught, who observes: "The term 'purpose' cannot be grasped apart from the notion of value. Only orientation toward value renders a movement purposeful. So purpose [may] be understood simply as the defining quality of any process aiming toward the realization of value."[4]

Admittedly, the word "purpose" can be misleading—it is provocative and even problematic, like evolution itself. So it is important to continually reemphasize that here "purpose" does not mean "preplanned." Although this conception of purpose connotes something less than a fixed or otherwise preplanned design, it nonetheless recognizes value generation that is more than passive, ephemeral, or epiphenomenal. To claim that evolution has purpose is to recognize that its growth produces both instrumental usefulness and intrinsic worth. When we analyze and understand the way evolution generates value, we find evidence of its purposiveness embodied in its directional unfolding and its storied achievements. Natural value may occasionally be created accidentally and without purpose. But when a process produces a progressive, interdependent structural chain of value, which increases in magnitude and intensity consistently across vast stretches of space and over huge spans of time, we must recognize it as purposive. Explaining this universal process as purposeless or otherwise accidental ignores the evolutionary evidence and ultimately defies reason.

Recall that purpose can be recognized in all forms of life, even those forms that have no apparent subjectivity or consciousness. Plants, for example, exhibit tenacious purpose in their growth. So recognizing purpose within the phenomenon of emergent evolution does not necessarily imply that the process results from the will of a super calculating intellect or a personal and intentional Deity. However, neither does our recognition of purpose rule out the possibility of a conscious Creator. Whether or not we recognize the presence of "God's will" within the purpose of evolution ultimately depends on our spiritual orientation. Conclusions about the Creator lie largely beyond the realm of philosophy. But what we can say philosophically by examining evolution's pattern is that there is unmistakable growth toward value and thus unmistakable *purpose in the process*. Again, the process is purposive because it aims at value. And the proof of evolution's "aiming at value" is found in the fact that it has been generating value—value that builds on itself and increases exponentially—for billions of years.

The immeasurable value created by evolution provides a strong argument for its purposiveness. However, beyond the increasing value found in evolution's dynamic structure, we can discover additional evidence of its purposiveness in the nature of its forward motion, to which we now turn.

## The Rising Flow of Creativity

Despite the contentions of many neo-Darwinists that the evolution of life is a random walk with no apparent direction, our analysis has shown how evolution's nested sequence of holarchical emergence demonstrates a clear directionality. And despite its diversity and occasional inconsistency, this directionality ties together the domains of cosmological, biological, and psychosocial development, wherein lower levels contribute to the viability of higher levels in every evolutionary holarchy. When we acknowledge this structure of emergence, we cannot help but see how there is an arrow of development that builds in a recognizable direction over time. In cosmological evolution, the driver of this developmental movement is said to be deterministic chemical reactions. And within biological evolution, the driver is said to be random mutations coupled with environmental pruning. Yet even if we were to concede that these processes are essentially mechanistic, or otherwise blind to purpose or direction, such explanations are completely inadequate when it comes to understanding the original *inception* of these domains of evolution themselves. So it is worth reemphasizing that the fine-tuned big bang cannot be explained mechanistically, and neither can the major emergences of life or human self-consciousness. In each case, evolutionary emergence demonstrates indisputable *original creativity*. And the staggering creativity which first initiated these major domains of evolution suggests that purely mechanistic explanations of the lesser events of emergence that occur within these domains are similarly inadequate.

The astonishing creativity of emergence points to "a directional charge within the universe," an upward current of development that has been unfolding from the beginning. This evolutionary current can be detected within all instances of emergence, but it begins to reveal itself most distinctly with the advent of life. The scientific context in which this directional charge is understood is well articulated by Kevin Kelly (quoted in the last chapter), who denied evolutionary progress and espoused the theory that all evolutionary entities are equally evolved. Yet despite his earlier embrace of this physicalist credo, Kelly nevertheless clearly acknowledges evolution's value generation in another form, which he calls the "rising flow":

> Many postdarwinians doubt that natural selection alone is powerful enough to offset Carnot's Second Law of Thermodynamics. Yet, we are here, so something has. They are not sure what they are looking for, but they intuitively feel that it can be stated as a complementary force to entropy. Some call it anti-entropy, some call it negentropy, and a few call it extropy. ... Two currents were thus born out of the white flash. One current runs downhill all the way. This force begins as a wild hot party and fizzes out into silent coldness. The second current runs in parallel, but with opposite effect. It diverts the heat before the heat disperses (since disperse it must) and extracts order out of disorder. It borrows the failing energy and raises the ante into a rising flow. The rising flow uses its short moment of order to snatch whatever dissipating power it can to build a platform upon which to extract the next round of order. It saves nothing and spends all. It invests all the order it has to amplify the next round of complexity, growth, and order. In this way it taps chaos to breed antichaos. We call it life.[5]

In light of these facts, as we continue our analysis of evolution's observable attributes and now bring in the dynamic action of this rising flow, we can see that this upward motion does not advance in a uniform or constant way; it exhibits sudden jumps—radical demonstrations of emergent novelty. That is, evolutionary growth often remains static or dormant for long periods, and then relatively suddenly, an astonishing new development appears. The unfolding course of evolution is thus marked by spurts of creativity that cannot be predicted or adequately explained. Gould's theory of punctuated equilibrium attempts to provide an account of these events of emergence, but the source of their creativity remains elusive, with purely mechanistic explanations increasingly strained. Indeed, it is the astounding creativity that really stands out in these emergent events. Even when we give full credit to the inherent creativity of natural selection, we still cannot deny the presence of unexplained artistry, ingenuity, virtuosity, and innovative originality found within these developments.

Ultimately, it is the creativity inherent in emergent evolution that takes us beyond Monod's long-standing dogma of "blind chance and necessity alone." Recognition of this creativity is not speculation; it is intensely evident in the products and processes of nature. This rising creativity is unmistakably present in evolution's problem solving and in the incredible diversity of its unfolding beauty. As Whitehead observed, "*Creativity* is the universal of universals characterizing ultimate matter of fact. It is that ultimate principle by which the many . . . become one and are increased by one."[6] Stated differently, the most foundational truth about the universe is not matter-energy, not spacetime, not quantum fields, not strings, but rather *creativity*—the emergent process through which the holarchical systems of evolving reality have come to be.

Scientific materialists have enthusiastically embraced the Darwinian explanation of random genetic changes and environmental selection as the sole cause of biological evolution because of the apparent purposelessness by which it functions. But when we bring the phenomenon of emergent creativity into our analysis, and when we situate the mechanisms of natural selection within the larger unified picture of evolution as a whole, we begin to see how explanations that rely exclusively on "chance and necessity" are no longer tenable.

Of all the marvelous achievements of evolution, arguably the most creative emergence of all is the purpose found within living things. Pre-biotic emergent systems such as tornados or hurricanes may apparently arise automatically and mechanistically, but living things contain purpose, and thus their purpose is demonstrated within their own being. And as we have seen, purpose quickens within life as it evolves, with the emergence of humans inaugurating a transcendent level of purposiveness that marks a new chapter in the evolutionary epic. The rising flow of creative evolution is thus not outside of us or beyond us; we experience the evolutionary impulse directly and regularly whenever we are motivated to improve our lives and help others. As biological anthropologist Terrence Deacon observes, "To be human is to know what it feels like to be evolution happening."[7] Because we can feel the evolutionary impulse within ourselves, we know accordingly from our own experience that the rising flow is inherently teleological and purposive. And we can feel the inherent creativity of this rising flow as the urge to be creative rises within us. Indeed, it is our ability to be creative—the ability to bring something entirely new and original into existence—that proves we are free agents of evolution. Thus, if we want to discover evolution's purpose, we need only look within ourselves. Our purposes are its purposes.

## Parallels between Personal and Universal Development

Following this insight, when we examine our own purposes in the hope of discovering the larger purposes of evolution as a whole, we can recognize a kind of connection or kinship between the way we develop as individuals and the structural features that mark the larger unfolding of evolution over time. This connection is found in the fact that the course of our personal development and the course of evolution overall are both characterized by clear dialectical polarities. In the case of macroevolution, as discussed above, this dialectical character of development is found in the dynamic polarity of part and whole that results in the holarchic structure which shapes all forms of evolution. And in the case of our personal development, this same dialectical pattern can be seen in the polarity of the individual and the larger community, which similarly appears in practically all human attempts to solve problems or pursue opportunities. In other words, as we are moved to make things better, we inevitably encounter the ever-present dialectic of self and other, which shows up whenever we set out to improve our conditions.

In order to grow and thrive as individuals over the long term, we not only have to take care of ourselves, we also have to provide service to something larger than ourselves. If we seek only our own growth, our efforts will eventually be retarded by the inertia of selfishness. As Rolston observed in the quote above, "Excellence does not consist in what a thing is merely for itself, but in what it is for others." Yet if we are completely selfless in our quest to make things better, this can exhaust us prematurely and lead to codependence. Even the United States Peace Corp requires that its applicants have "something in it for them," because this service organization has found that the volunteers whose motivations are entirely selfless often end up quitting before their term is complete. Thus, in the long run, progress in our personal development depends on our service to others, and our ability to be effective in our service to others depends, in turn, on our ongoing personal development. Stated yet another way, our ability to grow and continuously make things better is predicated on the pursuit of both self-improvement and the giving of ourselves to the larger community. There may be times when one or the other of these courses of action will be emphasized, but a degree of balance between them over time is the ideal.

For many of us, recognizing that the optimal course of personal development involves both working on ourselves and giving to others may seem like a platitude or an otherwise obvious feature of living in the world. However, when we come to see that this dialectical pattern of part and whole and self and other is actually a deep feature of our evolving universe, we can better appreciate its relevance and significance. This universal motif arises as part of a primordial current of value generation that has been influencing everything from the beginning. This pattern reflects the ever-present source of our origins coursing within us in every moment, calling us forward toward more perfect states of existence. And as we increasingly experience and understand this developmental impetus, we can perhaps sense that we are encountering an ancient and even sacred influence. This is the evolutionary impulse, the ultimate source of creativity in the universe.[8]

As we grow in our ability to experience the evolutionary impulse within ourselves, this helps confirm the universal nature of this underlying current of development. Our ability to experience evolution in this way shows us that the complementary headings of self and other that guide our personal development are the same headings of value creation for evolution overall. And this brings us back to the two kinds of purpose we identified above and in the last chapter: instrumental purpose and intrinsic purpose. This two-fold purpose that orients our personal development is grounded in evolution's essential organizing structure of wholes and parts, wherein every whole is also a part and vice a versa. Every evolutionary entity thus partakes of both kinds of purpose. So just as creativity and purpose give meaning to our lives, these powers also give meaning to evolution. Our ability to feel and know evolution's creativity and purpose from the inside thus provides evidence for the larger, external reality of these forces within the evolving universe as a whole.

## Consideration of the Purpose of the Whole

As a conclusion to these philosophical reflections on evolution's purpose, we now reconsider the essential types of purpose demonstrated by the character and motion of evolution at a macro scale. First, *instrumental purpose*.

### *Instrumental Purpose*

By way of review, the developmental structure of evolution's nested sequence of emergence reveals a chain of dependence in which earlier levels are enfolded within later appearing levels. Emergence produces increasingly more complex and accomplished systems through the technique of including and relying on the stable functions and competencies of preexisting evolutionary forms. Thus, whenever one system of evolution is taken up and used within a new encompassing form of emergence, this produces instrumental value within the system that is transcended and included by such an emergent event. By becoming useful in this way, the transcended system becomes more valuable. This impartation of instrumental value is particularly dramatic in the major events of emergence that produce entirely new forms of evolutionary development, which we see with the emergence of life and with the emergence of humanity. Using this understanding of the growth of instrumental value, we concluded that an instrumental purpose of the cosmological domain of development is to evolve toward conditions that will eventually support the emergence of life. Following this reasoning further, we also concluded that an instrumental purpose of the domain of life, in turn, is to evolve toward conditions that will support the emergence of creatures with self-conscious free will. And in these cases, the very fact of the instrumental use proves the purpose—as life depends on and uses matter, matter becomes endowed with a new form of purpose, and as our human minds depend on and use our animal bodies, we likewise add purpose to life.

However, recognizing these instrumental purposes does not negate, or even diminish, the inherent intrinsic value of the cosmological or biological domains of evolution. The intrinsic value of these domains is actually enhanced and reinforced through their instrumental use by transcendent levels that surpass and encompass them. By making a distinction between intrinsic and instrumental value in our analysis of evolution, and by recognizing how instrumental value is the complementary equal of intrinsic value, we come to see both kinds of value more clearly. By appreciating instrumental value in an evolutionary context, we can recognize that sustainable instrumental use is not exploitation or oppression, but rather *service*. And such an enhanced appreciation of instrumental value in turn helps make the inherent intrinsic value of every holon stand out in greater relief.

Postmodernism did well to dethrone anthropocentric values as the primary basis for assessing worth. Through the evolution of consciousness and culture many of us have come to see that we owe a moral duty to other organisms and to nature as a whole. But as we move beyond the postmodern antithesis toward an enlarged philosophical synthesis that fully includes both instrumental/fundamental and intrinsic/significant value, we come to realize that valuing the evolutionary significance of humans actually helps us better recognize the intrinsic significance of every evolutionary entity.

Acknowledging that the instrumental value or purpose of any given evolutionary system or domain is achieved when it becomes a foundational part of a larger encompassing level, what can we say about the instrumental value or purpose of the noosphere overall? Is the evolution of the noosphere leading to its eventual transcendence by a major new category of emergence? Given the history of evolutionary emergence, I think such an "omega event" is likely to happen someday. But rather than anticipate the "end of history," I think it is more realistic and productive to look for and expect more modest forms of emergence, such as new worldviews and new forms of culture within the currently existing noosphere.

Although no one can really know, it is my opinion that the vision of an epochal emergence that entirely transcends human cultural evolution and inaugurates a new category of evolutionary development is beyond our present horizon. Some have argued that the advent of genetic engineering or human-machine hybrids will constitute such a new category of evolution. However, while developments such as these would certainly change human history, they would likely be no more significant than other kinds of major technological changes, such as those seen during the industrial revolution. Others have speculated that the rise of self-replicating artificial intelligence will constitute an omega point for human history. However, scientists have not even been able to produce life from scratch, so I strongly doubt that they will ever produce artificial self-consciousness. Despite its currently fashionable acceptance within scientific circles, the prospect of technology "taking over" evolution is more of a science fiction fantasy than a realistic future scenario. Yet another candidate for the "end of history" posits the emergence of a "global brain" or a similar type of "species-subject" which will come to encompass all human individuals within a larger superorganism. However, this vision presents a troubling Orwellian scenario of totalitarian control wherein "the individual is only a cell." Moreover, such a hypothesis ignores the insights of integral philosophy, which recognize an important distinction between individual holons and social holons. This distinction, however, is somewhat technical and beyond the scope of our current discussion, so it is explained in this endnote.[9]

The anticipated future emergence of new worldviews or new stages of consciousness and culture may profoundly affect history, but such events will not constitute the appearance of a new category of evolution. For a form of emergence to have the cosmic significance of the original emergence of life from matter, or the emergence of human self-consciousness from animal consciousness, it seems to me that this would require a transformation equivalent to the appearance of heaven on earth. In other words, from what we now understand about emergence, we can conclude that cultural evolution's omega point is essentially beyond our ability to anticipate or predict. As explained in chapter 1, it is in the basic character of evolutionary emergence that it results in something entirely new and different—emergence produces ingressions of novelty that are not prefigured within pre-transcended levels, and cannot be anticipated by examining the characteristics of previous levels. Thus, if something does emerge beyond us, it will be more than we can imagine today.

Ultimately, asking about the instrumental purpose of the noosphere involves inquiring about the fundamental purpose of evolution as a whole. This is so because cosmological and biological evolution are instrumentally valuable to the noosphere, but generally not vice versa.[10] That is, as discussed in the previous chapter, the appearance of the human psychosocial domain of evolution is the outer encompassing layer that enfolds the whole within its emergence. And despite the mind-boggling implications of this inquiry about the instrumental value of the whole, it is possible to logically consider the evolving universe of time and space as a whole because the finite universe is a *bounded entity*. Notwithstanding the possibility that the known universe could be encompassed within a larger, infinite reality that science cannot detect, the material universe we live in—the universe in which evolution takes place—is not infinite in time, space, or in the number of its parts. As Rem Blanchard Edwards writes in his well-informed book, *What Caused the Big Bang?*:

> We need not be capable in practice of counting the number of things in the universe in order to make the concept of "the universe as a whole" intelligible. (1) Everything within our system of spacetime had a common, intensely concentrated, and totally unified origin. (2) All cones of causation within our contemporary universe are derived from an originally grandly unified Big Bang. (3) By extrapolating from pervasive laws of nature, we can trace the common evolutionary physical history of everything within our system of spacetime back to highly unified Big Bang origins. (4) This history goes back for approximately fifteen billion years and no further. . . . Since the notion of our universe as a whole really does make sense, and since traditional naturalists were wrong in insisting upon its infinite duration, the question of a transcendent cause or creation of the universe is intelligible after all.[11]

Still, while questions about the transcendent cause or purpose of the finite universe as a whole may be "intelligible," these questions pass beyond the realm of philosophy as I am defining it and enter the realm of theology, wherein our conclusions must necessarily be limited to informed speculation. We will nevertheless consider the theological implications of evolution's instrumental purpose in the next chapter. For now, however, we will move on to some conclusions about the *intrinsic purpose* of evolution considered philosophically.

## Intrinsic Purpose

Intrinsic purpose is largely synonymous with intrinsic value. And as discussed at length in chapters 3 and 4, the most intrinsic value can be identified as goodness, which is itself in a systemic relationship with beauty and truth. Goodness, truth, and beauty are what make any and every whole intrinsically valuable. Although these values are not possessed in equal measure by the holons of evolution, no holon is completely devoid of these values either. Wherever there is a whole entity of evolution, wherever instrumental value is being imparted in the holarchic chain, there is an intrinsic good in itself. The intrinsic value of every whole life form is dramatically demonstrated in the way organisms stand up for themselves and defend themselves when threatened. And when life forms go further by sacrificing themselves to defend their offspring or their group, they demonstrate their intrinsic value even more dramatically.

Moreover, emergent holons exhibit increasing intrinsic value as they grow in significance in the course of evolution's value generation. One of the markers of this growing significance can be found in the deepening originality—the one-of-a-kind uniqueness—borne in increasing measure by evolving entities. Indeed, the intrinsic value of humanity as a whole is demonstrated by the distinct, personal originality possessed by every individual human being.

And wherever there is goodness, we can always find traces of beauty and truth. Although not all wholes are recognizably beautiful, beauty is widely distributed within every domain of evolution. The beauty of a snowflake or a spiral galaxy, the beauty of a butterfly or a tiger, the beauty of a child's drawing or a mature artist's masterpiece, all attest to evolution's intrinsic value. When it comes to truth, we can see this aspect of intrinsic value in the fact that the evolving universe is intelligible and discoverable in the first place. That evolution reveals degrees of mathematical regularity and patterned order is testimony to its abiding truth. Indeed, every holon exemplifies the value of truth in the way that it participates in the narrative story of evolution. As Haught observes, "nature is narrative to the core," and the truth of this 13.7 billion year old story is told by each of the trillions and trillions of parts that comprise its totality. Haught continues: "At heart, evolutionary science is, after all, the telling of a grand story, in any of the various versions now being debated. It turns out that the recipe for evolution is first of all the recipe for nature-as-narrative. So we cannot hope to get to the bottom of evolution unless we risk asking why the universe would have a narrative character in the first place."[12]

The epic story told by the majestic unfolding of evolution helps us better understand and appreciate its intrinsic value overall. That is, the value of evolution is not static; its value is "alive, free, thrilling, and always moving." Evolution is a process of growth, and even the parts that are no longer growing or emerging are nevertheless contributing to the growth of the emergent levels which encompass those parts as a foundation for further growth.[13] Thus the intrinsic purpose of evolution can be discovered not only in the beauty, truth, and goodness it has already achieved; its purpose is also found in its ongoing growth toward these intrinsic values. Indeed, this is the essence of the entire process. In short, the intrinsic purpose of evolution is growth toward goodness, beauty, and truth. This is its purpose, and this is our purpose.

## *Purpose and Dialectical Synthesis*

In the final analysis, the polarity of parts and wholes that characterizes evolution's structure, the polarity of entropy and creativity that characterizes its motion, the polarity of self and other that characterizes its impulse, and the polarity of intrinsic and instrumental value that characterizes its purpose, are each expressions of evolution's master systemic pattern of continuous dialectical synthesis.

As a result of sustained reflection on the power of evolutionary growth, I have come to agree with Hegel that the rising flow that drives evolution toward ever greater realizations of value ultimately arises from the polar separation of thesis and antithesis, and thus finds fulfillment in the synthetic transcendence of these contrasting elements. Evolution's ultimate purpose, its final cause, can accordingly be found in the synthesis that includes both instrumental and intrinsic value. This synthesis is well described by Rolston:

> Intrinsic value, the value of an individual "for what it is in itself," becomes problematic in a holistic web. True, the system projects such values more and

more with its evolution of individuality and freedom. Yet to decouple this from the biotic, communal system is to make value too internal and elementary, to forget relatedness and externality. . . . Intrinsic value is a part in a whole, not to be fragmented by valuing it in isolation. . . . Intrinsic and instrumental values shuttle back and forth, parts-in-wholes and wholes-in-parts, local details of value embedded in global structures, gems in their settings, and their setting-situation a maternal matrix. To change the figure, intrinsic values are particles that are also waves, and instrumental values are waves that are also particles, as one shifts valuing perspective or coagulates events this way or that.[14]

As Rolston's analysis suggests, the dialectical separation of part and whole is an indelible feature of our evolving universe. However, despite the ever-present polarity of this separation, and despite the often painful partiality of our own incompleteness, the gravity of transcendent value continuously pulls us toward a better future. The dialectical tension of the incomplete can thus be understood as a kind of opening, a portal through which we may pass into more evolved states and stages. And as we are moved by evolution, as we grow in our ability to experience and create intrinsic value, we come to see how the purpose of evolution itself is still evolving—it cannot be discerned with finality because it is still in the process of being determined by the beings whose choices are required for its creation.

But despite its incomplete nature, I trust we have now grasped enough of evolution's meaning and value to confirm that the overall purpose of evolution is to increasingly grow toward perfection—to move toward ever-greater realizations of the beautiful, the true, and the good. This goal of evolution need not be conceived as a predetermined blueprint of perfection, but rather as a fresh and original form of perfection that is being creatively discerned and freely chosen by evolutionary creatures themselves.

There is more to say about the role of synthesis and increasing perfection in the purpose of evolution. But, as with our discussion of the instrumental value of the whole, further consideration of evolution's synthetic purpose takes us beyond the realm of philosophical argumentation and into the realm of theology. So this theme will be picked up again in the next chapter's discussion of the theological implications of this philosophy of evolution. But before finishing this more modest philosophical consideration of evolution's purpose, it is important to address the relationship between evolution's purpose and the presence of suffering and evil.

## The Purpose of Suffering

If we acknowledge that evolution is purposive, must we then also conclude that horrific suffering and evil are somehow contained within its purpose? I do not think this is the case. Rather, it seems that suffering is a consequence of emerging sentience within life, and evil is similarly an inevitable byproduct of the freedom and intentionality increasingly possessed by evolving human consciousness. Before I try to explain this, however, let me say first that evil and suffering are not rational or justified; rather, these horrors result from the relative absence of reason or justice. These afflictions arise from the reality of our incompleteness and give the evolutionary impulse its urgent impetus. The ongoing presence of evil and suffering in the world thus compels us to make further evolutionary progress and avoid regression.

The apparent purposelessness of affliction has been cited by many commentators as proof that evolution lacks purpose. Darwin himself was appalled by what he perceived as the cruelty and horror of the natural world. Yet the idea that the suffering of the world proves that the universe is indifferent to life is in large part a disappointed reaction to an underlying expectation of divine intervention and control. The original Victorian evolutionists were raised in a culture which taught that God designed and created the world as it is, that it is the result of a divine blueprint, and that every feature is God's handiwork. So as the facts of evolution came to light and contradicted this teaching, this caused many evolutionists to reject all forms of spiritual explanation whatsoever. Thus, the conclusion that the universe is devoid of purpose is an example of bad theology of one kind producing bad theology of an opposite kind.

Prior to the appearance of life, there was no real suffering; the only downside of evolution was destruction. The organization of matter can be destroyed, such as when a star is destroyed in a supernova, but we would not say that suffering is involved in the death of a star. Suffering only emerges with biological sentience. Likewise, the potential for evil and cruelty only really emerge with the human sense of morality. We do not expect animals to behave morally, so ascribing evil intentions to any of them is clearly an anthropomorphic projection. In other words, negative values or disvalues emerge only alongside the potential to recognize and choose values themselves. In the course of evolution, the awakening of consciousness to increasing realizations of morality is followed by the growing shadow of potential immorality. And this emergence of disvalues can be understood as the result of evolution's dialectical pattern under which progress is inevitably accompanied by pathology. However, rather than being proof of purposelessness, our growing awareness of pathology actually provides proof that consciousness is evolving toward greater realizations of value.

As biological systems evolve, the emergent potential to feel pain serves as a strong motivator for attention and action; the ability to feel pain is thus a powerful mechanism that promotes the survival of living things. Similarly, as psychosocial systems evolve, the emergent potential to be troubled by immorality, ignorance, and ugliness serves as a strong psychological motivator to improve the human condition. And the more developed our consciousness becomes, the more we become aware of the extent to which our development is partial and incomplete.

Suffering is a reality in the evolutionary realm of biological life, yet unlike the consequences of human evil, we need not conclude that suffering in nature is an immoral problem we need to fix. While we may have a moral duty to ameliorate the unjustified suffering of animals or the needless destruction of the natural environment when such harm is caused by humans, where humans have not caused harm or disruption, direct intervention in nature's course is usually uncalled for. In the realm of human affairs, however, the ongoing presence of both suffering and evil imparts a corresponding duty to do everything we can to improve the human condition.

As modernism reached its developmental climax in the twentieth century, these horrors were magnified by enormous proportions through world war and monstrous totalitarian regimes. And as noted earlier, these historical developments caused many to abandon the idea of cultural evolution altogether. Yet even as the negative side of modernism continues to challenge us, it is not a foregone conclusion that civilization will inevitably decline or collapse. Just as new solutions bring new problems, new problems stimulate further cultural development, which in turn results in another round of new solutions. So as we face the travails of history and the suffering and trouble we find in the world, we need not conclude that evolution is valueless or purposeless. The problem of evil is vexing and real, but our best response is to affirm the ongoing potential for the further evolution of consciousness and culture, rather than to deny that net progress is possible.

From an evolutionary perspective we can perhaps understand the ongoing presence of evil and suffering within a purposeful creation as the shadow of freedom. As Rolston observes, "One cannot enjoy a world in which one cannot suffer, any more than one can succeed in a world in which one cannot fail." This perspective helps us recognize the freedom we possess as "an empowering permission that places productive autonomy in the creation." We know that our bodies are physically real because they reflect light and cast a shadow, and we likewise know that our powers of choice are real because we can make mistakes and choose to do wrong. The shadow of potential error and evil is thus an inevitable result of the reality of free will. Yet progress can still be made: as we diminish the negative potential for error and evil in our choosing, we increasingly realize our positive potential for self-mastery and spiritual growth. We have the power to transform tragedy into something higher—to use our sensitivity to the horrors of the world as a source of energy and instruction for the amelioration through cultural evolution of much that is wrong with our troubled realm.

Just as there is more to say about the overall purpose of evolution, there is also more to say about the "purpose of suffering." But these further considerations are best discussed within a more spiritual frame of reference. So we will leave this discussion here for now, thus concluding our *philosophical* consideration of purpose in evolution. But in the next chapter we will continue reflecting on evolution's ultimate purpose within a *theological* context.

# CHAPTER 8

# Spiritual Reflections on Evolution's Purpose

FOR ME, THE SUBJECT OF SPIRITUALITY is deeply personal. Although I do not subscribe to any particular religion, I find spiritual experience in periods of silence and stillness, amid the beauty of nature, in tender moments with my family, and in reading the great books of spiritual masters from the past. I have also found a kind of spiritual experience in "reading the great book" of our universe's evolutionary history. That is, the more I learn and contemplate the scientific and historical story of our emergent origins, the more it becomes apparent that this history is a revelation of spiritual truth. Although this evolutionary story is founded on scientific facts, its truths ultimately connect with a sublime feeling of beauty and a deep sense of being "at home" in the creation. In other words, both the unfolding majesty we have discovered so far, and the intriguing mystery that remains, evokes a sense of awe and reverence for this marvelous journey we are all on. This feeling of the sacred nature of the universe arises not only from what has emerged so far, but also from a sense of our approaching destiny, the promise of an evolutionary future of transcendent achievement for consciousness and culture.

I set out to write a philosophy book that would help illuminate evolution's purposeful progression. But in the course of this writing I have come to see that our discussion would not be complete without a period of reflection on some of evolution's deeper potential significance. Up to this point, our philosophical investigation of the meaning and value of evolution has been grounded in scientific fact. However, just as this evolutionary philosophy would be of little worth were it not founded on science, it would also be of little value if it did not ultimately connect with spirituality. So in this chapter I hope to build on what we have concluded so far by briefly considering some of the possible spiritual implications that follow from this philosophical perspective.

As with the philosophy of evolution we have discussed in the book up to this point, the evolutionary theology[1] we now consider is rendered at a level of generality that makes it potentially acceptable to a wide variety of spiritual paths and orientations. As stated in the introduction, I am not arguing for, or otherwise promoting, a particular form of spirituality or belief. However, I acknowledge that there is little hope that these ideas will appeal to traditional religious conservatives or fundamentalists, who generally do not recognize the authority of science. Nor is there much chance of convincing the adherents of scientism, for whom talk of anything "extra-physical" is nonsense. But I do hope to appeal to religious naturalists—scientifically minded realists who are nevertheless able to recognize spirituality within life and the ceaseless creativity of the universe. I also hope to connect with those who have loyalties to Eastern nondual traditions, but who otherwise recognize the reality of evolution and the validity of scientific descriptions thereof. Again, even though I have argued that evolution demonstrates purpose, I have not insisted that this purposefulness necessarily implies a theistic Deity. This philosophy, however, does not preclude the conviction that a loving God is the ultimate creator and upholder of our evolving universe. I thus hope that the following theological reflections will also find acceptance with process theists, panentheists, and even traditional theists, who can see that evolution is, in the final analysis, a technique of creation.

This chapter, then, expands our examination of evolution's purpose, moving beyond the constraints of "minimal metaphysics" in order to consider the broader spiritual significance of this new philosophical understanding of the meaning and value of evolution. The theological discussion that follows is not being asserted as a philosophical argument subject to refutation; it is folly to try to "prove" matters that are essentially beyond scientifically grounded philosophy. These ideas about the "big picture" of the universe are thus presented, not as part of the philosophy I have argued for in our discussion so far, but rather as only one possible interpretation of the spiritual connotations of our evolving universe.

To make this heady discussion as clear as possible, I first state my theological thesis as a single (albeit long) sentence. Then I lay out the thesis in the form of ten tenets which follow a logical progression. After that, I discuss each of the tenets to bring out the issues raised thereby. Finally, in conclusion, I offer some personal thoughts on that which ultimately gives rise to evolution's purpose.

## A Dialectical Thesis of Experiential Perfection through Evolution

When we grasp the insight that dialectical development is evolution's overall master pattern and transcendent technique, we can begin to discern this pattern in the structure and function of evolution as a whole. And this suggests that the entire evolutionary process is itself a form of striving that is seeking some kind of transcendent synthetic achievement. We have seen how evolution's growth exhibits purpose in the way it aims at value, but what can we conclude about the underlying reason for this purposive movement? My conclusion is that evolution's ultimate end or purpose is the achievement of an *experiential form of perfection*. Although this conclusion is ultimately a personal spiritual conviction, it has been arrived at through the series of systematic theological steps that follow. The thesis underlying this theology can be summarized in the following statement:

> The cosmic interaction of the *thesis* of preexistent, existential perfection (eternal and infinite perfection) and the *antithesis* of time and space (the finite, material universe) gives rise to the emerging *synthesis* of experiential perfection—the evolutionary journey wherein the universe's creatures discover their Source.

This understanding of evolution's overall purpose reveals how we are each called upon to participate in the achievement of this experiential, transcendent synthesis by fulfilling our unique roles as agents of evolution. As Murdoch understood, "we are spiritual creatures, attracted by excellence and made for the good."

## Ten Tenets of Evolutionary Theology

The theological thesis stated above can be unpacked through a logical sequence of ten tenets, or premises, that arguably follow from the evolutionary philosophy presented in this book. These tenets employ certain phrases that require explanation and definition, but these terms will be clarified in the discussion that follows.

1. Our evolving universe had a distinct and dramatic beginning. This original emergence or emanation resulted from a primal cause—a primordial creative act.

2. This cause or creative act that initiated the universe can best be conceived as an "uncaused cause," or a *first cause*.

3. The first cause is necessarily prior to and transcendent of time, space, energy, matter, and evolution itself.

4. Because the first cause transcends the finite universe, it can be conceived as being infinite, eternal, and universal. In other words, the first cause is changeless and perfect. Thus, prior to the beginning of evolution, the universe as first cause was in a state of *existential perfection*.

5. The creative act that brought forth the finite universe can be partially understood as an act of separation, subtraction, or *kenosis*, wherein perfection is removed from a part of the universe, which nevertheless remains within the encompassing container of existential perfection.

6. The evolving universe that results from this creative act unfolds according to a self-similar pattern, process, and technique of dialectical development. And the pattern's self-similar structure suggests that this same pattern also configures the ongoing creative process of the universe as a whole.

7. From this we can hypothesize that the *thesis* of existential perfection is followed and partially negated by the *antithesis* of the finite universe, and that from the inherent tension of this thesis and antithesis, a *synthesis* is arising, which we recognize as evolution.

8. This synthesis emerges with life and matures through the psychosocial domain of evolution, wherein free will creatures increasingly develop toward perfection through widening realizations of value. This gradual realization of perfection is achieved through the experience and creation of beauty, truth, and goodness, and related sub-values.

9. The emerging synthesis of evolution adds to the thesis of existential perfection the *experience* of becoming perfect—freely and creatively. The antithesis of the finite universe is thus used as the domain wherein experiential perfection is achieved through dialectical evolution.

10. This evolutionary theology illuminates the instrumental purpose of the noosphere, helps explain the existence of evil and suffering, and connects the intrinsic purpose of each person with the intrinsic purpose of the universe's first cause.

## Discussion of the Ten Tenets

**Tenet 1:** *Our evolving universe had a distinct and dramatic beginning. This original emergence or emanation resulted from a primal cause—a primordial creative act.*

Prior to the scientific confirmation of the big bang in the 1960s most scientists held to the conviction that the universe had always existed in an eternal steady-state. Einstein was so committed to this idea that he even altered his equations to make them consistent with a steady-state cosmology. The idea of an eternal, unchanging universe also provided comfort for atheistic philosophers. Bertrand Russell summed up this position as: "The universe is just there, and that's all."[2] So when the facts came in that our universe actually "began" with a tremendous explosion, and that this event was not much older than the age of the earth itself, this was quite troubling for scientism, because it so clearly pointed to an act of creation. And when astrophysicists later discovered that the initial conditions and physical constants present in the first moments of the big bang were uncannily set to provide the exact conditions necessary for the later emergence of life, this was even more disturbing. Even atheistic physicist Stephen Hawking once conceded, "The odds against a universe like ours emerging out of something like the Big Bang are enormous. I think there are clearly religious implications."[3]

These discoveries have produced the rise of a cottage industry of speculation by theoretical physicists seeking a plausible explanation that can overcome or otherwise refute these unsettling "religious implications." However, despite the credibility given to such speculations within the scientific community, unfalsifiable theories such as the "multiverse hypothesis" seem to me to be little more than bad theology masquerading as science. Indeed, speculations about multiple universes or the "M theory" in physics do not negate the explanatory need for a first cause. Despite their naive claims, such speculations do not explain how "something came from nothing" and only push the need for a first cause back to the original creation of the hypothetical multiverse.

For those not familiar with the science in this area, it is worth emphasizing that the big bang is no longer merely a hypothesis. It is now an established scientific fact (confirmed by a variety of observational evidence) that our universe began 13.7 billion years ago (give or take 120 million years) with a primordial hot and dense initial condition, and has been expanding ever since. Scientists continue to debate the details, but the question of whether *our* universe began with the big bang is no longer subject to significant debate. The phrase "big bang" was initially used as a term of derision coined by those who doubted the original hypothesis, but it stuck. Although other terms have been proposed, such as the "primordial flaring forth," the "primordium," and the "Great Radiance," the term "big bang" has perhaps persisted with scientists because it is irreverent and semi-humorous, conveniently obscuring the truth that this event is saturated with sacred significance.

Tenet 1 points to the obvious implication that the big bang had some kind of cause. Although, as noted, the ordinary concept of cause and effect becomes somewhat untenable when we acknowledge that time did not exist prior to the big bang. This means that the "cause" of this event cannot be anything like the regular types of causation with which we are familiar. Nevertheless, this astonishing emergence did occur, and it stands in relation to the chain of subsequent emergences that have followed and built upon it in the course of evolution. The fact of the origin of our universe in the big bang is not meaningless; the only question is: What is its meaning? The discovery of this scientific fact creates a kind of conceptual vacuum into which one kind of metaphysics or another inevitably rushes in. To conclude that "no one will ever know" is a cop-out; if we can discover the fact scientifically, then we can also discover the meaning philosophically. The refusal to accept any metaphysical commitments may be aesthetically appealing to some, but this is just another kind of metaphysics, and an impoverished kind at that.

Our universe did not just "pop out of nothingness as the result of a causeless quantum transition." Before the big bang there was no time, space, energy, or matter, there was only what cosmologists call a "singularity." So even if there were other finite universes before this one, these previous universes were no longer in existence at the moment of the big bang. That is, our universe did not "come out of" a preexisting form of spacetime. Space-time *began* with our universe. Some theoretical physicists have asserted that the universe is self-organizing and self-creating, and that no "outside causes" were required for its emergence. However, this argument would have us assume that the supposedly preexisting laws of physics (such as gravity, as recently argued by Hawking) were capable of producing this emergence by themselves. Yet it strains credibility to argue that the stupendous outpouring of creativity represented by the big bang was wholly caused by gravity or some other preexisting mindless physical law. Indeed, if gravity is so marvel-ously creative, then what caused gravity to come into being? Further, the problems of such "causeless" explanations are compounded when we then add the evidence that the initial constants of physics which arose with the big bang were intricately fine-tuned for the later appearance of life. Under the accumulating weight of these facts, the assertion that the emergence of the big bang somehow occurred accidentally or automatically can be recognized as preposterous. And it is worth saying that the fact that the universe began with the big bang does not inevitably lead to the speculative conclusion that it must then end in some kind of "heat death."

In light of these arguments, the most plausible and parsimonious explanation for this stupendously dramatic event is that it was produced by some kind of primal, prior cause.

**Tenet 2:** *This cause or creative act that initiated the universe can best be conceived as an "uncaused cause," or a* first cause.

Some scientists have argued that inquiring about anything prior to the big bang is like asking what is north of the North Pole. But this is often science's response when faced with its own limitations—if science can't answer, then don't ask, because only science can deliver truth. It may be true that the finite human mind has difficulty with concepts that precede or transcend time, but this does not mean that we can know nothing at all of the original creative catalyst. We can reasonably surmise that the cause of this original, primordial emergence is somehow related to the cause of subsequent evolutionary emergences. And as we have seen, the evolutionary impulse responsible for these emergences can be directly experienced from the *inside* as it influences each of us.

Philosophical conceptions of a "first cause" can be traced to the ancient Greeks. Known as the "cosmological argument," the idea that something caused the universe to exist has persisted throughout the history of philosophy. And today, the scientific revelation of the big bang has given this old idea new relevance and authority.

Yet even if we accept a nontemporal first cause as the most plausible account of the big bang, this does not necessarily lead directly to theism; the concept of a first cause could turn out to be more of a principle than a personality, and is thus compatible with a variety of nontheistic notions regarding creativity in the cosmos. A first cause can also fit in with Hindu ideas of an impersonal Brahman, and even with some Buddhist conceptions of nondual emptiness.[4] The first cause can even find acceptance among "ground-of-being theologies," which reject the claim that the ultimate is a determinate entity of any kind. That is, it could simply be in the nature of being that it eventually results in the emergence of time and space. What "caused" the first cause is a question answered by the meaning of the concept itself—in philosophy, a first cause is an uncaused cause.

Obviously the first cause is unique and cannot be easily equated with any human experience of causation. However, the alternative explanation of the source of our origin—that the big bang had no cause or reason and somehow occurred accidentally or randomly—seems extremely weak and does not do justice to the dramatic facts of the big bang, nor to the ensuing sequence of creative emergences that have followed it. And even if the science of the big bang is substantially revised in the future, we will still be faced with the fact that there is something rather than nothing, and that this *something* is evolving. Thus a first cause will always remain the most likely answer to the question of how the universe came into being.

**Tenet 3:** *The first cause is necessarily prior to and transcendent of time, space, energy, matter, and evolution itself.*

As noted, according to the science of general relativity, the initial condition of the universe at the moment of the big bang was a *spacetime singularity.* A singularity is a mathematical concept of a "location" wherein matter is compressed to an "infinite density." This conclusion about the beginning of the universe has been "proven" by the Penrose-Hawking theorem, which also proves that the singularity of the big bang marks the beginning of time. What this means for our discussion is that the cause of this initial condition, the impetus that produced it, must be conceived as being prior to, or outside of, spacetime. In other words, that which caused, produced, created, gave rise to, or otherwise made the singularity, can be said to transcend time. Tenet 3 may seem obvious, but it is a necessary step in the logical sequence that leads to the important theological conclusions of the next tenet.

**Tenet 4:** *Because the first cause transcends the finite universe, it can be conceived as being infinite, eternal, and universal. In other words, the first cause is changeless and perfect. Thus, prior to the beginning of evolution, the universe as first cause was in a state of* existential perfection.

It is often said that the big bang "emerged out of nothing." But we could just as easily say that the big bang emerged out of *everything.* That is, that which existed "before" time can best be conceived as "eternal." And if we are willing to accept eternity as a feature of the first cause, then its infinite nature can also be recognized by natural association. For some, the notion that the cosmos existed in an eternal and infinite state prior to the big bang evokes the image of an ocean or featureless void. Yet it seems a stretch to envision a featureless void as possessing the necessary power and potency required to serve as a first cause of a universe of billions of galaxies. I thus prefer to envision the timeless and changeless entity or condition that produced the big bang as having the characteristic feature of *perfection*. That which encompasses and contains all being, that which lacks nothing and has no limits, that which is the source of all that is, shall we deny that this is perfect?

The idea of perfection may be difficult to conceive and thus requires a bit of definitional clarification. Perfection is a concept that is central to many forms of theology, but in the context of these theological tenets, perfection connotes both source and destiny. Perfection as source points to the existential state of the universe prior to the birth of time, a condition which we might characterize as the "first universe age." Perfection as destiny indicates a future state of evolutionary completion in which no further improvement is possible, a condition which we might characterize as evolution's "omega point."

Supplementing the theological concept of evolution's ultimate culmination or omega point is the idea of interim omega points, or events that signal the relative completion of an evolutionary era. In the previous discussion of progress in chapter 6 I explained how cosmological evolution reached a kind of omega point, or state of completion, with the initial emergence of life. Although cosmological evolution is continuing, the emergence of life marks the successful transcendence of one form of evolution by another. Similarly, I argued that biological evolution reached its omega point (although it too continues) here on earth with the emergence of self-conscious humans. This pattern of development thus suggests that psychosocial evolution may one day reach an omega point in which we actually achieve a form of permanent enlightenment—the emergence of a perfected state in which the need for further evolutionary progress essentially comes to an end. It may be difficult to imagine an end to cultural evolution through the advent of some kind of utopian "heaven on earth." However, if we allow for the possibility of an afterlife, then we can perhaps more easily envision such an ascendant destiny as the culmination of our own spiritual growth as individuals in the ages to come. The idea of perfection as both the source and destiny of evolution will be clarified further as our discussion continues.

I admit that Tenet 4's "affirmation of the existential perfection of the first cause" is merely a theological assertion. Arguments can certainly be made against such a conclusion. The theological propositions of Tenet 4, however, are supported and strengthened by the 6 additional tenets that follow. I therefore ask the reader to temporarily accept the idea of a state of perfection existing before the big bang, even if just for the sake of argument, and then reconsider it in light of the following discussion to see how it does good explanatory work.

**Tenet 5:** *The creative act that brought forth the finite universe can be partially understood as an act of separation, subtraction, or* kenosis, *wherein perfection is removed from a part of the universe, which nevertheless remains within the encompassing container of existential perfection.*

Tenet 5 is based on a rich theological tradition found in Christianity, Judaism, and also in a variety of non-traditional progressive spiritual teachings. Although this theology has been developed in theistic contexts, and thus attributes the creative act to God, the idea of "creation by subtraction" remains compatible with alternative conceptions of the ultimate.

In Christianity, the doctrine of *kenosis*, or self-emptying, originally concerned the practice of surrendering one's personal will to God's will. As Jesus said, referring to his Father in Heaven, "Not my will, but yours be done." This personal spiritual act of removing one's will from the field of action has subsequently been developed and expanded by a variety of progressive Christian theologians, including Philip Clayton and John Haught, into a description of creation itself as an act of self-emptying. Clayton explains: "For an infinite God to enter into relation with finite creatures . . . is for this God to have emptied Godself of certain divine attributes (since an all-powerful, always acting God would leave no place for separate agents to freely initiate independent actions on their own behalf)."[5] The characterization of the creation of the universe as an act of self-emptying has been adopted by evolutionary theologians such as Clayton (who has a Protestant background) and Haught (who is Roman Catholic) because they believe it best corresponds to the facts of evolutionary emergence. According to Clayton, creation as kenosis is "what a systematic theology would look like if developed out of the context of emergent thinking."

We find a similar idea in Jewish Kabbalistic thought, known as *Tzimtzum*, which has been translated as "contraction" or "constriction." According to this doctrine, God created the universe by "contracting his infinite light in order to allow for a 'conceptual space' in which a finite and seemingly independent world could exist. This contraction formed an 'empty space' (יונפה ללח) in which creation could begin."[6]

This mystical Jewish conception of creation by contraction has deeply influenced protestant theologian Jürgen Moltmann, who writes: "[God's] creative activity outwards is preceded by his humble divine self-restriction. . . . This self-restricting love is the beginning of that self-emptying of God which Philippians 2 sees as the divine mystery of the Messiah. Even in order to create heaven and earth, God emptied Himself of his all-plenishing omnipotence, and as Creator took . . . the form of a servant."[7]

Tenet 5's description of the creative removal of perfection from the finite universe is related to chapter 6's discussion of evolution as a gradual movement back toward perfection. As we have seen, human psychosocial evolution is a continuation of cosmological and biological evolution, yet its emergence also transcends previous categories of evolution. This transcendent form of development is demonstrated by humanity's evolutionary quest for beauty, truth, and goodness, which illuminates the meaning and purpose of evolution overall as the motion toward increasing perfection of value. That is, to move toward perfection is to become more beautiful, more true, and more good, and this is where evolution is heading despite frequent errors and dialectical setbacks.

Building on this reasoning, we can imagine that the features of the finite universe are, in a sense, what remains of reality when perfection has been subtracted. Within this allegorical conception, the subtraction of eternity creates time, the subtraction of infinity creates space, the subtraction of value creates energy, and the subtraction of mind creates matter.[8] This creative subtraction, however, leaves a vacuum, which evolution rushes into, restoring organized information, value, and consciousness, increasingly by emergent steps.

The final clause of Tenet 5, which states that the finite universe "remains within the encompassing container of existential perfection," explains the source of value gravity. Evolution is drawn toward perfection through the choices of consciousness because forms of perfection continue to permeate and pervade the universe, and ultimately "contain" it. "Containment" is used as an analogy in this context and must be understood as surrounding the evolving universe on both ends of its scale. In other words, the infinite perfection of spirit is found beyond the farthest reaches of space, and prior to the limits of the smallest subatomic particles. Existential perfection can thus be identified as both the center and circumference of the evolving universe.

Tenet 5 also provides support for a panentheistic theological position, which envisions the ever-present source of creation to be both transcendent and immanent. That is, spirit resides within the heart of being at the center of all things, yet it also encompasses the universe and thus exceeds its limits. Within this conception, the theological notion of creation by subtraction does not entail a Deistic notion of a creator who begins the process but does not interact with it after that. Rather, creation is continuous as perfection "shines through" the finite universe in the form of deep structures of value that permeate reality, continually luring us into more evolved states of being. This suggests that beauty, truth, and goodness are actually the *comprehensible elements of Deity*—the aspects of spirit that we can experience and help create. And the ongoing discovery of these intrinsic values demonstrates the efficacious power of existential perfection as evolution's ongoing final cause.

**Tenet 6:** *The evolving universe that results from this creative act unfolds according to a self-similar pattern, process, and technique of dialectical development. And the pattern's self-similar structure suggests that this same pattern also configures the ongoing creative process of the universe as a whole.*

The organization of the evolving universe exhibits many unity patterns, such as symmetry and harmony. But among these patterns of unity, perhaps the most profound is *self-similarity*, or unity across scale. Self-similarity is a mathematical relationship found in forms of organization wherein the shape or nature of a given whole mirrors the shape of its parts, and vice a versa. As an example, most readers are familiar with fractal geometry, which exhibits the patterns of self-similarity dramatically and beautifully. Many objects in nature exhibit exact self-similarity, such as certain plants, seashells, and coastlines. More often, however, natural forms reflect approximate self-similarity, wherein the parts express the organization of the whole in analogous ways. For example, each human cell is its own little organism, and each contains the DNA for the whole body. Even though cells are not exact replicas of the body, they nevertheless exhibit an approximately self-similar relation to it.

In 1922 Niels Bohr won a Nobel Prize in physics by showing the direct structural similarity between a hydrogen atom and a solar system. But further developments in physics eventually refuted Bohr's theory and cross-scale comparisons fell out of favor. However, more recent investigations have revived the theory by showing how comparisons between atoms in a high-energy state (Bohr's original theory compared low-energy state atoms) and solar systems reveal a striking correspondence in structure and behavior. This has led to the new science of "fractal cosmology," which has effectively employed the paradigm of self-similarity as a useful model for accurate astrophysical predictions and for physics in general.[9]

Perhaps the most pervasive example of self-similarity in evolution is its overall holarchical organization, wherein the pattern of nested whole/parts "transcend and include" each other across the entire scale of evolutionary complexity.

However, among all the self-similar features of evolutionary organization, it seems to me that the most striking and significant is the pattern of the dialectic. As discussed in chapter 3, the dialectical pattern/process can be found throughout cosmological evolution, biological evolution, and most distinctly in cultural evolution. This pattern is a fundamental technique of self-unfolding through which emergent evolution continuously transcends existing conditions and achieves new synthetic levels of organization. Thus, the crux of Tenet 6 is that the self-similar character of evolutionary development suggests that the ubiquitous pattern of the dialectic, which configures so many of evolution's parts and processes, is in fact, the overall functional structure of the evolutionary process as a whole. Put simply, the dialectical parts reveal the dialectical whole.

As with Tenet 4, the veracity of Tenet 6's proposition is supported and strengthened by the tenets that follow.

**Tenet 7:** *From this we can hypothesize that the thesis of existential perfection is followed and partially negated by the antithesis of the finite universe, and that from the inherent tension of this* thesis *and* antithesis, *a synthesis is arising, which we recognize as evolution.*

Proceeding from Tenet 6's conclusion regarding the dialectical relationship of the infinite and finite aspects of the universe, Tenet 7 presents a dialectical interpretation of the events described in Tenets 1 through 5. The emergence of the finite universe can be said to "negate" the preexisting state of existential perfection, or otherwise serve as its antithesis, because in this process, that which is whole is followed by that which is partial, that which is timeless and changeless is partially supplanted by that which is temporal and evolving—that which is pure being is transcended by that which is becoming. Yet because of the dynamic nature of the dialectic, the inherent polar tension of thesis and antithesis is not stable; the resulting synthesis that emerges out of this tension is thus "perched on the edge of chaos." To maintain an everelusive equilibrium, it must keep moving forward, continuously generating new accomplishments. This emerging synthesis serves as a "negation of the negation" by gradually returning to that which is whole, by responding to the pull of value gravity, and by seeking increasing achievements of experiential perfection in the form of beauty, truth, and goodness.

From this we can see how our universe's overall process of synthetic development arises out of the energetic and creative tension that exists between the infinite and finite aspects of the cosmos. And it is the action of this macro synthetic motion that ultimately produces the rising flow of creativity we call evolution.

**Tenet 8:** *This synthesis emerges with life and matures through the psychosocial domain of evolution, wherein free will creatures increasingly develop toward perfection through widening realizations of value. This gradual realization of perfection is achieved through the experience and creation of beauty, truth, and goodness, and related sub-values.*

Tenet 8 summarizes our discussion in chapters 3 and 4 where we examined how values serve as attractors of evolutionary development. As humans respond to the evolutionary impulse to improve themselves and their society, history and culture evolve through progressive stages of value realization, gradually leading to a better world. Then in chapter 7 we explored the idea that the evolutionary impulse we feel within us is the same force that is driving the development of all forms of evolution. This dialectical evolutionary impetus is what critical realist philosopher Roy Bhaskar calls the "pulse of freedom." Discussing the dialectical movement toward synthesis, Bhaskar writes, "Dialectic is the yearning for freedom and the transformative negation of constraints on it."[10] From this we can perhaps sense how the grand synthesis of evolution described in these theological tenets is not only universal; it is also intimate and personal. And we make it ours increasingly as we respond to it: by appreciating and expressing the highest forms of value that are within our capacity to know.

This conception also provides insight into the purpose of free will. We are not forced to evolve, and it is only through our voluntary choices that our response to value gravity can result in the evolution of our consciousness. Yet when we do choose to evolve, when we choose to do good, we become partners with the first cause in the evolutionary creation of the universe. The grand synthesis of evolution thus arises within each of us, calling us to become part of the universal family of conscious evolutionaries who have embarked on the "magnificent adventure of experiential perfection attainment." This evolutionary calling was expressed by Jesus when he admonished his followers: "Be you perfect, even as our Father in Heaven is perfect."

As we stand on the shoulders of our ancestors and work to improve the human condition, our planetary culture will continue to evolve and develop. And perhaps one day human history may even reach some kind of utopian omega point—thereby achieving a type of experiential perfection through cultural evolution. Indeed, this may well be the evolutionary destiny of billions of similar inhabited lifeworlds. But regardless of what happens in the future, we can each take pride in our life's contribution, big or small, to the ongoing development of our own evolving civilization. And for those of us whose spiritual orientation provides for a conception of an afterlife, our participation in the grand synthesis of experiential perfection can be envisioned as continuing beyond this world into untold evolutionary adventure and ongoing personal spiritual growth.

**Tenet 9:** *The emerging synthesis of evolution adds to the thesis of existential perfection the experience of becoming perfect—freely and creatively. The antithesis of the finite universe is thus used as the domain wherein experiential perfection is achieved through dialectical evolution.*

Tenet 9 provides an answer to the question of "why evolution?" This question is well-framed (although narrowed to refer to "God") by philosopher Michael Silberstein, who writes:

> If God exists, then why would he even bother creating a dizzying and complex *physical world* of forces, causal mechanisms, atoms, cells, brains, etc.? . . . If goodness, as opposed to say, a good storyline is his bottom line, then why not make creation exactly as it ought to be from the beginning? God simply does not need ontological emergence or any other naturalistic process or mechanism. . . . If the end-point of the universe's evolution is morally and spiritually ideal, then why not just make the world like that from the beginning?[11]

The "dialectical thesis of experiential perfection through evolution" presented here responds to Silberstein's challenge. This theological thesis argues that the advent of the evolving universe adds a new dimension to existential perfection which cannot be realized without the existence of time and the experience of free creatures. As the mystic poet Angelus Silesius understood, "In the bosom of time, God-without-beginning becomes what He has never been in all eternity." To phrase it in a colloquial manner: What does a universe of existential perfection do for an encore? It transcends itself through the development of creatures who can experience becoming perfect in time. That is, to achieve evolutionary perfection freely by choice, by effort, and even by occasional struggle, is to create an aspect of reality that did not exist in the state of existential perfection that we recognize as prevailing in the universe prior to the big bang. Once evolution comes into being as a result of the emergence of the finite domain, the ensuing motion "back toward a state of perfection" produces a novel form of synthetic, emergent perfection—not a perfection that has always been, but a form of perfection experienced in its becoming and personally achieved through the faithful travails of evolutionary free will creatures.[12]

Perhaps this conception stretches the idea of perfection beyond its limits. But if we can allow ourselves to envision the idea of the synthetic growth toward perfection through the emergence of the sacred relationship of finite creature and infinite Creator, we can catch a glimpse of the comprehensive purpose of evolution, at least as conceived theologically.

Ultimately, however, the truth of ideas such as this cannot be grasped with the eye of reason alone. Spiritual realities require the "eye of the spirit" for their full recognition, and this depends on faith. As the philosopher Pascal understood, "Human things must be known to be loved, but Divine things must be loved to be known."

**Tenet 10:** *This evolutionary theology illuminates the instrumental purpose of the noosphere, helps explain the existence of evil and suffering, and connects the intrinsic purpose of each person with the intrinsic purpose of the universe's first cause.*

This tenet connects back to the philosophical discussion of purpose in the last chapter where I briefly pondered the instrumental purpose of the noosphere, or psychosocial domain of evolution. There I concluded that questions regarding what the evolution of humanity was "good for" were ultimately beyond the reach of scientifically grounded philosophy. However, as this question is revisited here within the context of evolutionary theology, it becomes clear that self-conscious free will creatures play a central role in the cosmic economy by freely discerning and creatively choosing a new dimension of perfection—one which complements and supplements preexisting existential perfection. The instrumental purpose of the noosphere can thus be understood as the creative discernment of a new and transcendent form of self-organizing, experiential perfection—an original realization of the beautiful, the true, and the good achieved by creatures in time.

And because this realization of perfection is being achieved in and through time, it necessarily involves the overcoming of the inherent partiality of time. Thus, within this conception, in order for us to fulfill our overall purpose of gradually evolving toward perfection, we must emerge *out of* imperfection. In other words, in order for our experience of becoming perfect to be complete, we must start our journey at the lowest level possible, so that upon reaching the highest level, we will have woven a thread from "the dirt to paradise." Our earthly suffering then, can be understood as a kind of birth trauma—a passage through the material realm wherein we receive a taste of the nature of the incomplete and the inevitable pain that goes with it. If the finite universe really is the antithesis of existential perfection, then we might expect that our synthetic, evolutionary transcendence of this antithesis—our "negation of the negation"—would necessarily involve the unpleasant experience of that which we are called to transcend. That is, as life pushes off against a universe of dead matter, and as humanity in turn transcends the limitations of our animal origins in the quest for transcendent spiritual realities, we find ourselves "suffering through to something higher."

Our collective suffering can thus be seen as an indispensible aspect of the process of growth that helps make our transcendence of these lower levels an actual reality. And if we are willing to accept that our spiritual evolution continues in an afterlife, we can then perhaps sense how those who have borne a disproportionate share of this suffering will be ultimately compensated after death, wherein their experience of suffering in this life will become the inventory of their comparative joy in the next life. Through this theology we may thus come to appreciate that, in the scheme of evolution, "the greatest affliction is to have never been afflicted."

Finally, Tenet 10 concludes with the idea that every person shares in the ultimate purpose of the first cause. This is actually an idea that has been understood for thousands of years—as the ancient seers realized, "man is the measure of all things." When we therefore contemplate this saying in the context of evolutionary theology, we can begin to see how the life of each person is a microcosmic, self-similar enactment of the entire process of the evolving universe as a whole. As Teilhard de Chardin wrote, "the Universal and personal grow in the same direction and culminate simultaneously in each other." It thus bears repeating that the macro-purpose of the epic of evolution, and the micro-purpose of each evolutionary ascender, are ultimately one and the same.

## Last Thoughts on the First Cause

Admittedly, theological assertions of an existentially perfect first cause are not far from the concept of God. And in arguing for this as the primordial source of evolution, I may have lost the agreement of some readers. Nevertheless, the universe now disclosed by science does not really make sense without the recognition of some kind of creator or creative principle. Prior to the discovery of the big bang and the growing scientific recognition of strong emergence, it may have been tenable to hold that "the universe is just there, and that's all," or to otherwise believe in eternal "beginninglessness." However, if we give credence to the truths of science and want our reality frame to be consistent with the nature of the universe disclosed thereby, we now have to face the fact of a first cause. And once we accept that our evolving universe points to a first cause, this helps us recognize the continuous presence and influence of this first cause as the ongoing *final cause* of evolution. Writing in the 1980s about the then recently discovered fine-tuned big bang (which subsequent observations have failed to refute), religious scholar Huston Smith commented:

> It is going to be very interesting if the discipline that wrote the denial of final causes into its very charter emerges at the other end of its tunnel vision with the verdict that its findings require such a cause to round out its account. The conclusion would be formal; it would assert no more that that a Final Cause exists. But backed (as it would be) by the kind of knowledge that has come to persuade most, the finding would be momentous.[13]

As Smith presciently observed, it has indeed become "very interesting" that as the sciences of cosmology and biology have finally begun to reveal a comprehensive picture of the unfolding drama of universal evolution, these facts disclose a universe of progress and purpose—a universe wherein purpose is found externally and internally, and from beginning to end. Despite the vigorous rear-guard-action objections of materialists, recognition of an initial first cause and an ongoing final cause is becoming increasingly inescapable.[14] And when these facts are framed by a philosophy that can appropriately account for the effect of value gravity on evolutionary development, the presence of irreducible spiritual influences becomes unmistakable. Indeed, recent discoveries in cosmology and biology are now causing materialists to deny the evolutionary science for ideological reasons in ways that resemble the previous denials of creationists.

Throughout this chapter's theological reflections, I have done my best to leave room for a variety of conceptions regarding the nature of this first and final cause. But in concluding, I must briefly testify to my own faith in, and experience of, the loving, personal character of the Source of all that is. Again, recognition of a conscious Creator is not a required feature of either the philosophy or the theology presented here. And I do not wish to dissuade those who reject such a belief from otherwise accepting the idea that evolution is in fact a purposeful phenomenon. However, I do not want to hide or obscure my own spiritual convictions. Some progressive religionists deny that God is personal, but I cannot see how the first cause could be anything less than personal, since *we* are personal. Indeed, how could the part be greater than the whole? Although the infinite Source is certainly more than merely "one finite personality among others," and although the Being who is Being itself is certainly more than any human can fully comprehend, I can affirm that there are ways we *can* know God directly and experientially. And these experiences can be had through the spiritual forms we have identified as the beautiful, the true, and the good.

# CHAPTER 9

# The Promise of a New Evolutionary Worldview

HERE IN THE FINAL CHAPTER WE RETURN TO THE central problem identified at the beginning: our civilization needs to evolve. Although our culture has been evolving rapidly for the last 350 years, as a result of some of these very developments, the well-being of humanity as a whole is increasingly threatened. Yet these threats cannot be effectively addressed by returning to premodern forms of social organization. If we are going to honestly face the problems of the twenty-first century, the way forward lies in the direction of further cultural evolution. However, the question of what constitutes "further cultural evolution" does not have a straightforward answer. And even if there was widespread agreement regarding the directions of advance, we would still be faced with the question of how best to achieve further progress.

Unfortunately, neither modernism nor postmodernism adequately answer the crucial questions about where cultural evolution should be headed. So if we are to live up to the challenge of creating a just and sustainable civilization that works for everyone, at least some of us will need to transcend the developed world's current conflict between modernism and postmodernism by adopting a *new evolutionary worldview*—a fresh perspective that can effectively embrace the best of both of these seemingly antithetical preexisting worldviews. As with previous periods of emergent cultural evolution, all we need is the critical mass of a committed minority; positive change does not require that the entire population of the developed world adopt this new evolutionary perspective. For example, it has been estimated that only about ten percent of Americans had achieved a modernist center of gravity by the time of the American Revolution. Yet this minority had enough critical mass to bring about the momentous achievements of constitutional democracy and legally enforceable human rights.

This chapter explores the emerging contours of this new evolutionary perspective and attempts to answer the questions of where we are going and how we will get there. First, we revisit arguments for why postmodernism must be taken seriously as a historically significant worldview comparable to modernism and traditionalism. We consider evidence of postmodernism's achievements and appraise its shortcomings. Then we discuss competing visions for the next steps of cultural evolution. This leads to a presentation of the basic elements of the emerging evolutionary worldview as I understand it. We then explore how this evolutionary perspective can provide solutions to social and political problems that otherwise seem intractable. The chapter concludes by considering how this emerging worldview can also lead to a renewed culture of pluralistic, scientifically informed spirituality. Although we have been discussing *and using* this evolutionary perspective throughout the book, its full description has been saved until the end with the hope that its significance will be more evident, now that we have seen how powerful it can be for understanding the human condition.

## The Evolutionary Authenticity of the Postmodern Worldview

The first question in this analysis is whether postmodernism can even be considered an authentic and historically significant worldview comparable to modernism and traditionalism. Perhaps postmodernism (as I am defining it) is simply a countercurrent within modernism; it may be just a contrarian subculture that does not now, and never will, amount to the "next step" of cultural evolution beyond modernism. So perhaps the "historical significance" of this progressive set of values is being overestimated, and globalized modernism is really the "end of history," as Francis Fukuyama maintains. If this is the case, then the evolutionary worldview being described here is likewise misrepresented. That is, if the postmodern demographic does not represent authentic cultural evolution beyond modernism, if it does not really improve the human condition, then a worldview that uses postmodernism as a platform for its own "transcendence and inclusion" cannot truly represent the direction of our future historical development. The following arguments address these concerns by showing how the postmodern worldview does in fact represent a dialectical step forward in cultural evolution beyond modernism.

As noted in chapter 1, the academic field of developmental psychology has accumulated a large body of research on individuals, validating the idea that development in both children and adults unfolds according to distinct stages, which show a loose correspondence with historical worldviews. However, while this research has clearly revealed the existence of pre-traditional, traditional, and modernist stages of psychological or cognitive development, the findings usually end with the modernist stage. This can be explained by the fact that the researchers themselves are modernists, so it is unlikely they would be willing or able to identify development beyond their own level. While there are some notable exceptions, such as the research of Robert Kegan and Clare Graves, which does identify postmodern development and beyond, we cannot rely on developmental psychology alone to provide adequate evidence of the course of our future evolution.

Another body of empirical evidence from the social sciences that validates this stage conception of evolution is found in sociology. Many of us first came to recognize that the "postmodern worldview" was a distinct stage that could be compared and contrasted with modernism through the research of sociologist Paul Ray. In 1995 Ray published the findings of his national survey on the role of values in American life, which was sponsored by the Fetzer Institute and the Institute of Noetic Sciences. Ray's research drew upon more than 100,000 questionnaire responses and hundreds of focus groups, and clearly revealed the existence of three large cultural blocks in America, which he called "Traditionals, Moderns, and Cultural Creatives." Although the implicit postmodern orientation of both Ray and his sponsors resulted in a glorification of the "Cultural Creatives" that did not recognize the accompanying shortcomings of this emerging culture, his research nevertheless had a large social and economic influence. During the same period a less well-publicized but more comprehensive sociological study of values development was published by Ronald Inglehart of the University of Michigan. This multi-decade international survey cataloged the "basic values and beliefs" of people from 80 different countries, and found abundant evidence for the recent appearance of what was termed "post-material values" in developed countries. Known as *The World Values Survey*, this research corresponds with and generally confirms the findings of Ray and others. However, like the research of developmental psychology, research from the field of sociology is not sufficient, by itself, for the conclusion that cultural evolution in the developed world is moving toward postmodern values.

But what we can safely conclude from the research of the social sciences is that the distinct and dialectically separated stages identified as traditionalism, modernism, and postmodernism do exist as cultural systems of values, and that they have arisen in a historical sequence, with traditionalism being the oldest and postmodernism the most recent. However, when it comes to the conclusion that postmodernism is "more evolved" than modernism, we cannot rely on empirical research alone to make this value judgment for us; we also have to consider history. Thus, understanding how and why postmodernism represents authentic cultural evolution beyond modernism begins with the recognition of why modernism itself is more evolved than traditionalism.

As I trust our discussion so far has made clear, modernist culture, and the consciousness that goes with it, is not *absolutely* better than traditional culture in every possible sense. Modernists are not kinder or more generous, they are not more loyal or committed, they are not always smarter or even more educated. What makes modernism unquestionably more culturally evolved than traditionalism is that modernists have achieved a more developed level of values in a variety of crucial areas, and this emergence of higher values has led directly to forms of civilization for which people have shown a consistent preference during the last 350 years. As examples, modernism's more evolved understanding of truth has led to science and economic development, and modernism's more evolved conceptions of morality have led to democracy and the advent of human rights. As discussed in chapter 5, ongoing cultural development from traditionalism into modernism (but not vice versa) can be seen in the historical record since the Enlightenment. So regardless of our personal opinions of the merits of modernism, this achievement-oriented worldview has been, and continues to be, the goal of billions of people who perceive it as a way to improve their lives. Although not everyone feels this way, most people generally prefer democracy over dictatorships, they prefer scientific medicine over traditional forms of medicine, they prefer higher education over ignorance, and they prefer relative prosperity over poverty.

Modernism's evolutionary advance can sometimes be hard to see due to the presence of the dialectic of progress and pathology. But despite the horrific problems brought about by modernism, this form of culture is still what the majority of premodern people in the world seem to want. As also noted in chapter 5, postmodernists often deny this by contending that traditionalists only aspire to modernism because they have been seduced into embracing empty, materialistic values that will only make them unhappy in the end. Yet there are few educated modernists who are ready to give up their middleclass lifestyles and embrace a mythic worldview and a more traditional way of life.

Once we become clear as to how modernism is generally more evolved than traditionalism, we can then use these same criteria to reach the conclusion that postmodernism is similarly more evolved than modernism. Authentic postmodern culture has become a significant demographic only in regions where underlying modernist culture is most successful and well-established. Where people are relatively wealthy and well-educated, where they have already received most of what modernism has to offer, we find that significant numbers (especially the young) have consistently embraced countercultural, "post-material," postmodern perspectives.

Unlike traditionalism or modernism, the postmodern worldview can be hard to pin down. Because of its inherent pluralism, and because it consists of many disparate cultural currents, it can sometimes be difficult to recognize as a coherent system of values. Yet like traditionalism and modernism, postmodernism does provide identity and engender loyalty from those who make meaning using its perspectives. Moreover, the postmodern worldview defines who and what is valuable in ways that are clearly distinct from previous stages. Postmodern values can be recognized in the social movements of environmentalism, multiculturalism, feminism, and egalitarianism in general. Postmodernists are attracted to organic and natural foods, clothing, and related products, and they evince a strong preference for alternative medicine, alternative spirituality, progressive politics, and peace at all costs. And despite the diversity of views that are embraced within postmodern culture, what generally binds postmodernists together is their agreement regarding the abundant pathologies of modernism. Anti-modernism is thus the hallmark of postmodernism in practically all its forms.

Recognizing stages of values development in general, and postmodernism in particular, can also be tricky due to the fact that these systems are best conceived as types of consciousness within people, rather than types of people themselves. Most people living in the developed world are able to make meaning from more than one type of consciousness, depending on the context. Yet most also find that one of these major worldviews provides their "psychic center of gravity." Moreover, when considering these stages of cultural evolution it is important to continually reemphasize that the development of values and worldviews does not represent an absolute scale or single line of evolutionary growth. Consciousness develops along multiple lines, which can grow in ways that do not necessarily depend on the development of a person's worldview.

In fact, it is possible to achieve "self-actualization" within any of these worldview systems. For example, Pastor Rick Warren is certainly a self-actualized traditionalist, and businessman Bill Gates appears to be a self-actualized modernist. Thus, in our consideration of the evolution of consciousness and culture, we must acknowledge that the relative development of any given individual's values-based worldview cannot be used by itself as a simplistic measure of the degree of that person's evolution. However, as discussed in the upcoming section entitled "Value Dynamics within Cultural Evolution," developmental psychologists and integral philosophers are in general agreement that the "values line" *is* a leading line of development, and that the sophistication of a person's worldview *does* significantly influence the development of that person's consciousness overall. In the final analysis, estimates of the relative evolution of any single individual's consciousness can always be questioned or problemitized. So although consciousness and culture co-evolve together, my arguments for the developmental logic of these evolutionary structures rests on historical indicators of cultural progress, rather than on the assessment of the relative merits of any specific persons.

If you have never shopped at a natural foods store, attended a yoga class, or read a book of non-traditional spirituality, the distinct values of the post-modern worldview may be difficult to recognize or acknowledge. But for those who are familiar with the more progressive segments of the Western world, the culture of postmodernism is unmistakable. Yet even if we grant that postmodernism is a discrete worldview that can be distinguished from traditionalism and modernism, we have still not fully answered the question of whether this form of culture is somehow more evolved than the modernist culture from which it arises. So in answer to this question we can inquire: Is worldcentric morality more evolved than ethnocentric or nationalistic forms of morality? Is a deep concern for the environment more evolved than a general disregard thereof? Is an interest in the equality of women more evolved than paternalism or chauvinism? Is a holistic approach to science and medicine more evolved than a purely materialistic approach? It is easy to forget how prevalent were these latter views in the developed world of the 1950s, prior to the rise of the postmodern worldview. And obviously, the very framing of these questions reflects my personal affinity for postmodern values. As with millions of others in my generation, my life choices affirm that the countercultural perspectives of postmodernism are, in some important ways, authentically more evolved than the earlier values embodied in the modernist worldview.

Yet as a result of having previously maintained a postmodern identity for many years, I can also attest that this worldview contains some grave shortcomings and pathologies that show why, like modernism, postmodernism is not the "end of history." And it is postmodernism's very weaknesses and failures that point in the directions available for further cultural evolution. As previously mentioned, postmodern perspectives are plagued by "anything goes" relativism, narcissism, and magical thinking. Worse, postmodernists often fail to appreciate the traditionalist and modernist achievements that have built the civilization upon which their culture ultimately depends. Although postmodernists have done well in their identification and condemnation of increasing worldwide problems, such as climate change and environmental degradation, the often polarizing militancy of the postmodern political stance has rendered it largely impotent at solving the problems it identifies. Postmodernists are quick to scold modernist shortcomings, but their proposed solutions often amount to the admonition that "we all just need to come together and realize that we are all one people." And if it were evolutionarily possible for the world to suddenly come together like this it would indeed provide many solutions. However, these calls for a great awakening ring hollow because they are usually addressed to humanity as a whole, without regard to the fact the majority of humanity is not yet able to make meaning in the way that the postmodernists implore. Postmodernism's relative impotency to bring about further meaningful, large-scale social change is well expressed by Wilber, who writes:

> Simply asserting that we should all learn a worldcentric ecology, or embrace a global compassion, is a noble but pragmatically less-than-useful project, because worldcentric waves are the product of development, not exhortation. As noted, the "new paradigm" approaches exhort a goal without elucidating the path to that goal—they are cheerleaders for a cause that has no means of actualization, which perhaps explains the deep frustration among new-paradigm advocates who know they have a better ideal but are disappointed at how little the world responds to their calls.[1]

Postmodern culture *is* genuinely more evolved than either modernism or traditionalism, but it *is not evolved enough* to provide the leadership and solutions that will be required to solve the problems we are facing in the twenty-first century. And it is the presence of these growing global problems, together with the failure of postmodernism to effectively combat these threats, which provides a set of *powerfully problematic life conditions* that are animating the values of the emerging evolutionary worldview.

## Next Steps for Cultural Evolution

As we explored in chapter 5's discussion of progress in cultural evolution, psychosocial development is continuing in its various phases throughout the world, as pre-traditional cultures adopt traditional religious worldviews, as traditional societies embrace modernity, and as modernists become increasingly postmodern. Each of these ongoing historical steps of development has its own version of what constitutes progress based on specific problems encountered on the ground. Thus, one's definition of the next steps of cultural evolution depends on the values of the worldview that provides one's psychic center of gravity. For example, progress for modernists is often defined as further integration of the world's economy through globalization, pacification of terrorists, and progress in science and technology. Conversely, for postmodernists the next steps of cultural evolution are envisioned in the "re-localization" of the economy, the pacification of the developed world, and the growth of social services and entitlements. Although there are obviously many specific kinds of improvement that both modernists and postmodernists can agree on, there is nonetheless no clear general consensus in the developed world about what the overall next steps of cultural evolution can or should be.

The ongoing development of the postmodern worldview is certainly positive for the most part, but at the current rate of growth it will be generations before the majority of Americans have a postmodern center of gravity. Although postmodernists actively seek to persuade others to adopt their worldview, as noted above, many postmodernists harbor the expectation that the world will soon "wake up" en mass and adopt ecological and compassionate values in a kind of worldwide spiritual renaissance. However, by explaining how each of these worldview steps serve as an indispensible foundation for the emergence of the next, integral philosophy shows that the next steps of cultural evolution must include ongoing progress into all of the world's historically significant worldviews. And because these steps cannot generally be skipped or bypassed, the postmodern strategy for cultural evolution, which relies on the notion of a miraculous great awakening of humanity as a whole, can be recognized as naive and even misguided. At this point in history the challenge of achieving further cultural evolution is too important to be viewed through the lens of fantasy or wishful thinking.

Moreover, there are aspects of postmodern culture that retard, or even prevent, cultural evolution overall. The strident anti-modernist and anti-traditionalist rhetoric of postmodernists can make both modernists and traditionalists defensive, and this defensiveness serves to "pin people in place" culturally, as they develop a resistance to postmodern values of every kind. The irony is that, despite being the most evolved form of culture that has yet to appear, the postmodern worldview has in some ways become a kind of "cork in the bottle" that prevents many modernists and traditionalists from adopting the values of environmental sustainability and social justice. Modernists and traditionalists who might otherwise be persuaded by the attractive features of the postmodern agenda find themselves locked in a culture war wherein loyalty to the values of their respective worldviews places them in opposition to the progress offered by postmodernism, which is perceived as being a threat to modernist and traditional values.

Thus, because of the polarizing effects of its social agenda, definition of the next steps of cultural evolution cannot be left to postmodernism alone. Our global problems are becoming too urgent to allow progress in their amelioration to be stymied by the political stagnation that results from the developed world's culture war. For example, at the time of this writing, consensus about the need to fight global warming is actually declining due to sustained efforts by conservatives to discredit climate change science. This largely kneejerk reaction against the environmental movement stems from the deep animosity and distrust that conservatives feel toward anything that is dear to the hearts of postmodernists. And ironically, much of this acrimony began with postmodernism's own militant rejection of establishment values.

Therefore, socially and politically significant evolution in consciousness and culture in the developed world awaits the articulation of a new set of values that can harmonize these competing definitions of progress and bring peace to the culture war. And this needed vision is provided by the emerging evolutionary worldview, which offers solutions that are even *more progressive* than what passes for progressive culture today. Yet in this context, "more progressive" does not mean either "further left" or "further right"; this evolutionary perspective goes beyond the horizontal dimension of liberal and conservative by carrying forward the enduring strengths, while simultaneously pruning away the pathologies, of both positions. As we have seen, cultural evolution unfolds through the synthetic transcendence of thesis and antithesis, and this is exactly what the evolutionary perspective is attempting to do.

Although it may be a generation before this new evolutionary worldview has political power of its own, it can nevertheless make progress in our time by helping to reduce friction among the existing cultural structures of traditionalism, modernism, and postmodernism. And the evolutionary perspective can accomplish this by showing how the values of each of these historically significant worldviews have arisen within the dialectical structure of a larger internal cultural ecosystem. It can thus make clear how each of these worldviews is working to improve a distinct set of problematic life conditions that continue to plague us, and how each of these worldviews has an ongoing role to play in the structure of our civilization. In other words, modernism and traditionalism have not been negated or completely outmoded by the emergence of postmodern values. Indeed, the ongoing success of the healthy and enduring values of these earlier worldviews is essential for the viability of postmodernism itself.

Postmodernism became a significant political and social structure in the 1960s and 1970s, but its first appearance as an identifiable worldview can be traced back to the nineteenth century in the intellectual movement known as the "transcendentalists." Beginning in the 1830s, progressive writers such as Emerson and Thoreau extolled the virtues of the natural environment, Eastern spirituality, and better social services for the poor. Although the transcendentalists were significantly ahead of their time, we can see how they fully embodied practically all the major values of the later-appearing postmodern worldview, including the general rejection of modernism.

It may turn out that the evolutionary worldview we are anticipating is also significantly ahead of its time, like the transcendentalists of the nineteenth century. Yet as cultural evolution accelerates, it may not take decades for the evolutionary perspective to emerge as a historically significant social structure. Although the postmodern worldview itself is still young, and although its growth will be continuing throughout this century, there are signs that it has grown beyond its original emergent phase and is now maturing and consolidating as a system of values. And again, it is both the successes and the failures of postmodernism that provide the necessary life conditions for the emergence of this new evolutionary worldview. So even though the rise of the evolutionary perspective as a cultural force in the developed world may still be many years away, the usable values of this future worldview are becoming available today to those who are able to evolve their consciousness into this enlarged frame of reality.

## Elements of an Evolutionary Worldview

It bears repeating here that integral philosophy is essentially a philosophy of evolution; and it is integral philosophy's enlarged understanding of the evolution of consciousness and culture that reveals where evolution is headed and where our opportunities lie. Examining the historical record using this evolutionary perspective shows how modernism emerged out of traditionalism, and how postmodernism in turn evolved beyond modernism. And this perspective also shows the next stage of cultural evolution that is beginning to appear on the horizon of history.

The rise of the modernist worldview during the Enlightenment was the result of many factors, making a comprehensive analysis of this emergent event beyond the scope of our present discussion. Yet among the many causes of the Enlightenment, historians are in general agreement that the metaphysical philosophy of Rene Descartes was particularly significant. Beginning in the early seventeenth century, Galileo's demonstration of the heliocentric structure of the solar system had shown the superiority of scientific descriptions of reality over the mythical teachings of the Church. Spurred by these discoveries, Descartes developed an original philosophic foundation for the scientific revolution. His radical philosophy divided reality into a subjective, supernatural world of mind, and an objective, material world of matter. And by doing so he helped inaugurate a new era of reason and scientific discovery. By literally reframing reality using new metaphysical categories, Descartes helped open the eyes of scientists to the "objective" way of seeing and understanding the natural world.

## A New Ontology

Now in our time, integral philosophy is doing something very similar; it is reframing reality so as to open up the "ontology of interiors." Guided by the philosophy of Whitehead, Wilber, and others, as well as by the breakthroughs of system science, integral philosophy has discovered that the worldview structures that provide the steps of evolution for consciousness and culture are actually *dynamic systems of agreement* that resemble the dynamical systems (also known as "dissipative structures") found in nature. These worldview systems have both an exterior, physical expression, and also an interior dimension. On the external side, the features of these dynamic systems of culture are fairly straightforward; they can be found in the various forms of communication and social expression through which worldviews are transmitted and consolidated. Yet on the internal side, in addition to the subjective experience of individuals, integral philosophy has revealed a previously unrecognized *collective interior* aspect of worldview systems. And it is through its expanded recognition of the collective interiors of cultural evolution that integral philosophy reveals a new ontology.

As noted, historically significant worldviews are powerful, multi-generational, large-scale agreements that frame reality and provide identity for those who ascribe to them. And although these agreements are ultimately affirmed and maintained within the subjective consciousness of individuals, there is an element of such agreements that is neither wholly subjective nor completely objective. That is, worldview structures are partially objective, partially subjective, but also partially "intersubjective"—these dynamic systems occupy the "agreement space" that exists *in between* individuals. Put differently, evolutionarily significant, macro agreements about values occupy multiple domains simultaneously: these worldview systems subsist in objective forms of communication, subjective forms of assent and concurrence, and enduring intersubjective forms of connection that make up a large part of the "interior corpus" of these agreement structures.

This intersubjective aspect of worldview systems is not merely metaphorical. According to integral philosophy, the intersubjective realm is an interior dimension of reality that cannot be reduced to either objective or subjective categories. And it is by recognizing this collective interior dimension of cultural evolution that integral philosophy provides an expanded reality frame; a fresh perspective that helps us better understand the developmental structure of human consciousness and culture. Of course, cultural worldviews are not conscious entities, but they do exhibit enduring systemic behaviors that resemble other types of self-organizing evolutionary structures such as ecosystems.

Recognizing the similarities between worldview systems and biological systems helps us better understand the "metabolism of values" through which cultural structures maintain their systemic vitality. Just as cells are the micro-systems that make up an organism, agreements about specific values act similarly as the internal micro-systems that aggregate into historically significant worldviews that persist through time. Moreover, as discussed in the next two sections, this new understanding of value metabolism can help us better understand why some cultures are vibrant and healthy and why other cultures remain dysfunctional. This expanded ontological recognition of cultural evolution thus allows us to better see, contact, and work with these worldview systems as never before.

Furthermore, integral philosophy's expanded recognition of interiority avoids the problems of Cartesian dualism by explaining how the subjective category of consciousness (or interiority in general) is not "supernatural"; sentient subjectivity is as real and natural as the external aspects of reality. Building on Whitehead, integral philosophy argues that every naturally occurring form of evolutionary organization possesses an interior aspect. While this recognition of pervasive interiority does not imply that structures such as cells or molecules have consciousness per se, it does show how consciousness does not simply "pop out" at the top of the evolutionary scale. This reframing of reality thus helps avoid the *mind/body problem*, which has vexed materialistic forms of philosophy for over 300 years.[2]

Thus, just as Enlightenment philosophy opened up the *external* universe to a new era of investigation and discovery through objective science, integral philosophy now promises similar advances within the *internal* universe of consciousness and culture. And our growing recognition of the central role of organismal agency and value gravity in the evolution of the universe (discussed in chapter 3) provides an example of the kind of discoveries that can be made through the use of this new form of philosophy. Although a thorough description of integral philosophy's ontology of interiors is beyond the scope of our discussion, in the following sections we will consider examples of how this new understanding can also be used to diagnose and solve many of the cultural problems that currently plague our world.

## *A New Epistemology*

The "new way of seeing" that arose with the modernist worldview during the Enlightenment came about through the use of the emergent epistemological capacity of reason. Although premodern thinkers also used reason and logic, they lacked a systematic method of analyzing objective reality from a scientific perspective. Nor could they see how the mythical descriptions of the universe provided by their premodern worldviews were in fact inherently unreasonable, if not completely irrational. It was only through the new objective clarity provided by a thoroughly rational worldview that Europeans were able to "disenchant" their understanding of nature. And just as the rise of modernist consciousness provided a new epistemological capacity, the enlarged perspectives of the evolutionary worldview likewise provide the expanded vision of a new epistemological capacity. This new capacity, which Wilber calls "vision-logic," arises as we come to increasingly view the world through dialectical perspectives.

This dialectical way of knowing can be distinguished from both "formal operational thought" (originally described by Piaget), and "relativistic thought." Formal operational thinking, which is most often associated with modernist consciousness, usually perceives the world as presenting "right or wrong" choices within a closed system of lawful relationships. Relativistic thinking, which is most often associated with postmodern consciousness, can see the validity of more than one choice, but cannot usually see how such alternatives can be reconciled or synthesized. In contrast to both of these earlier ways of knowing, dialectical thinking always anticipates the possibility of development, and thus perceives the world as a fundamental process of changing dynamic relationships. This dialectical way of seeing thus recognizes how conflicting perspectives can actually work together, mutually supporting each other, even when in apparent opposition, in a manner that can be compared to the function of a tension strut in an architectural structure.

Developmental psychologist Michael Basseches illustrates dialectical thinking using the example of three college students who are each frustrated by standardized assignments and tests, and feel that their freedom and love of learning is being stifled. In this example, the first student (representing formal operational thinking) is angry about his situation, but resigns himself to the unfairness of the system and cynically decides to just give teachers what they want in order to get by. The second student (representing relativistic thinking) is confused; he knows his education would be improved if he had more curricular freedom, but he also "assumes that the college is run by experienced educators, who must have determined that the use of tests and assigned papers to measure and grades to motivate is the soundest educational method." However, the third student in Basseches's example (representing dialectical thinking), "reasons that this contradiction will only really be resolved when the basic relationship of the colleges and universities to society is transformed. He decides that he will devote his time at college to trying to learn all he can that might help him contribute to that kind of transformation of educational institutions. He accepts that in the meantime he will be given standardized assignments and grades and will have to make compromises . . . But he is resolved not to lose sight of his own educational goals."[3] This example thus suggests how dialectical thinkers can take conflicts in their stride, using them for further development. Additional examples are discussed in the sections that follow.

The emergent epistemological capacity of reason that arises with modernist consciousness is a *cognitive* capacity of the mind, which involves rational thinking. In contrast, the new epistemological capacity that arises with the evolutionary perspective is an emergent *volitional* capacity of the will, which comes about mostly through dialectical evaluation. That is, it is usually only by appropriately *valuing* the elements of a problematic situation that we can correctly perceive the crucial functions of such elements within the situation as a whole. This involves more than simply "weighing the alternatives" and assigning different values to various components; it is a way of understanding and appreciating that requires an intuitive sympathy achieved only by "getting in close"—by identifying with and actually entering into the alternative perspectives that generate opposing values. When we look at evolutionary processes without this ability, all we can see is conflict. But when we come to recognize the unfolding of internal structures through time, we can begin to better appreciate how they are working together within a larger developmental system, and this allows us to engage these structures more effectively. Recognizing this, developmental theorist Robert Kegan actually defines dialectical thinking as "the capacity to see conflict as a signal of our overidentification with a single system."[4]

## A New Set of Values

As we have seen, historically significant cultural worldviews are made up of discrete sets of values that are related to the problems faced by a given worldview's "time in history." Continuing this pattern, the emerging evolutionary worldview also has its own relatively unique values, such as the aspiration to harmonize science and spirituality, an enhanced sense of personal responsibility for the problems of the world, an enlarged appreciation of conflicting truths and dialectic reasoning, and a new appreciation of the significance of evolution in general, and cultural evolution in particular. But unlike older worldviews, this evolutionary perspective also recognizes that every previous worldview contains important values that are necessary for the ongoing functionality of society. As a result of this understanding, the evolutionary view is able to better appreciate and thus better *use* the healthy values of the entire spectrum of cultural development. And it is by including a wider range of values within its purview that the evolutionary perspective is able to transcend all previous worldviews. Earlier worldviews tend to see each other primarily for their pathologies, discounting the important cultural role that each worldview plays within the larger system of cultural evolution. But the evolutionary perspective can see existing cultural structures within a broader evolutionary context, and can thus more effectively "objectify" earlier values without being repulsed or embarrassed by them.

This process of cultural evolution through objectification is described by Kegan's well-known "subject-object theory." Kegan explains the progress of consciousness through the stages of development by observing that a person transcends a given stage when what was previously embedded in that person's subjective consciousness becomes objectified, or recognized from an external perspective. According to Kegan, "[T]ransforming our epistemologies, liberating ourselves from that in which we were embedded, making what was subject into object so that we can 'have it' rather than 'be had' by it—this is the most powerful way I know to conceptualize the growth of the mind."[5] For example, in the traditional stage of consciousness, one's religious belief system is a part of their subject—the traditionalist's subjective consciousness is embedded or contained within their belief system. The objective world is thus perceived and constructed to satisfy the demands of this belief system. However, when a person transcends the traditional stage and achieves the increased epistemological capacity of modernist consciousness, he may still hold the same essential religious beliefs, but these beliefs are now objectified; he can see beyond his beliefs, and thus gains a greater capacity to adopt the perspective of others and see the world through their beliefs as well as his own. As a person's consciousness evolves he can still "have his beliefs," but in more evolved stages those beliefs no longer "have him."

Kegan's description of the process of subjective evolution through expanding objectification also helps us understand how the evolutionary worldview makes progress. Unlike previous worldviews, the evolutionary perspective is able to objectify the *entire spectrum of established cultural development*, and is thus able to achieve an "expanded vertical perspective" that can recognize a new kind of depth. Yet not only does this evolutionary view better *objectify* previous stages, together with the larger system of which they are a part, it also better *subjectifies* previous stages by identifying with them more closely. As noted, it is only by "getting in close" to the values of these earlier worldviews that we can begin to separate their "dignities" from their "disasters." Recall that as a result of the dialectic of progress and pathology, successes are often tied to failures in cultural evolution. And this means that the positive values of a given worldview are accordingly tied together with that worldview's shortcomings. Recovering the useful and enduring values of previous worldviews thus requires careful attention and a sophisticated form of sympathy.

Using the traditional worldview as an example, we can see how the values that we continue to *need*—values such as honesty, decency, modesty, and personal responsibility—are connected with outlooks that we must now discard—such as sexism, racism, and religious fundamentalism. When we view the traditional worldview from the outside, it is these negative aspects that are often most apparent. But when we come to also see this worldview from the inside, by better identifying with it and partially making it our own, this allows us to better appreciate, and thus tease apart, the core values of this worldview from its remaining outmoded prejudices that continue to hold us back. And as we make common cause with the healthy values of every worldview, "they" become "us."

## A Second Enlightenment

As a result of its place within the sequence of historical development, the emerging evolutionary worldview is in many ways a synthesis of modernism and postmodernism. Without the sensitive and pluralistic values of postmodernism, the evolutionary perspective would be somewhat indistinguishable from cynical modernism. However, although it embraces many postmodern values, this evolutionary worldview also carries forward some of modernism's important strengths, such as its penchant for problem solving and its focus on progress. Thus, because the evolutionary perspective is a kind of "higher harmonic" of modernism, the historical context out of which this evolutionary view is emerging shows many similarities to the previous appearance of modernism during the Enlightenment. As mentioned, modernism came about through the rise of powerful new philosophical systems, which were rooted in the scientific advances of the seventeenth century. Similarly, this new evolutionary perspective is being catalyzed by philosophical advances in our understanding of emergent evolution, which reveal the influence of values and show how evolution is both driving and drawing the development of human consciousness and culture.

This parallel with the historical events of the Enlightenment can also be seen in the tension between academic philosophy and the new form of philosophy that is giving birth to the evolutionary worldview. In the late seventeenth and early eighteenth centuries, "the officially and legally sanctioned philosophy prevailing in universities and academies, and dominating philosophical and scientific discourse and textbooks" was Scholastic Aristotelianism, a philosophical system that supported the precepts of the Christian Church. Although Scholasticism had been a vibrant part of medieval thought, by the time of the Enlightenment, this academic philosophy had stagnated as a result of having become the handmaiden of religion. Now in our time we can observe a very similar situation wherein the officially sanctioned academic philosophy of our age has become stale. Yet the relative stagnation of contemporary professional philosophy has not resulted from its subservience to the traditional worldview; this time it is subservience to the modernist worldview that has caused the problem. In other words, just as Scholasticism had lost its potency by the time of the first Enlightenment as a result of being compromised by religion, now at the beginning of what may come to be recognized as a kind of "Second Enlightenment," much of professional philosophy, and especially the philosophy associated with life and evolution, has been similarly compromised by its subordination to science.

Thus, just as in the first Enlightenment, when philosophy was liberated from the static confines of the reigning establishment, leaping forward like a coiled spring, we can now anticipate a similar period of philosophical progress ahead. In the first Enlightenment, philosophy became separated from mythic religion, and now philosophy is becoming similarly liberated from the confines of scientific materialism.

Admittedly, the emergence of the modernist worldview and the rise of science was one of the most significant events in the history of humankind, so these comparisons with the Enlightenment may be overstated. Yet the emergence of this new evolutionary perspective could end up having a similarly dramatic impact on history as a result of its ability to produce social progress. Again, modernist science's power came from its ability to better understand and thus more effectively control the external, material universe. Similarly, the promise of this emerging evolutionary view is that it can better understand and thus more effectively achieve evolution within the internal universe of consciousness and culture. And a significant part of this enlarged ability to help bring about cultural evolution arises from integral philosophy's new insights about values.

## Value Dynamics within Cultural Evolution

By way of review, integral philosophy shows us more clearly than ever before why the development of human history is an authentic form of evolution in the universe. Although psychosocial evolution is not a seamless continuation of biological evolution, despite its discontinuities with earlier forms of development, cultural evolution does connect all the way back to the big bang through the nested sequence of emergences upon which it depends. In other words, the chain of transcendence and inclusion that links atoms to molecules to cells to organisms to us continues in human history through the sequence of emergent steps that have built our present civilization. And once we recognize the nature and behavior of the worldview structures that cohere into the larger internal ecosystem that forms our culture, we can then more clearly see how this ecosystem has evolved, and also how its evolution has sometimes been arrested or set back.

However, the habits and behaviors of these cultural structures, their "internal physics" if you will, cannot be completely understood from an external perspective. Although the social sciences of anthropology, sociology, and psychology have all contributed to our understanding of cultural evolution, these disciplines define themselves as sciences, so they cannot see into the internal universe of values with the clarity provided by this new philosophical perspective. Integral philosophy is able to surpass the social sciences in its ability to understand cultural evolution primarily because of its willingness to recognize the metaphysical and even spiritual aspects of values. And as we will now explore, it is through integral philosophy's expanded insight into the nature and behavior of values in human experience that the realm of cultural evolution is opened up to a new era of investigation and discovery.

## *Values as a Leading Line of Development*

Chapters 3 and 4 were devoted to an exploration of the role of values in evolution. There we saw how values attract evolutionary development through their influence on consciousness. Yet as we discussed, the evolution of consciousness and culture occurs as a result of both the *pull* of values and the *push* of unsatisfactory life conditions. Values are thus defined and animated by their relation to the real and pressing problems faced by people as they struggle to improve their lives. Recognizing how consciousness and culture evolve through both the internal influence of values and the external pressure of problematic conditions underlines the fact that interior consciousness almost always co-evolves with exterior circumstances. In other words, wherever we find the interior evolution of consciousness, we also find a corresponding evolution in the complexity of the exterior structures associated with such interior development.

The discussion in chapter 1 emphasized that the consciousness of animals generally evolves in lockstep with the evolution of their bodies, whereas the consciousness of humans can evolve in ways that are partially independent from the physical evolution of our biological brains. In the brief course of our historical evolution, humans have thus compensated for the relative absence of external biological development through the creation of artifacts such as language, tools, art, architecture, and social institutions. These external artifacts "stand in" for the lack of appreciable biological evolution and provide the physical counterparts of the mental evolution through which humans have developed beyond the animal level. The evolutionary emergence of human artifacts thus provides a rough exterior indicator of the interior evolution of consciousness. For example, the emergence of organized agriculture and writing are external indicators of traditional consciousness, and the emergence of industrial technology is an external indicator of modernist consciousness.

It thus appears that the interiors of consciousness and culture almost always co-evolve with exterior developments in institutions and technology. And just as emerging new forms of consciousness can give rise to new technologies, the growth of external artifacts and organizations can in turn raise the consciousness of the people who use them (at least in some cases). Indeed, one of the valid insights of Marxist philosophy was that the consciousness of people is significantly influenced by their "means of production." While the material determinism of Marxism ultimately goes too far in its emphasis on external, physical influences, the role of exterior factors in cultural evolution is well appreciated by integral philosophy.

Adding to the complexity of the co-evolution of interior consciousness and exterior artifacts is the fact that interior development cannot be reduced to a singular trajectory measured by the growth of one's values alone. As we also discussed in chapter 1 and above, consciousness evolves through a variety of cognitive and emotional lines of development, each of which can exhibit growth that is relatively independent from the development of one's values or worldview.

Yet even though the evolution of consciousness and culture is a subtle and complex phenomenon involving many influences, it appears that the development of values is nevertheless a particularly significant factor in the process. This is shown by the way new stages of history are most often initiated through the emergence of new truth, new beauty, and new ideals of morality. Although the values of new worldviews only become widely established socially when they result in the creation of new external institutions and technologies, new ideas and new ideals themselves first appear "on the inside," in the minds of innovators and thought leaders. And the reason why the development of values is perhaps the single most important factor in understanding cultural evolution overall is that *it is through the gravity of values that consciousness and culture are drawn toward ever-higher levels of evolutionary development.*

Once we recognize how the gravity of values pulls evolution forward, this clarifies our understanding of cultural evolution overall; it shows us where evolution is headed and how we can best align ourselves with evolution's positive trajectory of growth. Indeed, the central thrust of my argument for evolution's purposeful, teleological growth is the evident influence of values as attractors of evolutionary development. Therefore, if we can come to better understand why values have developed in some places and stagnated in others, this knowledge will prove very useful in promoting and sustaining humanity's continuing evolutionary progress across the entire spectrum of its ongoing development.

## The Internal Cultural Ecosystem

We have repeatedly discussed how cultural evolution develops through a series of emergent stages. And we have seen how these stages or levels are not simply stacked on top of one another like geologic strata; they are developmentally related to each other within a larger structure wherein the natural tension of dialectical separation contributes to the form and character of each emergent stage. In other words, each stage of cultural development comes to be shaped and defined by its place or position within the larger structure of human history overall.

A partial yet apt analogy for these stages of cultural development can be found in the spectrum of visible colors. When we look closely at the wavelengths of color in a rainbow, although we can perhaps identify thousands of subtle shades, and although we cannot draw hard lines between the colors, we can nevertheless identify seven specific hues. Each of the basic "rainbow colors" is a whole in itself, yet each one is formed in relation to its neighbors above and below on the spectrum. And we can see something very similar in the distinct stages found within the developmental spectrum of consciousness and culture.

Some may argue that this stage conception oversimplifies cultural evolution. Yet culture and consciousness do evolve, and this developmental unfolding does evince structural elements. Although from certain perspectives history's course of development may appear more like a "river" (that runs uphill) than like a series of discrete steps, even if we prefer a model that describes a continuous flow of intermixed development, we must nevertheless acknowledge that this "river's" course exhibits antithetical bends and dialectical meanders. So regardless of whether our metaphor points to discrete stages or continuous flows, there is clearly dialectical tension in the structure.

Although integral philosophy holds that historically significant worldviews are literally dynamic systems of values that can be compared in certain ways to ecosystems, it does not follow that psychosocial evolution can be conceived as, or reduced to, biological evolution. Unlike the apparently blind and partially mechanistic functioning of biological evolution, the cultural realm of evolution is governed more by internal *reasons* than by external causes. As we have seen, the gravitational influence of transcendent forms of value shapes the trajectory and structure of cultural evolution by *attracting* and *persuading* the outworking of human choices. And because value gravity only functions by agreement, because it requires the assent of consciousness to take effect, it cannot be understood as a deterministic law or a physical cause of cultural evolution.

But even though the evolution of culture is not entirely "law like," we can nevertheless detect the structuring influence of value gravity in the trajectory of its development. As discussed in chapters 4 and 5, because values are dialectical in their very nature, their gravitational influence on cultural evolution results in the large-scale historical pattern of dialectical development by stages. And within this stage structure of history, the success of each stage is crucial because the accomplishments of one level are necessarily taken up and used by the next appearing level. Recognition of this holarchic structure of cultural evolution thus reveals an important principle that can help us better understand and more effectively bring about further cultural evolution throughout the world.

## The "Holarchic Principle" of Cultural Evolution

Once we recognize this interdependent holarchic pattern of development within history, we can then see why stages cannot usually be skipped or bypassed, and why the success of later-appearing stages depends, at least partially, on the ongoing health and functionality of underlying earlier stages. Further, higher stages usually only emerge where lower stages have succeeded in producing the successful preconditions necessary for such a transcendent emergence.

An example that illustrates this holarchic principle of cultural evolution can be found in the recent history of Russia. When the Soviet Union collapsed in 1989, many in the West assumed that Russia was poised for significant economic growth, like that seen in Germany and Japan after World War II. As a result of this expectation, substantial foreign investments in the Russian economy were made in the early 1990s. These investors did not realize, however, that the *modernist culture* required for Western-style economic growth did not exist in large segments of the Russian populace at that time. Although Marxism may have originated at a higher level of cultural development than the traditional stage, by the second half of the twentieth century, Russian communism had come to resemble other forms of traditional, conformist culture. The communists effectively swept away the Russian Orthodox Church, but then simply replaced it with the

"Religion of the State." Then when communism itself was swept away, much of what remained consisted of the underlying structures of pre-traditional, egocentric consciousness. So instead of stimulating sustainable economic growth, foreign investment in Russia in the early 1990s only contributed to the rise of horrendous levels of organized crime. As we have discussed, the achievement-oriented values that are necessary for the development of modernist economies *use and depend on* the underlying values of "fair play" and respect for law, which are usually only found where healthy traditional structures are functioning within the society overall.

What distinguishes the individualistic orientation of the modernist level from the similarly individualistic worldview of the pre-traditional level is the *inclusion* of the intervening and moderating values of traditional culture. This intervening communally oriented stage serves to socialize and restrain the individual by providing a clear sense of right and wrong and by emphasizing the importance of law and order. Without a stable base of traditional culture of one form or another, attempts to evolve into modernism usually collapse back into the chaotic conditions of pre-traditional culture as a result of corruption and conflicts between rival groups. Thus, modernism in Russia did not develop (and still has not fully developed) as hoped, because a crucial stage of prerequisite development was partially missing from the ecosystemic structure of their culture.

As another example, we can see the obverse of Russia's developmental failure in Japan's developmental success. Japan was the first non-Western country able to evolve its own homegrown version of modernism because it had previously developed a strong and healthy version of traditional culture, which had been nurtured by two hundred years of self-imposed isolation and unfettered refinement, and which had never been colonized. So when the Japanese made the leap to modernism in the late nineteenth century, they were extremely successful (even after the devastation of World War II) because their strong base of traditional values served as a supporting foundation for their uniquely Japanese form of modernist culture.

These examples show why the success of earlier stages is generally required as a foundation or platform for the subsequent emergence of more developed stages. Just as in biological evolution, where later appearing levels depend on the accomplishments of earlier levels, this holarchic principle also functions in the realm of cultural evolution. And not only does this principle influence the relationship between traditionalism and modernism, it also shapes the relationship between modernism and post-modernism. Moreover, as the following example illustrates, the history of postmodernism's emergence from modernism reveals how a new level relies not only on the success of its previous stage; each new stage of cultural emergence also requires a degree of discontent, or evolutionary restlessness, stemming from the growing pathologies that are inevitably produced by the previous stage's successes.

Although postmodern cultural structures arose in a number of Western countries in the 1960s, America was the clear epicenter of this world-view's emergence. By the mid-sixties, after years of postwar prosperity and middleclass development, America had produced one of the world's most successful forms of modernist culture. And it was from the heart of America's well-educated modernist middleclass that the sixties youth revolution arose. Having grown up with all the advantages of modernist cultural development, the Baby Boom generation eventually became dissatisfied with the "establishment" and embraced the countercultural values of postmodernism in large numbers. Clearly, this dialectical move away from the achievement-oriented values of modernism was only made possible because of modernism's previous success. Postmodern youth came to reject the values of achieving wealth and status because most of them had been raised within a prosperous culture, and thus felt no need to strive for further upward mobility. They were therefore able to clearly recognize and reject the problems and limitations of modernist society because they had already received most of the benefits that modernism had to offer.

From these examples, we can begin to understand how this holarchic principle of dialectical "transcendence and inclusion" functions within the timeline of human history. And when we then remember that the state of human cultural development throughout the world remains spread out over the last 5,000 years of history, this shows us what we can do to help cultivate and stimulate the kinds of evolutionary emergence that we need to solve our global problems. This is not just a matter of better appreciating the needs and values of each stage, it also involves understanding the formative relationships that continue to exist between the stages. Yet once we come to understand the dynamics of this larger, holarchic structure of history that encompasses these various worldviews, we can then see how important the overall health of this larger structure is to the particular health of each individual worldview system. In other words, within this holarchic cultural ecosystem, if the evolution of a given stage has tried to move "too far ahead" in the timeline of development beyond its previous stage, if it gets ahead of itself by not appropriately *including* the values of its predecessor, it can fail to achieve evolutionary success. This can be seen in the example of Russia, above, where the situation calls for redevelopment of their traditional cultural structures as a prerequisite for the growth of vibrant forms of modernism. Conversely, if a given stage remains "too close" to its previous stage in the holarchic sequence, if it has not adequately *transcended* its predecessor, it can likewise fail.

A good example of social stagnation resulting from dialectically related stages of development remaining too close together can be found in the case of Islamic culture. One of the main reasons why most Islamic countries remain centered within their traditional culture—having failed to produce their own version of homegrown non-Western modernism, like Japan—is that the values of their traditional culture are intermixed with too many pre-traditional values. This can be seen in the significant influence that tribalism continues to exert upon Islamic societies in the Middle East, even after the recent political developments of the "Arab Spring." The intense fighting between small rival groups that characterizes pre-traditional cultural structures serves to undermine traditionalism's critical function of providing social unity and central authority. The excessive admixture of traditional and pre-traditional values within many Islamic societies can also be seen in the extreme pride that is often demonstrated by these cultures, which contributes to the virulent militancy that continues to plague Islam. While Islam's problems have certainly been exacerbated by Western imperialism and colonialism, this once-great civilization remains in the backwater of history primarily because its traditional form of culture is currently developmentally handicapped.

A similar set of circumstances afflicted Christianity prior to the Reformation. By the beginning of the sixteenth century, the Catholic Church had become corrupted and was thus sapped of much of its moral authority. This eventually led to the upheavals of the Reformation, which produced Protestant Christianity. This new kind of Christianity, which emerged from the struggles of the Reformation, had been largely purified of the negative aspects of pre-traditional values, making it a far more successful form of traditional religious culture. The demonstration of this success is seen in the fact that it was in Protestant countries where the Enlightenment first began to take root. And it is in these same historically Protestant countries where postmodernism is now most well developed.

Thus, when we view history through the lens of the evolutionary worldview, it provides a prescription for the cure of many of our current ills. We can see from the historical record how the evolutionary emergence of democracy, prosperity, and worldcentric morality depends on relatively healthy forms of underlying traditional culture to provide a foundation of responsible values. And this tells us that where traditional cultures remain stagnant or unhealthy, some kind of "reformation" will be needed before we can expect an "enlightenment."

As we come to better understand the nature of cultural development, this can help us become more effective at solving our world's problems by working to bring about the evolution of consciousness and culture. Although promoting cultural evolution is almost always a complex and difficult task, this discussion suggests an opening for a new approach. And obviously, this new approach has many potential political applications. With these insights in mind, we now turn to a brief consideration of "evolutionary politics."

## Evolutionary Politics

Any discussion of a "new approach to politics" must begin by acknowledging that some of the worst mischief in history has been wrought by "true believers" who were convinced they had a better idea. This risk is exacerbated in the case of the evolutionary worldview because of its willingness to recognize a vertical dimension of development. As noted, claims that some cultural groups are more developed or evolved than others can be problematic or even dangerous. Moreover, we must be mindful that previous efforts to apply evolutionary theory to politics resulted in severe mistakes, as seen in the case of both social Darwinism and Marxism. But these lessons of history are not lost on those who now advocate a new kind of evolutionary approach to politics.

This evolutionary method is better prepared to avoid the risks associated with attempting to bring about positive development because it includes the evolutionary achievements of the postmodern worldview within its perspective. The postmodern values of social justice and multiculturalism, together with the postmodern distrust of globalization and unrestrained economic expansion, serve as a safeguard that can help prevent this evolutionary political perspective from perpetuating the pathologies of modernism. Moreover, this evolutionary approach maintains a firm commitment to the proposition that "people have a right to be who they are." That is, there is no imperative to evolve, and people who live in less developed societies are certainly no less intrinsically valuable than those who dwell in postmodern cultural settings.

However, although people have a right to be who they are, as our world becomes increasingly interdependent, the problems of the few become the problems of the many. As carbon-intensive modernist economic development continues in places like China and India, the need for more effective forms of global politics becomes acute. Evolutionary politics accordingly seeks a synthetic approach that can help achieve worldwide social and cultural development while avoiding imperialism and neo-colonialism on one side, and by also avoiding the confusion and inaction that can result from strict multicultural relativism on the other side. Further, this evolutionary approach attempts to strike a balance between "realism" and "idealism," recognizing that politics is the art of the possible.

"What's wrong is not simple," and neither are the solutions to our problems. So the insights and goals of evolutionary politics are not being asserted as a panacea for every problem. However, sustainable solutions to our current global challenges will certainly require cultural evolution, and it is in this area that evolutionary politics can be particularly useful. Let's briefly consider some of the potentials.

## Near-Term Goals

Within America, the agenda of evolutionary politics encompasses both short-term and long-term goals for both national and international political evolution. In the relatively near term, the evolutionary approach seeks to move the overall cultural center of gravity of Americans forward in history. This goal is guided by the recognition that the American body politic can no longer be accurately conceived as simply "left and right." There are now actually four major political segments: religious traditionalists, conservative modernists, liberal modernists, and progressive postmodernists. These four distinct blocks often work at cross purposes with their allies along the political spectrum, and have thus produced the debilitating political stagnation witnessed at the time of this writing. Therefore, one of the short term pressing concerns of evolutionary politics is to break the current logjam and help build the necessary political will required to solve the growing problems of climate change, peak oil, unregulated globalization, war, hunger, poverty, and numerous other dilemmas. Yet despite the pressure of these threats, forming the political will necessary to make sacrifices and confront unpopular challenges remains extremely difficult because of America's ongoing culture war. Therefore, if the evolutionary approach to politics can help bring peace to the culture war, this will go a long way toward addressing many of the culturally complex problems we face.

We discussed above how postmodernism's often anti-modernist stance contributes to the culture war by making modernists and traditionalists defensive, which tends to increase stagnation and polarization. We also noted how evolutionary transitions to higher stages of development usually only occur where earlier stages have become *successful*. Thus, if we want to move America's cultural center of gravity forward in history, if we want consciousness to evolve along the margin from traditionalism into modernism and from modernism into postmodernism, then we would do well to start by helping the foundational values of traditionalism become a little more successful within American culture.

Prior to the rise of postmodernism and the resulting culture war, the values of the traditional worldview, both positive and negative, were very influential within American society as a whole. And by purging many of the negative aspects of traditionalism's oppressive moral hegemony, postmodernism was able to achieve a liberating form of cultural evolution. However, in the process of ridding our culture of the negative aspects of traditionalism, many of the positive and needed values of traditional culture were also discarded. So now, if we can use our understanding of the dialectic of progress and pathology to more clearly see the difference between traditionalism's enduring values and its outworn evolutionary scaffolding, we can then safely reintegrate some traditional values without regressing in the process. Making traditional culture more successful by allowing it to better fulfill its cultural mission will reduce the reactionary defensiveness that is presently preventing further cultural evolution. Although we cannot expect the most hardcore fundamentalists to move off of their positions, there are many who remain within a traditional center of gravity who would nevertheless become more sympathetic to postmodern proposals if they felt less threatened and more appreciated.

An important key to bringing peace to the culture war can thus be found in the task of reducing postmodern contempt for both traditionalism and modernism. As increasing numbers of progressive postmodernists adopt the evolutionary perspective and come to better appreciate the interdependence of all the stages of our cultural ecosystem, this will in turn help traditionalists and modernists to become more sympathetic to legitimate postmodern concerns. And as we carry forward their core values, we will find that we can also "carry forward" many of the modernists and traditionalists themselves into a new era of progressive agreement. This approach can thus help achieve progress in cultivating the political will that we now sorely lack.

Now, perhaps ironically, from this perspective the duty to evolve rests most squarely on the shoulders of postmodernists. It is they who must first "become the change" that they implore in others. If even a minority of postmodernists can soften their positions and evolve from their stance of staunch antithesis toward a more synthetic view of our cultural conditions, this can help bring peace to America's culture war and produce the political agreement needed to address our problems. Moreover, this kind of cultural evolution does not require a "great awakening." The close political margins by which elections are currently decided in the U.S. assures that even a small movement in our collective cultural center of gravity can make a big difference.

Because those who are beginning to adopt this emerging evolutionary understanding are coming primarily from postmodern perspectives, the rise of the evolutionary worldview is having its biggest impact on postmodernism. And because helping postmodernism to evolve—helping "uncork the bottle"—is a key to producing cultural evolution overall, even a relatively small demographic movement, such as the nascent evolutionary worldview, can nevertheless make positive progress in American politics in the near term.

As noted, the evolutionary perspective has the ability to "get in close" and identify with the healthy values of all the worldviews that make up our culture. By thus "metabolizing" a larger spectrum of values, evolutionaries become both *more postmodern and less postmodern*—more effective at working for environmental sustainability and social justice, but less handicapped by an anti-modernist resentment that rejects a large part of our civilization. Similarly, the evolutionary perspective allows us to be both *more traditional and less traditional*—more stalwart in protecting ourselves from those who would destroy our society, and at the same time less ethnocentric and imperialistic. This "values approach" to political evolution may at first seem vague or only marginally useful; but with the culture war costing us so dearly in terms of the decay of our collective political will, the potential of these kinds of culture-based solutions is immense at the domestic level of our politics.

Moving now from the consideration of domestic politics to American foreign policy, we can see how the evolutionary worldview provides unique solutions in this arena as well. As the ongoing "war on terror" continually demonstrates, war in the twenty-first century is being increasingly fought in the internal universe of culture. There is now broad consensus that our global conflicts have become primarily "battles for hearts and minds." And battles for hearts and minds are fought through compelling communications and demonstrations of value. Thus, improving our ability to understand the nature and behavior of the systemic structures that generate warring values becomes increasingly strategically significant. Yet the leaders of our security forces cannot achieve this kind of advance in *values intelligence* while they themselves remain centered within the values of the modernist worldview. The new epistemological capacity that can see conflict as part of a system of development only fully arises within those who have evolved their consciousness beyond both the formal operational perspectives of modernism and the relativistic perspectives of postmodernism.

It is important to emphasize that an evolutionary strategy for dealing with challenges such as militant Islam would not eliminate all current programs. Rather, an integral strategy might employ solutions from all worldviews simultaneously. For instance, we could continue to use a traditional approach by keeping the Navy in the Persian Gulf, we could also continue to use a modernist approach through the ongoing diplomacy of economic carrots and sticks. We could also begin to employ a postmodern approach by apologizing and making amends for some of our past actions. And to this multilevel strategy we could add an evolutionary element by working to strengthen and heal the unhealthy forms of traditional culture that are responsible for generating terrorist motivation.

Although there is much history to heal and much educational and economic development to be accomplished, we can also help make Islamic culture more healthy through simple gestures, such as memorials designed to restore pride and social solidarity. For example, we could sponsor a memorial in Baghdad commemorating Arab achievements in mathematics and celebrating the fact that "Arabic numerals" constitute the only truly global language. We could also strengthen moderate voices within Islamic culture by sponsoring prestigious prizes that could be awarded to writers who demonstrate that Islam is best interpreted as a religion of peace. Further, we could inaugurate programs to translate important books into Islamic languages and invest in their promotion and distribution. However, these efforts at cultural outreach and uplift will likely fail if they are led and administered primarily by modernists. Just as ham-handed attempts to "win hearts and minds" during the Vietnam war proved a dismal failure, attempts to reach out to Islamic culture will likewise fail unless these efforts are approached with the sympathy and sincerity possessed by higher levels of consciousness.

An evolutionary political approach to the war on terror seeks to help Islamic civilization evolve by working to recapitulate the emergent events of history through which other cultures have achieved evolution. And in this effort we have at least one partially successful example found in the history of Turkey. The Republic of Turkey is one of the few places where a native, democratic, prosperous modernist society has grown out of an Islamic culture. This resulted from the heroic leadership of Mustafa Kemal Atatürk, whose reforms of Turkish society after World War I were specifically designed to bring about the Enlightenment values of progress in science, education, and secular democracy. In other words, Turkey has evolved into a relatively modern country because its leaders and its people worked to consciously follow and repeat the developmental events of history. And the goal of evolutionary politics is to create similar kinds of success elsewhere in the world.

Yet both the success, and ongoing problems of Turkey also show that the only kind of Islamic modernism that will be healthy and sustainable in the long run is a modernism rooted in the soil of authentic Islamic culture; transplanted Western modernism will only serve to corrode underlying traditional structures and eventually undermine the foundation of traditional values that successful modernism requires.

## *Long-Term Goals*

One of the biggest strengths of evolutionary politics is its ability and willingness to take a long-term view of political evolution. And from this perspective we can see how the evolutionary trend of human social organization has been moving toward greater international interdependence and ever-larger political configurations, despite devolutionary countercurrents. This evolutionary trajectory tells us that an increasingly globalized world will eventually need to evolve limited, practical, and just forms of democratic global governance. Although democratic global governance may be as much as a century away, an evolutionary approach to politics recognizes that despite the dangers, as cultural evolution continues, a world federation of democracies will eventually become desirable, achievable, and inevitable.

The evolutionary perspective understands that each historically significant worldview has an accompanying form of political organization. Pre-traditional culture is usually organized around a chief or strong warlord. Then, with the emergence of traditional culture (both East and West) the structures of feudalism and class-bound systems of patronage appear. The subsequent emergence of modernism then results in the rise of constitutional democracies. And in the places where postmodern culture has achieved political success, forms of social democracy appear, as seen in many

Scandinavian countries. Thus, as human nature matures through cultural evolution, this results in more developed forms of political organization. This was recognized as early as the fourth century B.C. by Plato, who wrote:"The states are as the men are; they grow out of human characters."6 This principle, however, also works in reverse. As noted, attempts to bring about democratic forms of government often fail or become highly dysfunctional in places where the consciousness and culture that correspond to such structures remain absent. And this is well understood by those who advocate an evolutionary approach to politics, which recognizes that under the world's current cultural conditions any attempt to inaugurate a federation of democracies would be premature.

Thus, because the advent of democratically enacted, enforceable global law is still far in the future, and because any attempt to bring it about would be fraught with difficulty and danger, talk of even a minimal and limited form of world federation is currently seen by many as either too radical or too idealistic to deserve serious consideration in contemporary political discourse. But when we remember how quickly the European Union came into being, and when we also acknowledge that planetary conditions could change very quickly in the coming decades, a serious discussion of our future political evolution now seems warranted. Although neither modernist nor postmodern perspectives are evolved enough to serve as a foundation for a functional federal union of democratic nations, the rise of the evolutionary worldview can supply the necessary consciousness for such an advance.

As mentioned at the beginning of this chapter, it is estimated that at the time of the American Revolution, only about ten percent of the American population was able to make meaning at the modernist level of consciousness. Yet this was enough to bring about the rise of constitutional democracy. And similarly, we can anticipate that when the evolutionary worldview becomes adopted by approximately ten percent of the population of the developed world, the time could be propitious for the inauguration of a global federal union of democratic nation-states.

This is not a vision of a "world state," but rather a limited pooling of sovereignty under which existing national structures would remain relatively intact. Such a union could begin as a loose federation of modernist and postmodern democracies, with other willing nations being gradually admitted as probationary members until their development warranted full enfranchisement. And, of course, no nation would ever be coerced into joining such a union, as democratic consent would serve as a cornerstone of the structure.

The benefits of effective global governance would be abundant. Democratic oversight of the global economy would produce greater fairness for individuals and fragile local cultures, while at the same time producing more overall prosperity. A global federation of cooperating democracies would also be more effective at protecting human rights and our planet's environment, implementing the kinds of safeguards that are currently impossible in a world of competing independent nation-states.

Moreover, just as the design of the United States constitution was informed and guided by the wisdom of Enlightenment philosophy, the constitutional structures of global law could be likewise carefully crafted using the enlarged perspectives of integral philosophy. My previous book, *Integral Consciousness and the Future of Evolution*, described some of the ways in which integral philosophy could be used to design the structures and safeguards of a future world federal constitution.

This long-term vision for a new level of human political organization demonstrates the potential of the evolutionary worldview. Again, every historically significant worldview has produced an emergent new form of political organization, and the rise of the evolutionary worldview should be no exception. Without its championing of the long-term goal of democratic global governance, the evolutionary worldview would fail to offer the type of powerful new solutions that previously arising worldviews have provided. But when we realize just how much good a limited world federation could do, when we come to understand how we could realistically end war, hunger, and the environmental crisis, we can begin to feel the energy of an impending Second Enlightenment.

## Evolutionary Spirituality

Of course, a Second Enlightenment will not be brought about through politics alone. Any significant advance in cultural evolution will also require the emergence of new forms of spirituality. What do I mean by "spirituality?" Our relationship to spirit. And what is "spirit?" Well, to define something is to objectify it, and whatever spirit is, it is certainly not an object. But even though it cannot be adequately defined, this does not mean that spirit is obscure, indefinite, or wholly subjective. Although according to my understanding, spirituality is primarily a matter of direct personal experience, my experience confirms that its referent is real and not simply "in my head." So what is it? I believe it will take more than this lifetime to truly know. Most of those who have experienced spirit can perhaps agree that it is the presence of the infinite and eternal within the finite universe. Beyond this, however, agreement diminishes as we encounter a spectrum of paths and a wide variety of convictions regarding the nature of spiritual reality.

I briefly mentioned my own personal spiritual convictions in the introduction and at the end of chapter 8. This final section, however, will not include a further presentation of my specific version of spirituality. Rather, this section attempts to describe the inclusive agreement which is coming to frame the spiritual component of the emerging evolutionary worldview. It is clear that evolutionary spirituality is not simply a new kind of religion; it encompasses a variety of distinct religious paths (or "spiritual lines of development") and thus cannot be equated with any particular path or line. In fact, evolutionary spirituality begins with the recognition that religions or spiritual paths are not static institutions, but rather distinct trajectories of ongoing development within consciousness and culture. Although most of these lines are rooted in the traditional stage of psychosocial evolution, the progressive spiritual revival that has arisen with the postmodern worldview demonstrates that the world's great religions remain vibrant evolving entities. And as we will discuss, the rise of postmodern spirituality serves as a prerequisite for the subsequent emergence of evolutionary spirituality.

Prior to the rise of the postmodern demographic, most forms of spirituality remained within traditional culture. But as the counterculture emerged in the developed world, it brought a renewed appreciation of almost every kind of spirituality. And this revival of interest in spiritual teachings resulted in a kind of countercultural spiritual renaissance which has enriched the lives of millions and which continues to show ongoing vitality here at the beginning of the twenty-first century.

Defining the postmodern spiritual renewal as simply "New Age" would be too narrow. Although what most people would recognize as New Age spirituality certainly comprises a significant part of this movement, alternative spirituality also includes spiritual systems for which the New Age label does not fit, as well as many traditional forms of Eastern spirituality that have been transplanted to the West relatively intact. Thus, for the purposes of our discussion I will refer to this eclectic revival of religion within postmodern culture as "progressive spirituality."

Definitions of this sort are, of course, tricky because within the current culture of progressive spirituality we find religious forms from every level of development. For example, postmodern spiritual culture embraces pre-traditional shamanism, traditional Hinduism, modernist self-help programs, as well as uniquely postmodern forms, such as eco-spirituality. Although practically all the spiritual forms embraced by the cultural agreement of progressive spirituality are postmodern in some sense, the diverse mix of paths that comprises progressive spiritual culture spans the spectrum of development.

From an evolutionary perspective the postmodern worldview's quest to transcend the hyper-rational worldview of modernism has sometimes led to excess. For some, this has resulted in confusion and the inability to tell the difference between authentically "trans-rational" spirituality and older forms of "pre-rational" spirituality. As mentioned in chapter 3 this "pre/trans fallacy" was originally identified by Wilber in the 1970s through his analysis of the work of Carl Jung. However, although the adoption of certain forms of progressive spirituality has led some of those raised within a modernist culture to regress to a traditional level of consciousness, many practitioners of progressive spirituality have nevertheless achieved authentic evolution beyond both the traditional and modernist stages of cultural development.

The evolutionary accomplishments of progressive spirituality in the developed world include the rise of strong cultural mores for religious pluralism, and greater respect for most forms of spirituality. This cultural movement has also led to the large-scale discovery and integration of the wisdom teachings and practices of Eastern religions and esoteric forms of spirituality of all kinds. As a result of the advent of progressive spiritual culture, many people now define spirituality as a personal practice for achieving psychological development and "human potential," rather than as an inherited ethnic allegiance. Progressive spirituality thus provides a wide variety of choices regarding what it means to be spiritual. This enlarged freedom of choice includes not only which religion to practice; it also supports people in constructing their own eclectic versions of spirituality, mixing and matching disparate forms into a personal spiritual pastiche. Within postmodern spiritual contexts, institutional religious authority has been largely supplanted by the personal authority of each person to decide what they believe and how they will live a spiritual life.

Prior to the rise of progressive spirituality many Western intellectuals assumed that religion was in an irreversible decline and would soon die out. But the appearance of the now large and vibrant market for alternative forms of spirituality testifies to the ongoing vitality of the religious impulse, and to humanity's unquenchable thirst for spiritual truth. Thus, just as the first step in understanding the emerging evolutionary worldview as a whole begins with the recognition that the postmodern worldview is authentically more evolved than modernism, understanding evolutionary spirituality likewise begins by appreciating the significant evolution that has been achieved by postmodern spirituality in the last fifty years.

However, evolutionary spirituality—which might be termed "post-postmodern spirituality"—attempts to model the evolutionary technique of growth through transcendence and inclusion. Evolutionary spirituality thus seeks to build on the accomplishments of progressive spirituality, while simultaneously transcending its immaturities and debilitating pathologies. The shortcomings of progressive spirituality include the already mentioned "pre/trans fallacy" of magical thinking, "soft-headedness," superficiality, commercialism, and spiritual materialism. Despite its accomplishments, progressive spirituality has promoted an extensive amount of pseudoscience, co-opting and distorting science to prop up questionable belief systems. It has also contributed to a culture of narcissism and selfishness, promoting the idea that reality is simply whatever one wants it to be. And progressive spiritual culture has given rise to a wide variety of insular cults that isolate and control members to their significant detriment.

Although these problems are not unique to postmodern spirituality, they stand out in greater relief and are in many ways made worse because of their association with postmodernism's otherwise commendable evolutionary accomplishments. In other words, because postmodernism is generally the most evolved form of large-scale culture to appear in the timeline of human history, its spiritual pathologies have been magnified and its shortcomings rendered more difficult to overlook. An important task of evolutionary spirituality is thus to prune away the New Age sins of progressive spirituality and thereby produce a new form of spiritual culture that can provide more powerful forms of unifying leadership for our society.

In fact, progressive spirituality itself began with a similar round of cultural pruning. Arising as a significant demographic in the 1970s, and coming to full fruition in the 1990s, progressive spirituality's cultural agreement effectively expelled all forms of belief system exclusivity and claims for only "one true way." It banished teachings of fear, hell, and wrathful deities, and it did away with most forms of dogmatic literalism. Despite its welcoming pluralism and intensive relativism, progressive spirituality did achieve progress by purging some of the falsehoods propagated by earlier forms of religious culture.

Now as evolutionary spirituality continues with the next steps of this process of clarifying and purifying our understanding of spirit, it attempts another round of pruning. Evolutionary spirituality rejects claims that nature and history are a meaningless illusion or a pointless accident, that progress in civilization does not matter, or that everything is already perfect just as it is. Additionally, it rejects the idea that humans are no more valuable or evolved than other forms of life; it discards teachings that reality can be entirely created according to our wants or whims; it denies the notion that thinking and philosophy have no value in the spiritual quest, or that spiritual teachings have no obligation to be consistent with scientific facts; and it questions the claim that all spiritual paths are equally valid. Although evolutionary spirituality can recognize truth in paradox, and can see degrees of truth even in what it rejects, it nevertheless pushes off against the limitations of progressive spirituality in its quest to make a dialectical advance into the next era of humanity's spiritual evolution. Yet evolutionary spirituality does not distinguish itself from progressive spirituality by attempting to nullify or vilify this previous level of development. In our use of the dialectical evolutionary technique we must be careful to include the important aspects of what we are otherwise attempting to transcend. And of course, this dialectical technique applies to earlier levels of development as well. Thus, an important element of evolutionary spirituality is its attempt to reintegrate at a higher level the rigor and clarity of truth provided by modernist science and philosophy.

Evolutionary spirituality is primarily forward looking, so it can be understood more by what it affirms than by what it denies. Although the "spiritual teachings" of evolution are not a fixed doctrine—although our understanding of evolution's spiritual message is itself evolving and always subject to a variety of interpretations—most evolutionaries will agree that evolutionary spirituality affirms a universe of progress and purpose; that it acknowledges the essential interconnectedness and interdependence of all beings while simultaneously affirming the unique originality of every individual; that it recognizes a universal form of spirituality in our evolving conceptions of beauty, truth, and goodness; and that it confirms the freedom of human will and the open-ended potential of our ongoing spiritual growth. Evolutionary spirituality also sees most forms of spirituality as evolving lines of development that will inevitably continue to grow beyond the historically situated evolutionary worldview itself.

Further, evolutionary spirituality recognizes that religion fulfills an essential and ongoing function in cultural evolution by providing explanations and practices that go beyond science or philosophy. Most forms of evolutionary spirituality thus transcend science and philosophy by describing the essential nature of the self, by explaining the character of the ultimate or absolute, by providing hope in some kind of an afterlife, and by offering practices through which these realities can be at least partially experienced. Even though the different lines of religious development that are welcomed within evolutionary spirituality's cultural agreement often offer conflicting explanations of these things, faith in some form of higher truth cannot be dispensed with if one is to live an authentic spiritual life. That is, at a very minimum, all forms of genuine spirituality require that we ultimately recognize something larger than ourselves.

Moreover, because the evolutionary view understands the importance of having some kind of definite (even if open-ended) beliefs and convictions about the nature of spiritual reality, this perspective can better appreciate the *entire developmental line* formed by the evolutionary trajectory of each great world religion, rather than just the most recent growing tip of these lines. In other words, the value of any given form of spirituality is found in both its current blossoms and its historical roots. Although the root teachings of the world's great religions include myths and pathologies, these erroneous conceptions do not completely invalidate the larger eternal truths taught by these ancient lines of spiritual development. The evolutionary perspective thus recognizes most religious pathologies as the worn out cultural scaffolding of previous eras, and is thus better able to distinguish the enduring truths that remain within these historical religious forms.

As I have argued, the newly emerging picture of evolution now being disclosed by science and philosophy—the great story of cosmological, biological, and psychosocial evolution—presents a spiritual teaching. Although it has many facets, the essence of this teaching is that evolution is moving toward ever-greater realizations of beauty, truth, and goodness. And it is this growing recognition of evolution's spiritual message that serves as a foundation for evolutionary spirituality. Yet the best view of evolution's spiritual truth regards it not as a *substitute* for existing forms of religion, but rather as a *supplement* that can enhance almost every kind of spirituality. In fact, the spiritual teachings of evolution confirm much of what existing religions have been teaching all along.

For example, our discussion in chapter 6 showed how evolution generates value in opposing yet complementary directions—increasing the intrinsic value of its emerging new wholes while simultaneously adding to the instrumental value of its encompassed parts. And an understanding of this method of evolutionary development helps us better appreciate how the spiritual development of our individual character—the growth of our personal intrinsic value—is linked to the instrumental service value that we provide to others. Stated differently, when we see how evolution grows in value overall, this teaches us that the gifts we give to the world actually provide the rungs of the ladder of our own ascent, and that our individual spiritual status can be partially measured by our usefulness in giving value to our fellows. This newly recognized truth about evolution thus confirms an ancient religious teaching. As Jesus said, "By their fruits you shall know them."

As the evolutionary worldview develops as a new form of culture, its enlarged understanding of the spiritual nature of evolution will become a touchstone that uplifts all the various forms of spirituality it encompasses. The spiritual lessons of evolution will thus serve as a "true tone" or "concert pitch" that can help "tune up" all the spiritual lines of development that will come to "play in the orchestra" of emerging evolutionary spiritual culture.

And as the evolutionary perspective endeavors to discern the spiritual teachings of evolution, it attempts to learn from all the myriad forms of beauty, truth, and goodness that can be found within the evolutionary epic. But among the many spiritual lessons of evolution, the truths of the evolutionary impulse are among the most important. As discussed in chapter 7, the internal spectrum of desire that spans the range from our most basic biological urges to our most sublime spiritual aspirations provides a personal microcosmic experience of the creative unfolding of the universe as a whole—from matter, to life, to mind, to spirit. We can thus each connect to evolution's macrocosmic purpose through the personal purpose that courses within our own minds and hearts. By working to feel and cultivate this impulse as a spiritual practice, we find that the pull of value gravity becomes intensified, and our ability to give our gifts to the world becomes ever stronger. And it is through this practice of working with the evolutionary impulse that we become increasingly assured that we are spiritual beings living in a universe of ongoing spiritual growth.

Yet this last point brings up a kind of dividing line that can be found within the growing agreement of evolutionary spirituality. This concerns the question of whether or not there is an afterlife. The emerging evolutionary worldview as a whole includes those who are willing to acknowledge that the story of evolution contains a spiritual teaching, but who otherwise reject the idea of life after death as too supernatural to be credible. While I think evolutionary spirituality is broad and flexible enough to welcome such views within its cultural agreement structure, in my experience, the full benefits of evolutionary spirituality cannot be had without faith in an afterlife of some kind.

The evidence from near-death experiences notwithstanding, neither science nor philosophy can confirm the common intuition that the growth of our consciousness will continue after death. Assurances of an afterlife require the teachings of religion. And practically all the great religions contain a teaching about one kind of afterlife or another. However, if we adopt an evolutionary view of the afterlife we may be led to modify these teachings so as to emphasize continuity between this life and the next. That is, when we begin to better understand how consciousness evolves, we may no longer expect that after death we will either become immediately perfected in heaven (the traditional Christian view), or that our progress in this life will only survive as karma in the next (the traditional Buddhist view). Rather, from an evolutionary perspective we might expect that in the afterlife we will "begin over there right where we leave off down here."

This faith-based commitment to some kind of "soul survival" helps us realize that our evolutionary journey is limitless, and that the personal progress we make on earth does not go for naught. Although this is not the place to make a detailed argument for belief in an afterlife, I will say that this kind of faith can make a significant positive difference in the here and now. Moreover, I personally feel that our evolving universe does not really make sense unless there is continuing spiritual growth of human consciousness beyond this life.

• • •

In conclusion, the goal of the evolutionary worldview is to provide the kind of cultural leadership that can help bring about some of the further evolution we now urgently need. Again, even though it will likely be quite some time before the evolutionary worldview becomes a significant social structure, this emerging perspective can nevertheless make progress in the short term by helping to improve postmodernism, so that postmodernism can in turn better improve modernism. And as discussed in this chapter, the most effective way to improve postmodern culture is by transcending it, by convincingly demonstrating what comes after postmodernism in the course of cultural evolution.

Although a deeper understanding of evolution can be used to solve many social and political problems, I believe it is by coming to see the spiritual aspects of evolution that we can make the most progress. Recognition of the spiritual teachings of evolution can eventually lead to a new form of liberating cultural solidarity, a new phase of culture united by the understanding that evolution does have a purpose, and that this purpose points to the evolving realities of freedom, goodness, truth, and beauty. And as this new form of cultural solidarity begins to take hold in the developed world, it could result in a more functional future civilization wherein the experience of transcendence plays a larger role in public life. However, the minimal metaphysics of this spiritual philosophy of evolution need not become the officially sanctioned view. The growing recognition of the reality of purpose and progress in nature and history can significantly improve our culture by simply supplanting materialism within the spheres of public life where it remains the dominant form of metaphysics, such as in academia in general, and in science in particular.

By using hard-edged, scientifically grounded arguments to demonstrate evolution's purposeful progression, we can outgrow the limitations of materialistic modernism, and in the process bring many former modernists along with us into this new evolutionary worldview. And by doing this we will also have transcended postmodernism by achieving what it has been unable to achieve, by bringing an end to what philosopher Charles Taylor calls "the secular age." Although modernism will undoubtedly continue as the dominant worldview of the developed world for many years to come, we can eventually curtail modernism's cultural power and minimize its more negative aspects by exposing the fallacy of scientific materialism and by showing how this purely physicalist view of the universe is now as outdated as the myths of the traditional worldview. So it is perhaps ironic, but nevertheless dialectically fitting, that the revelation of evolution will have served as both a major factor in the ascendency of materialism, and the primary agency through which its dominance is brought to an end.

# NOTES

## Introduction

1. Mary Midgley, *Evolution as a Religion* (London: Methuen, 1985), p. 1.

2. See, e.g., Robert Inglehart, ed. *Human Values and Social Change* (New York: Brill, 2003); Paul Ray and Sherry Anderson. *The Cultural Creatives, How 50 Million People are Changing the World* (New York: Harmony Books, 2000). See also, James Mark Baldwin. *Genetic Theory of Reality* (New York: G.P. Putnam's Sons, 1915); Jean Piaget. *The Child's Conception of the World* (New York: Routledge, 1928); Lawrence Kohlberg. *From Is to Ought* (New York: Academic Press, 1971); Clare W. Graves, "Levels of Existence: An Open System Theory of Values," *Journal of Humanistic Psychology* (November, 1970); Jenny Wade. *Changes of Mind: A Holonomic Theory of the Evolution of Consciousness* (Albany, NY: SUNY Press, 1996); and Jeremy Rifkin. *The Empathic Civilization* (New York: Tarcher Putnam, 2009).

## Chapter 1

1. Quoted in Robert Wright, *Nonzero, the Logic of Human Destiny* (New York: Pantheon, 2000), p. 14.

2. Douglas Futuyama, *Evolutionary Biology* (Sunderland, MA: Sinauer Associates, 1979), p. 4.

3. Loyal Rue, *Everybody's Story* (Albany, NY: SUNY Press 1999), p. 42-43.

4. Harold Morowitz, *The Emergence of Everything* (Oxford: Oxford University Press, 2002), back cover.

5. Terrence Deacon, "The Hierarchic Logic of Emergence: Untangling the Interdependence of Evolution and Self-Organization," *in* Weber and Depew, eds. *Evolution and Learning: The Baldwin Effect Reconsidered*, (Cambridge, MA: MIT Press, 2003), p. 273.

6. Peter Corning, *Holistic Darwinism: Synergy, Cybernetics, and the Bioeconomics of Evolution* (Chicago: University of Chicago Press, 2005) (initial definition quoted from J. Goldstein), p 7.

7. Philip Clayton, *Adventures in the Spirit* (Minneapolis, MN: Fortress Press, 2008), p. 90.

8. Holmes Rolston III, *Genes, Genesis and God* (Cambridge, UK: Cambridge University Press, 1999), p. 357.

9. Rod Swenson, "Epistemic Ordering and Development of Spacetime: Intentionality as a Universal Entailment," in *Semiotica, Biosemiotica*, 127 Special Issue (1999), p. 567-598. The quote from Darwin that appears above this quote from Swenson is from page 152 of *The Origin of Species* (London: Hurst, 1911).

10. Certain laws of physics, such as gravity, may have existed "prior to" the big bang. But because the big bang marks the beginning of time, it is difficult to conceive of anything having a temporal pre-existence to it.

11. Robert Godwin, *One Cosmos Under God* (Minneapolis, MN: Paragon House 2004), p. 71. The immensity of the difference between cosmological and biological evolution is underscored by biologist Lynn Margulis, who writes: "To go from a bacterium to people is less of a step than to go from a mixture of amino acids to that bacterium." (quoted in Holmes Rolston, *Three Big Bangs* (New York: Columbia University Press, 2010), p. 43.

12. Arthur Koestler, *Janus: A Summing Up* (New York: Random House, 1978), p. 275.

13. Alfred Russel Wallace, *Natural Selection and Tropical Nature* (London: Macmillan, 1895), p. 202.

14. See A.R. Luria, *Cognitive Development: Its Cultural and Social Foundations* (Cambridge, MA: Harvard University Press, 1976); M.J. Lundberg, *The Incomplete Adult: Social Class Constraints on Personal Development* (Westport, CT: Greenwood Press, 1974); S. Scribner, & M. Cole, *The Psychology of Literacy* (Cambridge, MA: Harvard University Press, 1981); H. Werner, *Comparative Psychology of Mental Development* (Madison, CT: International University Press, 1980) (Originally published 1940); L. Levy-Bruhl, *How Natives Think.* (Princeton, NJ: Princeton University Press, 1985) (Originally published 1910). See also Jenny Wade, *Changes of Mind: A Holonomic Theory of the Evolution of Consciousness* (Albany, NY: SUNY, 1996), p. 77-96, and Ken Wilber, *Sex, Ecology, Spirituality* (Boston, MA: Shambhala 1995), p. 169-176.

15. Admittedly, animal culture also evinces degrees of evolution, as documented in the book: *The Evolution of the Culture of Animals*, by John Tyler Bonner (Princeton, NJ: Princeton University Press, 1983). And from certain perspectives, almost any distinction we can make between humans and animals is arguably more a matter of degree than of kind. Yet the evolutionary achievements of human consciousness and culture are clearly "unlike" anything found in the animal kingdom. As biologist Marc Hauser observes: ". . . cognitively, the difference between humans and chimps is greater than that between chimps and worms." (quoted in Holmes Rolston, *Three Big Bangs* (New York: Columbia University Press), p. 105). See also chapter 3, note 16.

16. Merlin Donald, "The Virtues of Rigorous Interdisciplinarity," *in* Joan M. Lucariello et al, eds. *The Development of the Mediated Mind* (London: Psychology Press, 2004), p. 254.

17. Jürgen Habermas, *Communication and the Evolution of Society* (Boston, MA: Beacon Press, 1979), pp. 98-99.

18. Robert Kegan, *In Over Our Heads* (Cambridge, MA: Harvard University Press, 1994), p. 34.

## Chapter 2

1. John Heil, *From an Ontological Point of View* (Oxford: Oxford University Press, 2003), p. 1.

2. Jacques Derrida, *Structure, Sign and Play in the Discourse of the Human Sciences. in Writing and Difference* (Chicago: University of Chicago Press, 1978), pp. 278-93.

3. Robert Elliott Allinson, *A Metaphysics for the Future* (Burlington VT: Ashgate, 2001), p. 50.

4. F.H. Bradley, *Appearance and Reality* (Oxford: Oxford University Press, 1930), p. x.

5. In connection with this broad definition of metaphysics it should be noted that since 1988, social theorist Jürgen Habermas has been claiming that his philosophy is "postmetaphysical" because it focuses on the "deep structures" of language and does not rely on ontological concepts in reaching its conclusions. Similarly, Ken Wilber has recently adopted Habermas' terminology (but not Habermas' methods or self-imposed limitations) and has also begun using the term "postmetaphysical" to characterize his philosophy. However, Wilber's version of postmetaphysics is designed to support claims that his spiritual system is beyond mere belief and is thus a kind of "spiritual science." Accordingly, Wilber's thinking cannot be categorized as "postmetaphysical" in the Habermasian sense because unlike the strictly materialistic philosophy of Habermas, Wilber's philosophy is robustly spiritual. Wilber's version of postmetaphysical philosophy is nevertheless an interesting attempt to overcome the "myth of the given" in the realm of spiritual truth claims, but in the final analysis, it remains a form of metaphysics.

6. Although the contemporary version of the modernist worldview has its origins primarily in the Enlightenment, we can see earlier but ultimately unsustainable emergences of this perspective in previous historical periods. As I wrote in *Integral Consciousness*: "The first significant emergence of modernist culture appeared in the fifth century B.C. during the Golden Age of ancient Greece. The triumph of reason over myth was evident in Greek philosophy, mathematics, engineering, politics, and art. Indeed, the appearance of realism and perspective in art is always a good marker of emerging modernist consciousness. However, although the Golden Age of ancient Greece has served as a kind of 'Platonic essence of civilization,' a romantic ideal that has captured the imagination of latter-day modernists for the past five hundred years, this level of civilization was premature; it could not be sustained. And even though traces of modernist

culture can be seen in the Roman empire up to its final collapse (and to a degree in ancient Islamic, Indian, and Chinese civilization), modernist consciousness did not emerge in a sustainable form until the European Renaissance, with it then coming to complete fruition during the Enlightenment of the 17th and 18th centuries." Steve McIntosh, *Integral Consciousness and the Future of Evolution* (Minneapolis, MN: Paragon House 2007), pp. 48-49.

7. Douglas Futuyama, *Evolutionary Biology* (Sunderland, MA: Sinauer Associates, 1979), p. 449.

8. David Griffin, *Religion and Scientific Naturalism, Overcoming the Conflicts* (Albany, NY: SUNY Press, 2000), pp. 252 -254.

9. Charles Darwin, *The Origin of Species* (New York: Mentor Books, 1958), p. 171.

10. See Niles Eldridge, *Reinventing Darwin: The Great Debate at the High Table of Evolutionary Theory* (Hoboken, NJ: John Wiley and Sons, 1995), p. 67.

11. Stephen Jay Gould, *Ever Since Darwin* (New York: W.W. Norton, 1977), p. 36.

12. Robert Wesson, *Beyond Natural Selection* (Cambridge, MA: MIT Press, 1991) p. 20.

13. *Ibid*, p. 4.

14. Alex Rosenberg and Robert Arp, eds. *Philosophy of Biology: An Anthology* (Malden, MA: Wiley-Blackwell, 2010), p. 10.

15. Philip Clayton, *Adventures in the Spirit* (Minneapolis, MN: Fortress Press, 2008), p. 37.

16. Holmes Rolston, III, *Genes, Genesis and God* (Cambridge, MA: Cambridge University Press, 1999), p. 355.

17. Simon Conway Morris, *Life's Solution, Inevitable Humans in a Lonely Universe* (Cambridge, UK: Cambridge University Press, 2004), p. 327.

18. John Holland, *Emergence: From Chaos to Order* (New York: Basic Books, 1999), (quoted in Morowitz, *The Emergence of Everything*, p. 25).

19. Holmes Rolston III, *Genes, Genesis and God* (Cambridge, UK: Cambridge University Press, 1999), p. 359.

20. See, Johnjoe McFadden, *Quantum evolution* (New York: W.W. Norton & Co, 2000), and Amit Goswami, *Creative evolution* (Wheaton, IL: Quest Books, 2008).

21. Allan Combs, *The Radiance of Being* (Minneapolis, MN: Paragon House, 2005), p. 117.

22. Quoted from Wikipedia, an online encyclopedia; http://en.wikipedia.org/wiki/Intelligent_Design, accessed July 15, 2010.

23. Stuart Kauffman, *Reinventing the Sacred* (New York: Basic Books, 2008), pp. 86-87.

24. Holmes Rolston III, *Environmental Ethics, Duties to and Values in the Natural World* (Philadelphia, PA: Temple University Press, 1988), pp. 108-109.

25. Stuart Kauffman, *Reinventing the Sacred* (New York: Basic Books, 2008), p. 12. Regarding Kauffman's statement that human life is a part of the biosphere, I should point out that because the noosphere transcends and includes the biosphere, it is more accurate to say that the biosphere is a "part" of the noosphere rather than the other way around. This idea is discussed further in chapter 6.

26. Decision-making has been generally associated with the functioning of the neo-cortex, but its exact neurophysiological mechanisms remain unexplained. Recently, the ventromedial prefrontal cortex has been identified as playing an active role in integrating emotions into decision-making through its connection with the amygdala. However, the physiology of decision-making is still largely a mystery to science. See further, Philip Clayton, *In Quest of Freedom The Emergence of Spirit in the Natural World* (Göttingen, Germany: Vandenhoeck & Ruprecht, 2009). On pages 29-39, Clayton discusses the experiments of Benjamin Libet, which seem to show that a human subject becomes aware of his choice only after it has been previously made by the brain. Clayton, however, concludes that this does not negate freedom of the will, which he defends through a theory of "broad naturalism" that recognizes free will as an emergent property that exerts authentic downward causation on brain states.

27. Despite the arguments of "compatibilists" such as Daniel Dennet, who argue that free will and material determinism are not inconsistent, this position is essential incoherent. See Clayton, *Ibid*, 31-39

28. Abraham Maslow, *Motivation and Personality* (New York: HarperCollins, 1987), p. 162.

## Chapter 3

1. Ludwig Wittgenstein, *Tractatus Logico-Philosophicus* (New York: Routedge, 1961), p. 476.

2. Stewart Kauffman, *Reinventing the Sacred* (New York: Basic Books, 2008), p. 8.

3. *Ibid*, p. 9.

4. Iris Murdoch, *The Sovereignty of the Good* (New York: Routledge and Kegan Paul, 1970), p. 97.

5. *Ibid* p. 93.

6. Alister McGrath, *The Open Secret, A New Vision for Natural Theology* (Oxford: Blackwell, 2008), pp. 26-27. McGrath lists three general definitions of the transcendent: 1) "The idea of self-transcendence . . . mastering natural limitations. . . . 2) A realm beyond ordinary experience [with] ontological significance . . . 3) Experiences which are interpreted to relate to a transcendent reality . . . used psychologically to refer to an experience." *Ibid.*, pp. 25-26.

7. Frederick Turner, *Natural Religion* (New Brunswick, NJ: Transaction Publishers, 2006), p. 83.

8. *Ibid.*, p. 96.

9. Holmes Rolston III, *Environmental Ethics, Duties to and Values in the Natural World* (Philadelphia, PA: Temple University Press, 1988), pp. 211-213.

10. *Ibid*, p. 215.

11. J. L. Mackey, *Ethics: Inventing Right and Wrong* (New York: Penguin, 1977), p. 38.

12. This is a quote from David Griffin, who is interpreting Whitehead's thought from *Adventures of Ideas*. See David Griffin, *Religion and Scientific Naturalism, Overcoming the Conflicts*, (Albany, NY: SUNY Press, 2000), p. 294.

13. See D. Blumenfeld, "Leibniz's theory of the striving possibles." *in* R. Woolhouse, ed., *Leibniz: Metaphysics and philosophy of science* (Oxford: Oxford University Press, 1981), pp. 77-88.

14. In psychology, and especially Jungian psychology, a person's "shadow" is the part of their unconscious mind that consists of disowned or repressed impulses, shortcomings or weaknesses, which often become projected onto others. Ken Wilber describes the negative attraction power of one's repressed shadow issues as follows: "Whenever I disown and project my own qualities, they appear 'out there,' where they frighten me, irritate me, depress me, obsess me. . . . recent studies [show] men who were anti-gay-pornography crusaders were themselves attracted to gay sex but, finding that unacceptable in themselves, spent their lives trying to eradicate it in others, while claiming they had no such nasty desires themselves." *Integral Spirituality* (Boston, MA: Shambhala, 2006), p. 120-121.

15. Iris Murdoch, *The Sovereignty of the Good* (New York: Routledge and Kegan Paul, London, 1970), p. 103.

16. In connection with our comparison of the capacity of value perception in animals and humans, it should be noted that animals in general, and mammals in particular, do apparently experience love through affection for their mates and offspring. They also experience a form of beauty as evidenced by their discrimination in the selection of reproductive partners. Darwin himself recognized the functioning of this aesthetic sense in animals, finding it "astonishing" that even reptiles, fish and insects "would be endowed with sufficient taste for . . . sexual selection." Charles Darwin, *The Descent of Man*, (New York: Plume 2007), p. 400. And as discussed in chapters 2 and 3, the value of "survival" itself can be recognized as a primitive form of goodness valued by all forms of life. So on the one hand, animals appear to possess traces of almost all the traits by which humans have traditionally been distinguished from animals, including language, toolmaking, and even self-awareness. And from this perspective, the differences between animals and humans seem to be more a matter of degree than of kind. Yet on the other hand, the human ability to recognize sophisticated forms of value stems

from an evolutionary emergence in consciousness that clearly transcends all forms of animal consciousness, as evidenced by the fact that the emergence of humanity results in a entirely new category of evolution—humans are not only animals, we represent a transcendent kind of being. This is especially evident in the case of language. Prominent linguist Noam Chomsky observers: "There seems to be no substance to the view that human language is simply a more complex instance of something to be found elsewhere in the animal world. This poses problems for the biologist, since, if true, it is an example of true 'emergence'—the appearance of a qualitatively different phenomenon at a specific stage of complexity of organization." Noam Chomsky, *Language and Mind*, (Cambridge, UK: Cambridge University Press 2006), p. 70.

17. The characterization of evolution's dialectical movement through the use of the three terms "thesis, antithesis, and synthesis" has been criticized as a "vulgarization" of the dialectic's subtlety. It has been pointed out that the reduction of the dialectic into three separate terms suggests a mechanical process, or that the explication of this triad somehow implies that these contradictions come from outside of things. However, I think we can make effective use of the idea of thesis, antithesis, and synthesis if we keep in mind Hegel's explanation of how the dialectical tension between thesis and antithesis is internal and inherent in the very nature of things and beings. That is, in a universe populated by imperfect, partial entities, we can almost always find an existential conflict resident in the separation between the real and the ideal. And it is partially out of the intrinsic energy of the inherent tension of this conflict that systems of development arise.

18. See, Gregory L. Fricchione, "Separation, Attachment and Altruistic Love" *in* Stephen Garrard Post, ed., *Altruism & Altruistic love*, (Oxford: Oxford University Press 2002), where Fricchione discusses what he calls "the separation–attachment dialectic." This is described as: "A dialectical process involving the inseparable interconnectedness of two opposing forces," which is seen as the synthesis. Fricchione traces this attachment dialectic through cosmology, chemistry, biology, consciousness, language and culture, p. 348.

19. Michael C. Corey, *Back to Darwin, the Scientific Case for Deistic Evolution* (Lanham, MA: University Press of America, 1994), p. 243.

20. Richard Lewontin and Richard Levins, *The Dialectical Biologist* (Cambridge, MA: Harvard University Press, 1985).

## Chapter 4

1. Alister McGrath, *The Open Secret* (Oxford: Blackwell Publishing, 2008), pp. 228-229.

2. Mortimer Adler and William Gorman, eds., *The Syntopicon: An Index to the Great Ideas* (Chicago: Encyclopaedia Britannica 1952).

3. Sri Aurobindo Ghose, *The Future Evolution of Man* (Twin Lakes, WI: Lotus Press 2003), p. 16.

4. Pitirim Sorokin, "Integralism is My Philosophy," *in* Whit Burnett, ed. *This is My Philosophy,* (New York: Harper and Brothers, 1957), p. 184, quoted in: Barry Johnston, *Pitirim A. Sorokin, An Intellectual Biography* (Lawrence, KS: University Press of Kansas 1995).

5. John Haught, *God After Darwin* (Boulder, CO: Westview Press, 2007), pp. 139-140.

6. Alfred North Whitehead, *Adventures of Ideas* (New York: Free Press, 1933), p.11.

## Chapter 5

1. Jürgen Habermas, *Communication and the Evolution of Society* (Boston, MA: Beacon Press, 1979), p. 164.

2. Thomas McCarthy, *Race, Empire and the Idea of Human Development* (Cambridge, UK: Cambridge University Press, 2009), p. 242. Although McCarthy's point is well taken, unlike the diverse varieties of traditional culture, modernism is primarily a singular, international culture because it is based on science, which is likewise cross-cultural and international in its scope.

## Chapter 6

1. Stephen Jay Gould, "On Replacing the Idea of Progress with an Operational Notion of Directionality," *in* Matthew Nitecki, ed., *Evolutionary Progress*, (Chicago: University of Chicago Press, 1988), p. 319.

2. Retrieved from: http://www.talkorigins.org/faqs/faq-intro-to-biology.html, July 20, 2010.

3. Daniel McShea and Alex Rosenberg, *Philosophy of Biology, A Contemporary Introduction* (New York: Routledge 2008), pp. 143-144.

4. William Provine, "Progress in Evolution and the Meaning of Life," *in* Matthew Nitecki, ed., *Evolutionary Progress* (Chicago: University of Chicago Press, 1988), p. 63.

5. Daniel McShea and Alex Rosenberg, *Philosophy of Biology, A Contemporary Introduction* (New York: Routledge, 2008), p. 142.

6. Jeffrey Schloss, "Evolutionary Theory and Religious Belief," *in* Philip Clayton, ed., *The Oxford Handbook of Religion and Science* (Oxford: Oxford University Press, 2006), p. 201.

7. I am not arguing that increasing complexity can be unambiguously equated with progress in evolution. While the direction of increasing organismal complexity is an observable trait that lends itself to scientific analysis, evolutionary progress is sometimes achieved by moving in the opposite direction of simplification. Indeed, it appears that complexification and simplification represent an indestructible polarity that conditions evolution's overall dialectical trajectory

of improvement. This concept of dialectical polarity was explored in chapters 3 and 4.

8. Gregg Easterbrook, *The Progress Paradox, How Life Gets Better While People Feel Worse* (New York: Random House, 2004), pp. 252-253.

9. Kevin Kelly, *Out of Control* (New York: Basic Books, 1994), pp. 406-407. Kevin Kelly seems to have modified his position on progress since 1994, but this paragraph nevertheless vividly describes the position of biocentric egalitarianism, which is still held by many, and which is discussed further in the text of this chapter 6.

10. Ken Wilber, *Sex, Ecology, Spirituality* (Boston, MA: Shambhala, 1995), pp. 28-29.

11. Holmes Rolston III, *Environmental Ethics, Duties to and Values in the Natural World* (Philadelphia, PA: Temple University Press, 1988), p. 187.

12. Ken Wilber, *Sex, Ecology, Spirituality* (Boston, MA: Shambhala, 1995), pp. 544-545.

13. *Ibid,* p. 546.

14. See Arne Næss, *Ecology, Community and Lifestyle: Outline of an Ecosophy.* (Cambridge, UK: Cambridge University Press 1989); Warwick Fox, *Towards a Transpersonal Ecology* (Boston, MA: Shambhala 1990); and Aldo Leopold, *A Sand County Almanac* (Oxford: Oxford University Press 1949).

15. Ken Wilber, *Sex, Ecology, Spirituality* (Boston, MA: Shambhala, 1995), p. 546.

16. Lynn Margulis, *What is Life?* (Berkeley, CA: University of California Press, 2000), p. 44.

17. Holmes Rolston, III, *Environmental Ethics, Duties to and Values in the Natural World* (Philadelphia, PA: Temple University Press, 1988), p. 207.

18. See Harold Morowitz, *The Emergence of Everything* (Oxford: Oxford University Press, 2002). However, there is nothing concrete about 15 levels because emergence has an essentially fractal quality. Every species is an instance of emergence, but the uniquely emergent features of every species are obviously not included in the chain of transcendence and inclusion that leads to higher levels. Further, with respect to the structural trajectory of emergence, it should be noted that emergence unfolds simultaneously in at least "four quadrants," as charted in Ken Wilber's well known four-quadrant model of evolution. Building on Teilhard de Chardin's law of "complexity-consciousness," Wilber's model shows how evolutionary emergence occurs simultaneously in both the exterior structures and interior sentience of every organism (as organisms become more complex they generally exhibit greater consciousness). Moreover, Wilber's model charts the unfolding of emergence not only in individual organisms, it also shows how this same sequence of emergence occurs simultaneously in collective dimensions of evolution, such as through the increasing complexity of ecosystems that support

the emergence of more complex organisms. Thus, the structural sequence of evolutionary emergence produces a complex web of interactive relationships that are far from linear or simplistic and that reveal a clear trajectory of progress. For more on Wilber's four-quadrant model, see Ken Wilber, *Sex, Ecology, Spirituality* (Boston, MA: Shambhala,1995).

19. Source: Wikipedia, an online encyclopedia; http://en.wikipedia.org/wiki/ Fine-tuned_Universe, accessed July 14, 2010.

20. See B. J. Carr and M. J. Rees: "The Anthropic Principle and the Structure of the Physical World," in *Nature* 278 (April 12, 1979).

21. Paul C.W. Davies, "How bio-friendly is the universe?" in *International Journal of Astrobiology, vol. 2, no. 2* (2003), p. 115.

22. Holmes Rolston, III, *Science and Religion, A Critical Survey* (West Conshohocken, PA: Templeton Foundation Press, 2006), p. 71. In his discussion of the anthropic principle, Rolston also quotes evolutionary biochemist and Nobel laureate George Wald, who writes: "Life is a precarious development wherever it occurs. The universe is fit for it; we can imagine others that would not be. Indeed this universe is only *just* fit for it. . . . Sometimes it is as though Nature were trying to tell us something, almost to shake us into listening." Quoted from: George Wald, "Fitness in the Universe: Choices and Necessities," *in* J Oro et al., eds., *Cosmochemical Evolution and the Origin of Life* (Dordrecht, Netherlands: D. Reidel Publishing Co., 1974), pp. 8-9.

23. Paul C.W. Davies, *Accidental Universe* (Cambridge,UK: Cambridge University Press, 1982), p. 110.

## Chapter 7

1. This point is documented by Philip Clayton in *Adventures in the Spirit* (Minneapolis, MN: Fortress Press 2008). While all dynamic systems are non-computational to some degree, the point is that the purposes of organisms are not entirely mechanical or predictable, living things always possess an element of spontaneity and relative freedom.

2. This quote is from Richard Tarnas' description of Platonic philosophy in *The Passion of the Western Mind*, (New York: Ballantine, 1991), p. 14.

3. Holmes Rolston III, *Environmental Ethics, Duties to and Values in the Natural World* (Philadelphia, PA: Temple University Press, 1988), p. 223.

4. John Haught, *Nature and Purpose* (Lanham, MD: University of America Press, 1980), p. 70.

5. Kevin Kelly, *Out of Control* (New York: Basic Books, 1994), p. 405.

6. Alfred North Whitehead, *Process and Reality* (New York: Free Press, 1978), p. 21. (This quote is a simplified composite. But it is true to the meaning of the original quote nonetheless).

7. Terrence Deacon, "The Hierarchic Logic of Emergence," *in* Bruce H. Weber and David J. Depew*, eds., Evolution and Learning: The Baldwin Effect Reconsidered,* (Cambridge, MA: MIT Press, 2003), p. 306.

8. In connection with this discussion of the evolutionary impulse, I want to acknowledge the work of spiritual teacher Andrew Cohen. Although references to the "evolutionary impulse" as a stimulus to spiritual growth can be found in a variety of previous spiritual sources, Cohen's central emphasis of this impulse in his teaching has had a significant influence within the integral movement. See Andrew Cohen, *Evolutionary Enlightenment* (New York: Select Books, 2011).

9. Individual holons are entities such as cells and multicellular complex organisms. In contrast, social holons are entities such as flocks, herds, or ecosystems, which lack subjectivity or agency. In the course of the unfolding of the accumulating sequence of emergence, individual holons tend to grow larger, whereas social holons grow smaller as they increase in depth. For more on these distinctions, see: Sean Hargens and Michael Zimmerman, *Integral Ecology* (Boston, MA: Integral Books/Shambhala, 2009), pp. 91-103.

10. Obviously, exceptions can be found in the species of plants and animals that have used the activities of humans as a survival strategy of their own, as well documented by Michael Pollan in his book, *The Botany of Desire* (New York: Random House, 2002). But in general, if the noosphere were to disappear, it would have little effect on the ongoing survival of the biosphere.

11. Rem Blanchard Edwards, *What Caused the Big Bang?* (New York: Rodopi Press, 2001), p. 344.

12. John Haught, "God and Evolution," *in* Philip Clayton, ed., *The Oxford Handbook of Religion and Science* (Oxford: Oxford University Press, 2006), p. 705.

13. As a technical matter, we could say that evolution never stops—that evolution will continue in the domains of cosmological, biological and cultural evolution, unless these domains themselves somehow become extinguished. Nevertheless, the leading edge of evolutionary emergence on our planet is now occurring in the realm of cultural evolution, which moves at a faster pace than cosmological or biological evolution. And as a result of cultural evolution, the biological evolution of the human race is, for the most part, no longer subject to the pressures of natural selection. So for humans at least, our future biological evolution will be largely determined by developments in the realm of culture. As we have seen, cultural evolution is not automatic, it does not advance inexorably like biological evolution through random mutations and environmental selection, it requires human effort and intention to move forward. Put differently, the future of evolution is in our hands; the advance of emergence now depends on us.

14. Holmes Rolston III, *Environmental Ethics, Duties to and Values in the Natural World* (Philadelphia, PA: Temple University Press, 1988), pp. 217-128.

## Chapter 8

1. The term "theology" is obviously connected to theism, and although I do not wish to frame this discussion in exclusively theistic terms, there is, unfortunately, no ready synonym. However, this term has been catching on within the larger field of "philosophy of religion," where even "Buddhist theology" has become a phrase in usage within this context. I thus acknowledge the difficulties and ask the reader to allow for a broad and inclusive definition of the term "theology."

2. Bertrand Russell and Frederick Copleston, "The Existence of God," in John Hick and Paul Edwards, eds., The Existence of God, Problems of Philosophy Series (New York: Macmillan & Co., 1964), p. 175.

3. Quoted in John Boslough, Stephen Hawking's Universe (New York: William Morrow, 1985), p. 121. The arguments in Hawking's latest book, The Grand Design (New York: Bantam, 2010), apparently contradict his earlier conclusion about the "religious implications" of the big bang, but his previous position is worth citing nonetheless.

4. See, e. g., Trinh Xuan Thuan and Matthieu Ricard, The Quantum and the Lotus (New York: Crown, 2001). Despite the dramatic beginning demonstrated by the big bang, the Buddhist teaching that the universe is "beginningless" can be grounded in the eternal nature of the first cause described in Tenet 4. Admittedly, "some forms of Buddhism regard thinking about ultimate realities as a kind of distraction from which we must detach ourselves if we are to achieve enlightenment." But I obviously disagree. Valuing nature and history in their particulars, and in their wholeness, is an important practice for any spiritual path.

5. Philip Clayton, Adventures in the Spirit (Minneapolis, MN: Fortress Press, 2008), p. 104.

6. Quoted from Wikipedia, an online encyclopedia; http://en.wikipedia.org/wiki/Tzimtzum, accessed November 12, 2009.

7. Jürgen Moltmann, God in Creation (New York: Harper & Row, 1985), p. 88.

8. The idea that the "subtraction" of value leaves energy is taken from integral philosophy's recognition that values work within internal evolutionary systems in a manner that is similar to the way energy functions in external evolutionary systems. This idea is discussed in chapter 9. Further, as mentioned in chapter 3, the objective and subjective poles of value can be compared to the positive and negative poles of an electric current, hence the idea that energy is the physical shadow of value. Obviously, we cannot put too much weight on these kinds of analogies, but I hope that my description of such things in the text can at least be appreciated from an allegorical perspective.

9. See, for example, the work of "fractal cosmologist" Robert L. Oldershaw, at: http://www3.amherst.edu/~rloldershaw/menu.html

10. Roy Bhaskar, Dialectic: The Pulse of Freedom (London: Verso, 1993), p. 378.

11. Michael Silberstein, "Emergence, Theology, and the Manifest Image," *in* Philip Clayton, ed., *The Oxford Handbook of Religion and Science* (Oxford: Oxford University Press 2006), p. 794.

12. Tenets 8 and 9 emphasize the important role played by human free will in determining the future course of evolution's unfolding. And in this context it should be noted that this point partially contradicts Sri Aurobindo's teaching regarding *involution*. The concept of involution describes the evolution of the universe as the unfolding of preexisting potentials that have already been planted or inscribed within the evolutionary process. However, if the future course of evolution has already been previously enfolded or laid down through involution, then the importance of our human participation as free agents of evolution is clearly diminished. Thus, while I agree that the potentials of perfection are, in a way, already present in the evolving universe through the "shining through" of the infinite into the finite, I also hold that agency and free will play an indispensable role in determining where evolution is headed.

13. Houston Smith and David Griffin, *Primordial Truth and Postmodern Theology* (Albany, NY: SUNY Press, 1989), p. 184.

14. My argument for the influence of a final cause or purpose in evolution rests primarily on the evident role of consciousness and value in the evolutionary process. The presence of formal and final causes can, however, also be detected in the unexplained phenomenon of emergence, and especially in the major emergences of the big bang, life, and human consciousness. It thus bears mentioning that this partial reliance on emergence's "scientific mystery" to bolster my claim could be mistaken for a "God of the gaps" style argument. God of the gaps arguments have been used by creationists in cases where science has failed to explain some natural phenomenon. Arguments of this kind, of course, must be regarded as suspect in the face of science's ongoing success in discovering material explanations for nature's mysteries. However, even in the unlikely event that a completely physical explanation for ontological emergence is discovered, this will not negate the presence of consciousness and value, which constitute the real evidence for evolution's purpose. In order to establish why we need a better philosophy of evolution in the first place, it has been necessary to show where evolutionary science has either explained away its gaps or filled them in with materialist metaphysics. And while I trust that some of these gaps may eventually be closed by new scientific discoveries, consciousness and value will never be reduced to mere matter and energy. Further, while I hold that the science of evolution now points to the presence of formal and final causes in the universe, I have not argued for a philosophy that necessarily requires God or Spirit to fill science's explanatory "gaps."

## Chapter 9

1. Ken Wilber, *Excerpt D,* Part IV, in: *Part 2 of The Kosmos Trilogy,* published on: http://wilber.shambhala.com, accessed June 3, 2009.

2. As I wrote in *Integral Consciousness*: "From the perspective of the integral worldview, the mind/body problem is seen as merely a conundrum that arises from the limitations of a materialist metaphysics. That is, the very idea that the universe is purely material, that all phenomena can be explained by or reduced to the laws of physics, is itself highly metaphysical because it is ultimately a proposition that must be taken on faith. . . . Yet materialism [has] stubbornly persisted even as it was demonstrated that a reality frame claiming that the universe was nothing more than 'matter in motion' was just as extra-scientific as any other kind of metaphysics. As the materialists continued to struggle with the mind/body problem, as they continued to ask: 'how can conscious experience arise from the electrical activity of the brain?,' they couldn't quite see that starting their inquiry with the false certainties of physical matter was still a thoroughly metaphysical starting place. This dilemma arises from what Whitehead famously identified as 'the fallacy of misplaced concreteness.'" Steve McIntosh, *Integral Consciousness and the Future of Evolution* (Minneapolis, MN: Paragon House, 2007), p. 10 and p. 203.

3. Michael Basseches, "The Development of Dialectical Thinking as an Approach to Integration," in *Integral Review Journal*, vol. 1, 2005.

4. Robert Kegan, *In Over Our Heads* (Cambridge, MA: Harvard University Press, 1994), p. 351.

5. *Ibid*, p. 34.

6. Plato, *The Republic* (New York: Penguin Classics, 2007), p. 468.

# SELECTED BIBLIOGRAPHY

Allinson, Robert Elliott. *A Metaphysics for the Future* (Farnham, UK: Ashgate, 2001).

Aurobindo, Ghose. *The Future Evolution of Man: The Divine Life upon Earth* (Wheaton, IL: Quest Books, 1974).

_____. *The Life Divine* (Twin Lakes, WI: Lotus Press, 1985).

Barbour, Ian. *Religion and Science: Historical and Contemporary Issues* (New York: HarperCollins, 1997).

Barlow, Connie, ed. *Evolution Extended: Biological Debates on the Meaning of Life* (Cambridge, MA: MIT Press, 1994).

Basseches, Michael. *Dialectical thinking and adult development* (New York: Ablex Pub. Corp., 1984).

Beck, Don and Cowan, Christopher. *Spiral Dynamics: Mastering Values, Leadership and Change* (Malden, MA: Blackwell, 1996).

Bergson, Henri. *Creative Evolution* (New York: Macmillan, 1928).

Bhaskar, Roy. *Dialectic: the Pulse of Freedom* (London: Verso, 1993).

Bradley, F.H. *Appearance and Reality* (Oxford: Oxford University Press, 1930).

Carroll, Sean. *Endless Forms Most Beautiful: The New Science of Evo Devo and the Making of the Animal Kingdom* (New York: W.W. Norton & Co., 2005).

Clayton, Philip. *Adventures in the Spirit* (Minneapolis, MN: Fortress Press, 2008).

_____. *In Quest of Freedom* (Göttingen, Germany: Vandenhoeck & Ruprecht, 2009).

_____. ed. *The Oxford Handbook of Religion and Science* (Oxford: Oxford University Press, 2006).

Clayton, Philip and Davies, Paul C.W. *The Reemergence of Emergence* (Oxford: Oxford University Press, 2008).

Cobb, John Jr., ed. *Back to Darwin: A Richer Account of Evolution* (Grand Rapids, MN: William B. Eerdmans Pub. Co., 2008).

Cohen, Andrew. *Evolutionary Enlightenment* (New York: Select Books, 2011).

Combs, Allen. *The Radiance of Being* (Minneapolis, MN: Paragon House, 2002).

_____. *Consciousness Explained Better* (Minneapolis, MN: Paragon House, 2009).

Cooper, Laurence. *Eros in Plato, Rousseau, and Nietzsche: The Politics of Infinity* (University Park, PA: Pennsylvania State University Press, 2008).

Corey, Michael C. *Back to Darwin, the Scientific Case for Deistic Evolution* (Lanham, MA: University Press of America, 1994).

Corning, Peter. *Holistic Darwinism: Synergy, Cybernetics, and the Bioeconomics of Evolution* (Chicago: University of Chicago Press, 2005).

Cronk, Lee. *That Complex Whole: Culture and the Evolution of Human Behavior* (Boulder, CO: Westview Press, 1999).

Cunningham, Connor. *Darwin's Pious Idea* (Grand Rapids, MN: William B. Eerdmans Pub. Co, 2010).

Darwin, Charles. *On the Origin of Species by Means of Natural Selection: Or, The Preservation of Favoured Races in the Struggle for Life* (London: Hurst, 1911 (1859)).

_____. *The Descent of Man: The Concise Edition* (New York: Plume, 2007 (1871)).

Davies, Paul C.W. *Cosmic Jackpot: Why Our Universe is Just Right for Life* (New York: Houghton Mifflin, 2007).

Davies, Paul Sheldon. *Subjects of the World: Darwin's Rhetoric and the Study of Agency in Nature* (Chicago: University of Chicago Press, 2009).

Dawkins, Richard. *The Greatest Show on Earth: The Evidence for Evolution* (New York: Free Press, 2009).

Deacon, Terrence. "The Hierarchic Logic of Emergence: Untangling the Interdependence of Evolution and Self-Organization," *in* Weber and Depew, eds. *Evolution and Learning: The Baldwin Effect Reconsidered*, (Cambridge, MA: MIT Press, 2003).

Derrida, Jacques. *Structure, Sign and Play in the Discourse of the Human Sciences,* in *Writing and Difference* (Chicago: University of Chicago Press, 1978).

Diamond, Jared. *Guns, Germs, and Steel* (New York: W. W. Norton & Company, 2005).

Dick, Steven and Lupisella, Mark, eds. *Cosmos & culture: Cultural Evolution in a Cosmic Context* (Washington, D.C.: National Aeronautics and Space Administration, Office of External Relations, History Division, 2009).

Dowd, Michael. *Thank God for Evolution* (New York: Penguin, 2009).

Dunbar, Robin, Power, and Camila, eds. *The Evolution of Culture: an Interdisciplinary View* (Piscataway, NJ: Rutgers University Press, 1999).

Easterbrook, Gregg. *The Progress Paradox, How Life Gets Better While People Feel Worse* (New York: Random House, 2004).

Edwards, Rem Blanchard. *What Caused the Big Bang?* (New York: Rodopi Press, 2001).

Eldridge, Niles. *Reinventing Darwin: The Great Debate at the High Table of Evolutionary Theory* (Hoboken, NJ: John Wiley and Sons, 1995).

Feinman, Gary and Manzanilla, Linda, eds. *Cultural Evolution: Contemporary Viewpoints* (New York: Kluwer Academic/Plenum Publishers, 2000).

Futuyama, Douglas. *Evolutionary Biology* (Sunderland, MA: Sinauer Associates, 1979).

Gardner, Howard. *Truth, Beauty, and Goodness Reframed* (New York: Basic Books, 2011).

Gebser, Jean. *The Ever-Present Origin* (Athens, OH: Ohio University Press, 1985).

Godwin, Robert. *One Cosmos Under God* (Minneapolis, MA: Paragon House, 2004).

Gould, Stephen Jay. *Ever Since Darwin* (New York: W.W. Norton & Co, 1977).

_____. *The Panda's Thumb: More Reflections in Natural History* (New York: W.W. Norton & Co, 1992).

Griffin, David. *Religion and Scientific Naturalism: Overcoming the Conflicts* (Albany, NY: SUNY Press, 2000).

Habermas, Jürgen. *Communication and the Evolution of Society* (Boston, MA: Beacon Press, 1979).

_____. *The Philosophical Discourse of Modernity* (Cambridge, MA: MIT Press, 1987).

Hargens, Sean and Zimmerman, Michael. *Integral Ecology* (Boston, MA: Integral Books/Shambhala, 2009).

Harper, Charles L. Jr., ed. *Spiritual Information: 100 Perspectives on Science and Religion* (Philadelphia, PA: Templeton Foundation Press, 2005).

Haught, John. *Nature and Purpose* (Lanham, MD: University Press of America, 1980).

_____. *Deeper than Darwin: The Prospect for Religion in the Age of Evolution* (Boulder, CO: Westview Press, 2003).

_____. *God after Darwin: A Theology of Evolution* (Boulder, CO: Westview Press, 2008).

Hawking, Stephen and Mlodinow, Leonard. *The Grand Design* (New York: Bantam, 2010).

Hegel, Georg W. F. *The Phenomenology of Spirit* (Oxford: Oxford University Press, 1979).

_____ . *Reason in History* (New York: Prentice Hall, 1995).

Heil, John. *From an Ontological Point of View* (Oxford: Oxford University Press, 2003).

Holbrook, David. *Evolution and the Humanities* (New York: St. Martin's Press, 1987).

Holland, John. *Emergence: From Chaos to Order* (New York: Basic Books, 1999).

Hulswit, Menno. *From Cause to Causation: A Peircean Perspective* (New York: Kluwer Academic Publishers, 2002).

Inglehart, Ronald. *Modernization and Postmodernization: Cultural, Economic, and Political Change in 43 Societies* (Princeton, NJ: Princeton University Press, 1997).

_____ . *Human Values and Social Change* (Boston, MA: Brill Academic Publishers, 2003).

Jantsch, Erich. *The Self-Organizing Universe* (Oxford: Pergamon Press, 1980).

Johnson, Barry. *Polarity Management: Identifying and Solving Unsolvable Problems* (Amherst, MA: HRD Press, 1992).

Kaufman, Stuart. *Reinventing the Sacred* (New York: Basic Books, 2008).

Kegan, Robert. *The Evolving Self* (Cambridge, MA: Harvard University Press, 1982).

_____ . *In Over Our Heads* (Cambridge, MA: Harvard University Press, 1994).

Kelly, Kevin. *Out of Control*, (New York: Basic Books, 1994).

Klapwijk, Jacob. *Purpose in the Living World?: Creation and Emergent Evolution* / translated and edited by Harry Cook, (Cambridge, UK: Cambridge University Press, 2008).

Koestler, Arthur. *Janus: A Summing Up* (New York: Random House, 1978).

Laszlo, Ervin. *Evolution: The Grand Synthesis* (Boston, MA: Shambhala, 1987).

_____ . *The Systems View of the World* (New York: Hampton Press, 1996).

_____ . *The Chaos Point: The World at the Crossroads* (Newburyport, MA: Hampton Roads Pub., 2006).

Laubichler, Manfred and Maienschein, Jane, eds. *From Embryology to Evo-devo: a history of developmental evolution* (Cambridge, MA: MIT Press, 2007).

Leopold, Aldo. *A Sand County Almanac* (Oxford: Oxford University Press, 1949).

Lewontin, Richard and Levins Richard. *The Dialectical Biologist* (Cambridge, MA: Harvard University Press, 1985).

Mackey, J. L. *Ethics: Inventing Right and Wrong* (New York: Penguin, 1977).

MacLean, Paul. *The Triune Brain in Evolution* (New York: Springer, 1990).

Margulis, Lynn and Punset, Eduardo, eds. *Mind, Life, and Universe: conversations with great scientists of our time* (White River Junction, VT: Chelsea Green Pub., 2007).

Margulis, Lynn and Sagan, Dorion. *What Is Life?* (New York: Simon & Schuster, 1995).

Maslow, Abraham. *Motivation and Personality* (New York: HarperCollins, 1987).

Mayer, Ernst. *What Evolution Is* (New York: Basic Books, 2002).

McFadden, Johnjoe. *Quantum Evolution.* (New York: W. W. Norton & Co, 2000).

McGrath, Alister. *The Open Secret: A New Vision for Natural Theology* (Malden, MA: Blackwell, 2008).

McIntosh, Steve. *Integral Consciousness and the Future of Evolution* (Minneapolis, MA: Paragon House, 2007).

McShea, Daniel and Rosenberg, Alex. *Philosophy of Biology: A Contemporary Introduction* (New York: Routledge, 2008).

Meacher, Michael. *Destination of the Species: The Riddle of Human Existence* (London: O Books, 2010).

Midgley, Mary. *Evolution as a Religion* (London: Methuen, 1985).

_____ . *The Myths We Live By* (New York: Routledge, 2004).

Moltmann, Jürgen. *God in Creation* (New York: Harper & Row, 1985).

Morin, Edgar. *On Complexity* / translated by Robin Postel (New York: Hampton Press, 2008).

Morowitz, Harold. *The Emergence of Everything* (Oxford: Oxford University Press, 2002).

Morris, Simon Conway. *Life's Solution: Inevitable Humans in a Lonely Universe* (Cambridge, UK: Cambridge University Press, 2003).

Murdoch, Iris. *The Sovereignty of the Good* (New York: Routledge and Kegan Paul, 1970).

Næss, Arne. *Ecology, Community and Lifestyle: Outline of an Ecosophy* (Cambridge, UK: Cambridge University Press, 1989).

Neumann, Erich. *The Origins and History of Consciousness* (Princeton, NJ: Princeton University Press, 1970).

Nitecki, Matthew, ed., *Evolutionary Progress* (Chicago: University of Chicago Press, 1988).

Nygren, Anders. *Agape and Eros* / translated by Philip S. Watson (Boulder, CO: Westminster Press, 1953).

Owen, David. *Between Reason and History: Habermas and the Idea of Progress* (Albany, NY: SUNY Press, 2002).

Phipps, Carter. *Evolutionaries* (New York: Harper Perennial, 2012).

Plato. *The Republic* (New York: Penguin Classics, 2007).

Polanyi, Michael. *Personal Knowledge: Towards a Post-critical Philosophy* (New York: Harper & Row, 1964).

Prothero, Donald. *Evolution: What the Fossils Say and Why It Matters* (New York: Columbia University Press, 2007).

Ray, Paul and Anderson, Sherry. *The Cultural Creatives: How 50 Million People are Changing the World* (New York: Harmony Books, 2000).

Richerson, Peter and Boyd, Robert. *Not By Genes Alone: How Culture Transformed Human Evolution* (Chicago: University of Chicago Press, 2005).

Rhodes, James. *Eros, Wisdom, and Silence: Plato's Erotic Dialogues* (Columbia, MO: University of Missouri Press, 2003).

Rice, Hugh. *God and Goodness* (Oxford: Oxford University Press, 2000).

Rifkin, Jeremy. *The Empathic Civilization* (New York: Tarcher Putnam, 2009).

Rolston, Holmes III. *Environmental Ethics: Duties to and Values in the Natural World* (Philadelphia, PA: Temple University Press, 1988).

_____. *Science and Religion: A Critical Survey* (West Conshohocken, PA: Templeton Foundation Press, 2006).

_____. *Genes, Genesis and God: Values and Their Origins in Natural and Human History* (Cambridge, UK: Cambridge University Press, 1999).

_____. *Three Big Bangs: Matter-Energy, Life, Mind* (New York: Columbia University Press, 2010).

Rosenberg, Alex and Arp, Robert, eds. *Philosophy of Biology: An Anthology* (Malden, MA: Wiley-Blackwell, 2010).

Rothenberg, David and Pryor, Wandee, eds. *Writing the Future: Progress and Evolution* (Cambridge, MA: MIT Press, 2004).

Rue, Loyal. *Everybody's Story* (Albany, NY: SUNY Press, 1999).

Ruse, Michael. *Evolutionary Naturalism: Selected Essays* (New York: Routledge, 1995).

_____. *Darwin and Design: Does Evolution Have a Purpose?* (Cambridge, MA: Harvard University Press, 2003).

Salvadori, Massimo. *Progress: Can We Do Without It?* / translated by Patrick Camiller, (London: Zed Books Ltd., 2008).

Schwartz, Frederick and Polanyi, Michael, eds. *Scientific Thought and Social Reality: essays* (Madison, CT: International Universities Press, 1974).

Shayegan, Daryush. *Cultural Schizophrenia: Islamic Societies Confronting the West* / translated by John Howe (Syracuse, NY: Syracuse University Press, 1992).

Sheldrake, Rupert. *A New Science of Life* (New York: Park Street Press, 1995).

Smith, Houston and Griffin, David. *Primordial Truth and Postmodern Theology* (Albany, NY: SUNY Press, 1989).

Smith, John Maynard and Szathmáry, Eors. *The Major Transitions in Evolution* (Oxford: Oxford University Press, 1998).

_____. *The Origins of Life: From the Birth of Life to the Origin of Language* (Oxford: Oxford University Press, 2000).

Spencer, Herbert. *First Principles* (London: Williams and Norgate, 1863).

Sternberg, Robert and Kaufman, James, eds. *The Evolution of Intelligence* (Hillsdale, NY: L. Erlbaum Associates, 2002).

Stewart, John. *Evolution's Arrow* (Canberra, AU: Chapman Press, 2000).

Swimme, Brian and Berry, Thomas. *The Universe Story* (San Francisco, CA: Harper San Francisco, 1992).

Tarnas, Richard. *The Passion of the Western Mind* (New York: Ballantine, 1991).

Taylor, Charles. *A Secular Age* (Cambridge, MA: Harvard University Press, 2007).

Teilhard de Chardin, Pierre. *The Phenomenon of Man* (New York: Harper & Row, 1955).

_____. *The Future of Man* (New York: Harper & Row, 1964).

_____. *The Vision of the Past* (New York: Harper & Row, 1966).

Thuan, Trinh Xuan and Ricard, Matthieu. *The Quantum and the Lotus* (New York: Crown, 2001).

Turner, Frederick. *Natural Religion* (New Brunswick, NJ: Transaction Publishers, 2006).

Urantia Foundation. *The Urantia Book* (Chicago: Urantia Foundation, 1955).

Wade, Jenny. *Changes of Mind: A Holonomic Theory of the Evolution of Consciousness* (Albany, NY: SUNY Press, 1996).

Wallace, Alfred Russel. *The World of Life: A Manifestation of Creative Power, Directive Mind and Ultimate Purpose* (London: Moffat, Yard & Co., 1911).

Wesson, Robert. *Beyond Natural Selection* (Cambridge, MA: MIT Press, 1991).

Whitehead, Alfred North. *Science and the Modern World* (New York: Macmillan, 1925).

_____. *Adventures of Ideas* (New York: Macmillan, 1933).

_____. *Process and Reality* (New York: Free Press, 1978).

Wilber, Ken. *Sex, Ecology, Spirituality* (Boston, MA: Shambhala, 1995).

_____. *A Theory of Everything* (Boston, MA: Shambhala, 2000).

_____. *Integral Spirituality* (Boston, MA: Integral Books/Shambhala, 2006).

Wilson, Edward O. *Consilience: The Unity of Knowledge* (New York: Vintage, 1998).

Wright, Robert. *Nonzero: The Logic of Human Destiny* (New York: Pantheon, 2000).

Wynn, Mark. *God and Goodness: a natural theological perspective* (New York: Routledge, 1999).

# INDEX

# O

# P

# ABOUT THE AUTHOR

STEVE MCINTOSH, J.D. is a leader in the integral philosophy movement and author of *Integral Consciousness and the Future of Evolution*. He currently works as a Founding Partner of the new social policy foundation, The Institute for Cultural Evolution. In addition to this think tank, and his work in philosophy, McIntosh has had a variety of other successful careers, including founding the consumer products company Now & Zen, practicing law with one of America's largest firms, working as an executive with Celestial Seasonings Tea Company, and Olympic-class bicycle racing. He is a graduate of the University of Virginia Law School and the University of Southern California Business School. He now lives in Boulder, Colorado with his wife and two sons.

For more information visit: www.stevemcintosh.com.